DETERGENCY

THEORY AND TEST METHODS

SURFACTANT SCIENCE SERIES

CONSULTING EDITORS

MARTIN J. SCHICK

*Diamond Shamrock Chemical
Company
Process Chemicals Division
Morristown, New Jersey*

FREDERICK M. FOWKES

*Chairman of the Department
of Chemistry
Lehigh University
Bethlehem, Pennsylvania*

OTHER VOLUMES IN PREPARATION

DETERGENCY

THEORY AND TEST METHODS

(in three parts)

PART II

edited by W. G. CUTLER and R. C. Davis

Whirlpool Corporation
Research and Engineering Center
Benton Harbor, Michigan

MARCEL DEKKER, INC.   New York

MARCEL DEKKER, INC.
270 Madison Avenue, New York, New York 10016

LIBRARY OF CONGRESS CATALOG CARD NUMBER: 79-163921

ISBN: 0-8247-1114-9

CURRENT PRINTING (last digit):   10 9 8 7 6 5 4 3 2 1

PRINTED IN THE UNITED STATES OF AMERICA

PREFACE

The detergent process is very widely used today. Despite its acceptance and wide usage, it is a process not completely defined and understood. There is no general agreement as to test methods for measuring the effectiveness of the detergent process. This volume of the Surfactant Science Series is intended to provide to both industrial and academic research workers a compilation of test methods in use today and background information as to the theoretical basis of these tests. Perhaps such a volume will stimulate new interest in further investigation in the field of detergency.

The author list has been chosen to provide representatives from detergent and detergent-component producers, those specialized in applications of detergents, and universities. There has been no attempt to conform to a group presentation or to render a group opinion. Each author has been left free, within the constraint of a general outline, to present and interpret data from his viewpoint and experience.

For the convenience of the reader and to expedite publication, this volume of the Surfactant Science Series is being presented in three parts. Part I treats the fundamentals of the soil removal process, soil redeposition, and test methods for soil removal and soil redeposition. Part I is concerned with the soil removal process primarily as it applies to fibers.

The current part, Part II, consists of topics related to a more complete understanding of the detergency process. The emphasis on the detergency process as related to fibers continues with such topics as the rinsing process, bleaching, physical damage, the action of enzymes, and ancillary tests. Topics of considerable current interest are sequestration and test methods in toxicology and dermatology. Departing from the fiber emphasis, a chapter summarizing the cleaning of metals is provided.

Part III completes this volume of the Surfactant Science Series. It contains a detailed explanation of fluorescent whitening agents with appropriate test methods, an examination of the relation of detergents to the environment, and a treatment of the topic of dishwashing as an example of the role of detergents in hard surface cleaning. Part III also contains the indexes to the entire volume. These indexes permit the reader to examine contributions to the theory of detergency in the scientific literature and serve to identify those researchers who have made contributions to this theory.

A number of people have contributed to Part II. The editors wish to thank the contributing authors and their companies. The support of the Whirlpool Corporation in permitting the editors to undertake the task of compiling this volume is also acknowledged. Special thanks are also due to Dr. Martin Schick for his many suggestions and critical review of the book outline and to Mrs. Carol Hauch for the secretarial assistance so necessary to this undertaking.

Benton Harbor, Michigan   W. G. Cutler
                                                           R. C. Davis

CONTRIBUTORS TO PART II

THEODORE CAYLE, Wallerstein Company, Division of Travenol Laboratories, Inc., Morton Grove, Illinois*

J. A. DAYVAULT, Celanese Fibers Marketing Company, Charlotte, North Carolina

CHRISTIAN GLOXHUBER, Toxicological Laboratories, Henkel & Cie. GmbH, Düsseldorf, West Germany

CHARLES P. McCLAIN, Purex Corporation, Applications Research, Grocery Products, Carson, California

WALTER L. MARPLE, Whirlpool Research and Engineering Center, Benton Harbor, Michigan**

WILLIAM W. MORGENTHALER, Monsanto Company, St. Louis, Missouri

E. B. SAUBESTRE, Enthone, Inc., New Haven, Connecticut[†]

K. H. SCHULZ, Dermatology Clinic, University of Hamburg, Hamburg, West Germany

PAUL SOSIS, Conoco Chemicals, Saddle Brook, New Jersey[††]

LEONARD J. VINSON, Lever Brothers Company, Research and Development Division, Edgewater, New Jersey

---

*Present address: CCF Consulting Corporation, Highland Park, Illinois.

**Now retired.

[†]Deceased.

[††]Present address: Witco Chemical Corporation, Ultra Division, Paterson, New Jersey.

CONTENTS OF PART II

CONTENTS OF PART I

CONTENTS OF PART III

DETERGENCY

THEORY AND TEST METHODS

Chapter 11

SEQUESTRATION

William W. Morgenthaler
Monsanto Company
St. Louis, Missouri

I. INTRODUCTION

A sequestering agent or sequestrant is a chemical reagent that can combine with metal ions in solution to form water-soluble complex ions. The metal ion involved in the binding process has been sequestered or "inactivated." Sequestration, chelation, and complexation have been commonly used to describe this reaction, and the choice of one term over another seems to be largely a matter of the author's preference. Sequestration is used exclusively throughout this chapter to describe complex formation between a sequestrant and a metal ion.

The purpose of this chapter is to (a) provide the uninitiated with a brief theoretical background on sequestration, (b) describe some of the techniques for measuring sequestration, and (c) define the role of sequestrants in detergent products.

II. SEQUESTRATION

Sequestration can be defined as the phenomenon of binding metal ions in soluble complexes and thereby preventing the formation of undesirable precipitates or the occurrence of other detrimental side reactions. In the more recent literature the sequestering agent or sequestrant is commonly referred to as the ligand.

A ligand usually, but not necessarily, has at least one electron pair in an orbital of σ symmetry, which is not already directly involved in the bonding. This allows the ligand to form a coordinate bond with the metal ion. Ligands are frequently classified by the number of coordinate bonds that can form with the metal ion. When one bond can form with the metal, the ligand is called unidentate, such as H_2O, NH_3, and CN^-. If two positions are available for bonding, the ligand is bidentate, and so on up to the six coordinating positions found in the ethylenediaminetetraacetate (EDTA) ion. Ligands must contain at least two bonding positions from different parts of the molecule, or ion, to form a stable ring or cage type of structure. Therefore, it is understood that reference to ligands will be to the various multidentate types.

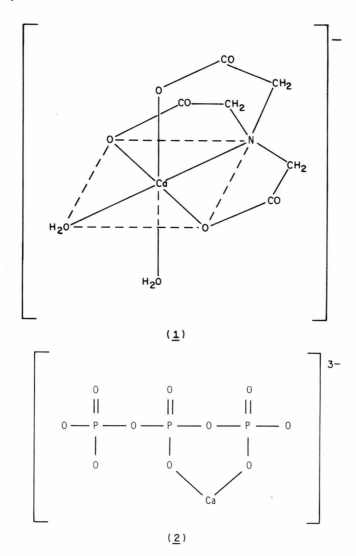

(**1**)

(**2**)

Structure (**1**) shows the complex between calcium(II) ion and nitrilotriacetate ion. The cage type of structure is readily apparent. A typical
ring type of structure has been hypothesized [1] for the calcium(II) and tripolyphosphate complex, as shown in structure (**2**).

A. Coordination Groups

Recalling that a ligand usually has sites with nonbonded (lone pair)
electrons available for donation, it is not surprising to note that coordina-

tion with a metal through nitrogen, oxygen, or both is the most prevalent. Groups having important coordinating functions were listed by Van Uitert and Fernelius [2] in the order of decreasing affinity for metal ions as follows:

$$-O^- \quad > \quad NH_2 \quad > \quad -N=N- \quad > \quad \underset{|}{N} \quad > \quad \quad -COO^- \quad > \quad -O- \quad >> \quad C=O$$

Enolate   Amine   Azo   Ring   Carboxylate   Ether   Carbonyl
ion   N

A listing of the commercially available organic sequestering agents shows that the amino and carboxylate ions are most common while the polyphosphate anions are the principal inorganic ligands of commerce. However, other groups which are capable of donating electrons such as phosphonic acid, $-PO(OH)_2$, and hydroxy ($-OH$) may be present and usable in the molecule. Chaberek and Martell [3] have proposed that the structural types given here should (and in fact do) provide good sequestration performance on the basis of possessing the most desirable functionality in a molecule. Most of the organic compounds discussed herein are of these basic types.

$$>\!N-(CH_2)_n-COOH \qquad\qquad\qquad \text{Aminocarboxylic acid}$$

$$HO-(CH_2)_n-N-(CH_2)_m-COOH \qquad \text{Hydroxylalkylaminocarboxylic acid}$$

$$>\!N-(CH_2)_n-\overset{\displaystyle O}{\overset{\displaystyle \|}{P}}\!\!<\!\!\begin{array}{l} OH \\ OH \end{array} \qquad \text{Aminophosphonic acid}$$

$$\begin{array}{l} H_2C-COOH \\ | \\ HO-C-COOH \\ | \\ H_2C-COOH \end{array} \qquad \begin{array}{l} \text{Polycarboxylic acid} \\ \text{(e.g., citric acid)} \end{array}$$

B. Factors Affecting Sequestration

In many applications, including detergency, the prime function of a sequestrant is to complex metal ions so that undesirable precipitates do not form. This establishes competition between the sequestrant and the precipating anion for the metal cation. This can be represented by the following equations:

$$M^{n+} + L^{m-} \; \rightleftharpoons \; ML^{(n-m)} \tag{1}$$

$$M^{n+} + A^- \; \rightleftharpoons \; MA^{(n-1)} \tag{2}$$

In the above, M^{n+} is the metal ion, L^{m-} is the sequestering agent, and A^- is the precipitating agent. One of the most useful methods of evaluating the sequestering ability of a compound utilizes this competitive situation and turbidity or light transmittance measurements to obtain sequestration values.

Since this is a competitive type of reaction, the sequestration values obtained are dependent on several variables. These variables are reported [4] to be

1. Attainment of equilibrium
2. Specific metal cation and its concentration
3. Specific sequestering anion and its concentration
4. Specific precipitating anion and its concentration
5. Presence of other metal ions
6. Total ionic strength
7. Solution pH
8. Solution temperature

In addition, the method of measurement and assumptions for calculation can alter the apparent sequestration values. Consequently one must exercise caution in evaluating data on alternative sequestrants to ensure that experimental conditions are such that direct comparison is justified and realistic. The problems that can be encountered in comparing data under different conditions will become evident as the various factors affecting sequestration are detailed.

1. Attainment of Equilibrium

The objective in making turbidimetric measurements is to obtain an end point that is independent of time and mode of addition of the components or their relative concentration. The most foolproof method of getting the correct (equilibrium) result is to approach the precipitate end point from both ends. Several solutions with controlled pH values having various amounts of metal ion, but the same amount of ligand and precipitating anion, can be prepared and stirred for several days. Then the point of incipient precipitation can be determined from light intensity measurements. In this case, solutions that were initially clear because of supersaturation can become turbid with time. Obtaining an end point from the opposite direction is accomplished by setting up a number of solutions that contain excess metal ion so that a precipitate forms. Then various amounts of ligand are added and the solutions stirred for several days. Again, the end point is noted from light intensity determinations. The end point obtained by each approach should agree within experimental error. It may then be concluded that equilibrium has been established. While this technique generally provides a reliable and reproducible measure of sequestration, it is recognized that the procedure is time-consuming and assumes no degradation of the ligand over the time span of the experiment.

The importance of attaining equilibrium cannot be overemphasized since sequestration values that were different by factors as high as 10 have been reported [5,6] depending on the time of equilibration.

2. Specific Metal Cation and Its Concentration

In most cases, any given ligand sequesters different metal ions in various amounts on a weight basis. On a mole basis, the common assumption is that 1 mole of sequestering agent reacts with 1 mole of metal ion. If the assumption is proved valid for a metal ion such as calcium(II) at given conditions, it is reasonable to assert that the same ratio will hold true for similar metal ions, for example magnesium(II). Table 1 shows the calculated theoretical amounts of several metal ions complexed by 100 g of a broad spectrum sequestering agent, EDTA.

TABLE 1

Sequestration of Various Metal Ions by EDTA[a]

Metal	$g\ M^{n+}/100\ g\ EDTA$[b]
Magnesium(II)	6.4
Aluminum(III)	7.1
Calcium(II)	10.5
Manganese(II)	14.4
Iron(II) or iron(III)	14.7
Cobalt(II)	15.5
Nickel(II)	15.4
Copper(II)	16.7
Zinc(II)	17.2
Cadmium(II)	29.6
Barium(II)	36.1
Lead(II)	54.5

[a] Assuming 1:1 mole ratio complex for calculation.
[b] Tetrasodium salt basis.

It is important to point out that sequestration can only be accomplished with ionized metals. Sequestration directly from the free metallic state has not been observed, and apparent direct sequestration must go through solubilization and ionization steps before complex formation.

The concentration dependence is linear, in that the higher the concentration of metal ion, the higher must be the concentration of ligand to provide effective control or sequestration. Assuming sufficient sequestrant is present at any metal ion level, there remains in solution a small and, in most cases, insignificant amount of free metal ion. Since this is an equilibrium process, the amount of free metal ion can be calculated from the stability constant.

In general, the most stable complexes are formed with multivalent metal ions. However, with certain ligands such as tripolyphosphate weak binding of sodium(I) has been observed [7].

3. Specific Sequestering Anion and Its Concentration

As was the case with metal ions, the basis (weight or mole) of calculation or determination must be established. While a number of sequestering anions may form 1:1 complexes with a metal ion, the difference in molecular weights may be quite large when comparing simple ligands with elaborate organic molecules. For example, the fully ionized pyrophosphate anion $P_2O_7^{4-}$ has a molecular weight of 173.9 whereas the monoprotonated diethylenetriaminepentaacetate anion (the principal species at pH about 10) has a molecular weight of 389.1 or about 2.25 times greater. Therefore, on a weight basis the pyrophosphate holds a clear-cut advantage over DTPA, assuming 1:1 complexes in both cases.

Another consideration, which is covered more fully under pH effects, is the ionic state of the sequestering anion which varies with pH. Generally, the more highly ionized sequestering anions are more efficient as ligands. Therefore, while 1:1 mole ratio sequestration usually occurs with a fully ionized ligand, the less efficient 1:2 metal-ligand species may be the primary complex at lower pH (less ionized sequestering anion) conditions. In other cases, such as with the calcium-NTA complex, nearly equivalent amounts of 1:1 and 1:2 complex are present at the turbidimetric end point [8]. These findings point out that the 1:1 assumption can be in error and in lieu of supporting data should only be used as a first approximation.

When the sequestering anion is a rather long-chain polymer (more than approximately six repeating units), the prediction of calcium sequestration efficiency is quite difficult since it may require any number of sites to bind one calcium. Ratios of approximately 4 moles of phosphorus per bound calcium have been found for several polymeric phosphorus-containing compounds [8].

The concentration effects of sequestering anions parallel those described for the metal ion. As more ligand is added, more metal is complexed (if metal ion is present in excess) until a point is reached where the metal ion concentration is at the equilibrium value calculated from the stability constant.

4. Specific Precipitating Anion and Its Concentration

The definition of a sequestering agent, as previously given, may be restated as a substance exhibiting a complexing anion that is sufficiently strong to dissolve common precipitates of the metal ion being complexed. Practically speaking, this means that the complexing ability of a sequestering agent must be compared with the insolubility of the metal precipitate from which the metal is sequestered. This can be done on the basis of free metal ion concentration in equilibrium with either the complex or the precipitate. If the free metal ion concentration is lower for the complex than for the precipitate, the precipitate dissolves and sequestration occurs. Conversely, if the free metal ion concentration is lower for the precipitate, no dissolution occurs and hence no sequestration. The free calcium ion concentration in equilibrium with a 0.01 M solution of several sequestering agents and with various precipitated calcium salts was calculated and is depicted graphically in Fig. 1. Any sequestering agent shown on this figure dissolves all of the precipitates located higher on the scale. Since sodium tripolyphosphate, sodium nitrilotriacetate, and EDTA are situated lower on the scale than the commonly encountered calcium salts, these materials will dissolve these calcium salts. It should be pointed out that EDTA is substantially lower on the scale than the tripolyphosphate which simply means it is a much stronger complexing agent for calcium ion. However, in most practical situations this added strength is not necessary since the lower cost tripolyphosphate or nitrilotriacetate materials are sufficiently strong to provide effective sequestration.

Figure 1, then, illustrates that the choice of precipitating anion can greatly influence a sequestration result. Poorer sequestrants can be made to appear quite efficient if a fairly soluble calcium salt, such as the sulfate, were used as the precipitating anion. Similarly, good sequestering agents in most systems can appear to be poor if a highly insoluble precipitant such as stearic acid, $CH_3(CH_2)_{16}COOH$, were used since the stearate anion provides strong competition for calcium. Also, if the solubility of a calcium salt is too high, the presence of a sequestrant can prevent precipitation completely. This phenomenon was observed during a study of the solubility of calcium soaps of linear carboxylic acids [9].

The identity and precipitating or calcium-fixing strength of the competing anion(s) is a detergent-soil system comprise an interesting but as yet unanswered question. A correlation between detergency and the sequestration ability of builders using a particular competing anion, such as

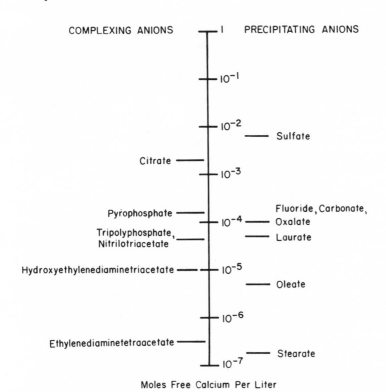

FIG. 1. Competition of complexing agents with precipitating agents for calcium. (The free calcium for the complexing agent is computed for the dissociation of a 0.01 M solution of the 1:1 calcium complex.)

oxalate, might be obtained if a good approximation of the sequestration competition encountered in the wash tank could be made. A correlation of this type would allow the effectiveness of new sequestrants as potential detergent builders to be predicted directly from relatively fast and simple sequestration measurements. Current unpublished data suggest that such a correlation does exist, at least in certain active systems, and builder effectiveness has been effectively predicted.

Increasing the concentration of a precipitating agent gives data similar to those obtained at lower concentration except the sequestration value (on a weight basis) is reduced due to the increased tendency for precipitate formation. Lowering the precipitant concentration conversely provides higher sequestration values due to a decreased tendency to form a precipitate.

5. Presence of Other Metal Ions

Any effect from other metal ions is dependent on the stability of the respective complexes and the concentration of the various metals. In other words, the stability of the complex between a given sequestering agent and a specific metal can be strong enough so that complexing will occur despite the presence of low levels of "foreign" metal ions. If the metal concentrations are similar, but the stability constants are sufficiently different (about three orders of magnitude), preferential complexing will occur. Similarly, a weak complex can be displaced by a stronger one. This is observed in the tripolyphosphate system wherein weak sodium complexes are displaced with calcium(II) or magnesium(II) in detergent solutions.

6. Total Ionic Strength

Due to the fact that sequestration involves ionic equilibria, it is not unexpected that the gross concentration of ionic species not participating in the reaction may have an effect on the efficiency of sequestration. In general, the effect of high concentrations of various anions and cations commonly found in detergent solutions such as sulfate, silicate, sodium, potassium, and so on, tends to lower the stability constant. It is for this reason that the ionic strength is generally reported along with the stability constant in the literature. Reasonably stable complexes (K = ~ 5-7) are affected only slightly by a tenfold increase in ionic strength.

7. pH of Solution

The effect of pH on sequestration is of primary importance. In an equilibrium situation any reagent that can react with another species participating in the system will cause perturbations. Hydrogen ion concentration influences sequestration, as sequestering anions and metal ions change in character depending on the solution pH. At high pH values (pH 11-12) a ligand generally exists in a free or fully ionized state. Lowering the solution pH adds protons to the ligand stepwise until a point is reached where there is no ionic species capable of sequestration. This stepwise addition of protons is measured quantitatively by successive acidity constants. These values can be used to calculate ionic species distributions as a function of pH. Hence, the hydrogen ion, which is of course a cation, can compete for the ligand. Therefore, the sequestration value depends on the outcome of the competition between the hydrogen ion and the metal ion for the ligand.

The ionic species distribution of sodium tripolyphosphate [10-12] and sodium nitrilotriacetate [13] as a function of solution pH is shown in Figs. 2 and 3. Since the most efficient sequestration is obtained from a fully ionized ligand, these figures show that STP is expected to be most efficient at pH 9 or higher, whereas NTA should perform best at a pH near 10 or higher. Figure 4 shows the calcium sequestration values [14, 15] for NTA

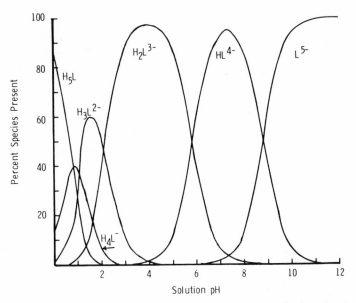

FIG. 2. The distribution of ionic species in tripolyphosphoric acid solution as a function of pH at 25°C.

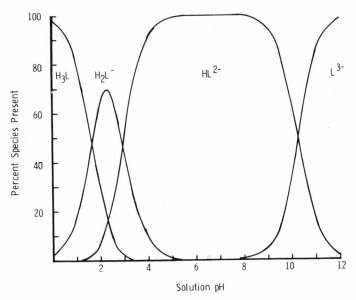

FIG. 3. The distribution of ionic species in nitrilotriacetic acid solution as a function of pH at 25°C.

W. W. MORGENTHALER

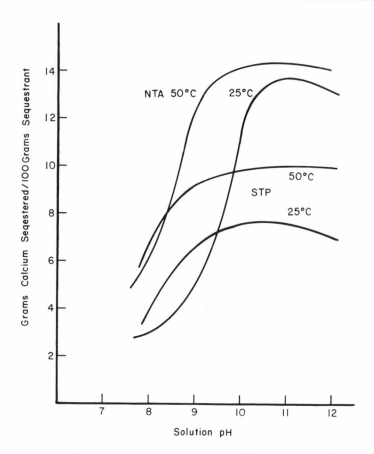

FIG. 4. Calcium sequestration by sodium tripolyphosphate and tri-sodium nitrilotriacetate monohydrate.

and STP. In both cases, the reduction in sequestration corresponds closely to decreasing amounts of fully ionized ligand, either L^{3-} or L^{5-} for NTA and STP, respectively, as the solution pH is reduced. This correlation should be used only as a guide to anticipated sequestration behavior since complicating factors such as the formation of complexes other than 1:1 will not allow linear correlations to be obtained. However, in the STP case a fairly good correlation was observed and is shown in Fig. 5 [16]. The theoretical line was developed by taking percentages of the sequestration values obtained when essentially 100% of a given species was present, adding the respective contributions and plotting at the proper distribution of species.

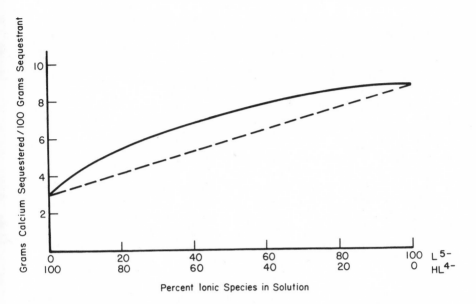

FIG. 5. Calcium sequestration by sodium tripolyphosphate as a function of ionic species at 25°C.

The actual data fall higher than the predicted. This is believed to be due to the formation of a small amount of a higher complex of STP, that is, Ca (STP)$_2$ with the reported 1:1 complexes for Ca(P$_3$O$_{10}$)$^{3-}$ and for Ca(HP$_3$O$_{10}$)$^{2-}$. This explanation is consistent with prior unpublished data wherein an average of 3.1 phosphorus atoms per bound calcium was reported for STP [17].

Hence, a knowledge of the ionic species can give a rough approximation of the pH sensitivity of a sequestrant. Deviations from the correlations will probably be in the positive direction due to underestimated participation of protonated ligands or formation of other than 1:1 complexes. Thus values obtained by this technique always provide a minimum estimate and the actual values can be higher.

Although most efficient sequestration is obtained at high pH values, another competitive situation must be considered, that is, the tendency of a metal ion to interact with hydroxide ion. Therefore, a sequestrant that may be quite efficient at pH 11 may show very poor complexing ability in 1-2% sodium hydroxide solution due to the insolubility of the metal hydroxide compared to the stability of the complex.

In practical situations fairly large changes in solution pH can affect sequestration capacity detrimentally. Thus buffering is normally required to maintain the pH in the most efficient range. In detergent applications the usual pH change is downward because of soil acids and proton release from partially protonated ligands involved in sequestration.

8. Temperature Effect

Increases in solution temperature decrease the effectiveness of some ligands by lowering the stability constant and thus the sequestration values [18]. Normally, the loss in sequestering efficiency is rather small when working in the optimum pH range for a given ligand, over the temperature range practicable in detergent usage. Alkaline-earth-polyphosphate complexes, however, have been shown [19, 20] to be independent of temperature. The higher sequestration values shown for STP in Fig. 4 are due to the increased solubility of calcium oxalate with increasing temperatures. Since its solubility is higher, there is effectively less resistance to dissolving the precipitate at higher temperature and the sequestration values appear higher.

The difference in temperature stability appears to be related to the type of complex structure, that is, ring or cage type. The less complicated ring structure is the preferred configuration from a temperature stability viewpoint.

C. Summary

The foregoing discussion serves to reemphasize the earlier comment that sequestration is dependent on many factors. Hopefully, it clarifies the need to be aware of the conditions under which sequestration measurements are made and to avoid comparison of data obtained under different conditions. Sequestration data, properly obtained and evaluated, are an invaluable aid to investigators working in the detergent area.

III.   SEQUESTRATION MEASUREMENTS

Several qualitative and quantitative techniques are available for measuring the formation of complex ions formed from sequestrants and metal ions. These include nephelometric titrations, acid-base titrations, competitive titrations with sequestering agents, spectrophotometric measurements, ion exchange studies, conductivity measurements, and polarographic experiments, in approximate order of frequency of use. Information on the use of these procedures is given in several works [3, 21-23] on chelating agents and a good review [7] on their application to phosphate complexes has been published. The first two techniques have enjoyed widespread utility and are discussed in some detail herein.

A. Nephelometric Titrations

Perhaps the most useful technique for determining quantitatively the sequestration of hardness ions, for example calcium and magnesium, is by nephelometric titrations. A nephelometer is defined by Webster as "an instrument for studying the character of suspensions by means of diffuse transmitted or reflected light." Nephelometric and turbidimetric determinations for the purposes of this discussion are synonymous and are used interchangeably.

An oxalate titration is reported to be the specification method for determining the sequestration value for EDTA [24]. A solution containing a weighed amount of EDTA and ammonium oxalate is titrated with calcium chloride to the first visual permanent turbidity at pH 11. This procedure is quite precise and accurate with visual observation of the end point since the calcium-EDTA complex is quite stable and a sharp end point is obtained. However, in the majority of cases the detection of the end point is not so obvious and a more general nephelometric method based on instrumental measurements of light transmittance through the solution was developed [4, 19]. With this technique, the nephelometric titrations are performed by recording the light transmittance of a solution containing the sequestrant and competing anion (precipitant). The titrant solution, containing the metal ion(s) of interest, is automatically added in increments to unstirred solutions, followed by agitation. This method of titration provides a high localized concentration of metal ion in the quiescent solution and precipitation occurs. Subsequently, agitation is resumed and equilibrium is attained from the precipitate end so that supersaturation is unlikely. Since the precipitates are fresh, their rate of solution in the presence of sequestering agent is rapid. The automatic titrating cycle is repeated until the end point is passed, as noted from the decrease in light transmittance caused by a permanent precipitate.

The housing and sensing elements of a Sargent-Malmstadt photometric titrator [25] are employed as the heart of the apparatus. The voltage output of the photoelectric cell is reduced through a 0.5-meg helipot and fed into a recorder with a fast response (1 sec) and a 0-100 mV range full scale. A 25-ml automatic buret is fastened over the titrator and the input of a solenoid valve that regulates flow of titrant is connected to one lead of a relay timer. The other lead of the relay timer is attached to the input of the 2000-rpm stirring motor in the titrator. The stirring cycle of the timer is 2 min, while the titrant addition time is varied between 2 and 10 sec, as required for a particular experiment. Capillary delivery tips of various diameters are inserted at the end of the buret to further control the rate of titrant delivery. These precautions allow each titrant addition to be constant over the top several milliliters of the buret. Noting the buret reading after each addition ensures accurate titrant volume records.

In a typical calcium sequestration experiment, aliquot volumes of the sequestrant solution and calcium-precipitating anion solution (e.g., sodium oxalate) are pipetted into a 400-ml beaker, containing about 200 ml of distilled water. The solution pH is then adjusted with acid or base, if required, and the total volume of the solution is adjusted to 250 ml with additional water. The beaker containing the solution is placed in the titrator and brought to the desired temperature with a temperature control unit. The light source, recorder, and relay-timer switches are turned on and a percent light transmittance baseline of 90-95% is established during a stirring cycle. Then, in automatic sequence, the stirrer shuts off, the solenoid opens and allows titrant to enter the solution, the solenoid shuts off in a few seconds, and stirring resumes for a period of about 2 min. The formation of the calcium oxalate precipitate in the unstirred solution causes the recorder pen to move down scale. Resumption of stirring in the presence of excess ligand causes dissolution of the precipitate and the pen moves back up scale to the baseline and remains there until the next addition of titrant. After a number of cycles, dependent on the sequestering agent, the absence of additional sequestration capacity is indicated on the recorder by a new equilibrium light transmittance reading below the original baseline. A few cycles beyond the appearance of the first permanent turbidity is enough to establish the end point, that is the point of incipient precipitation. If desired, the pH can be adjusted between each titrant addition or followed and noted during the course of an experiment. Figure 6 is a reproduction of a typical recorder trace obtained during such a run. The recorder readings are then replotted versus the number of cycles (if constant volume delivery) or volume of titrant for each addition, as shown in Fig. 7. The intersection of the lines drawn through the points is taken as the end point and sequestration calculations are made using this value of titrant volume per known amount of ligand.

This procedure has been successfully used to obtain sequestration values as well as stability constant data. In the latter case, where very careful experimental work is desired, care can be taken to avoid the presence of possible interference from sodium ions by neutralizing acid salts with cations that are known not to form complexes such as the tetramethyl-ammonium ion, and adjusting the ionic strength to a predetermined level.

This technique has also been used in the opposite manner [9, 26]; that is, instead of determining sequestration information, knowing the solubility of the precipitant, one obtains the solubility product for a metal salt knowing the stability constant of the sequestrant quite precisely.

B. pH Titrations

The species distribution information discussed earlier shows that ligands are associated, to various extents, with hydrogen ions across a wide

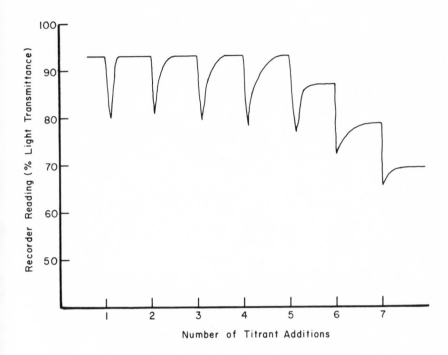

FIG. 6. Typical recorder chart during nephelometric titration.

pH range. Although most efficient sequestration occurs with a fully ionized ligand, binding by protonated ligands is prevalent also. Therefore, the sequestration reaction frequently involves a displacement of hydrogen ion(s) from a ligand by the metal ion. One of the many possible combinations is as follows:

$$M^{n+} + HA^{m-} = MA^{n-m-1} + H^+$$

or in the case of one of the calcium tripolyphosphate complexes

$$Ca^{2+} + HP_3O_{10}^{4-} = CaP_3O_{10}^{3-} + H^+$$

Many ligands, such as NTA, contain several acidic groups. Thus a relatively large quantity of hydrogen ions may be displaced during the course of the reaction. Therefore, it can be stated that complex formation usually results in a decrease in the pH of a solution. Since complex formation can occur with facility when ionized ligands are in solution, there are certain pH (usually rather high) ranges wherein no pH lowering is observed.

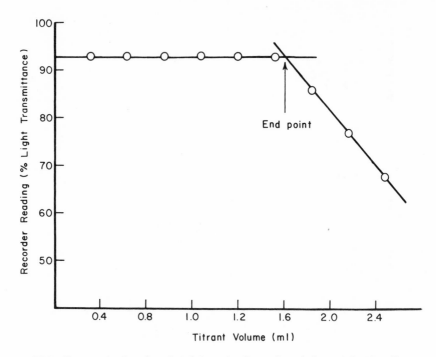

FIG. 7.   Typical end-point determination of nephelometric titration.

It is possible to use pH lowering to determine sequestration values but this is not as expedient as the nephelometric technique previously described. This approach can be used for rapid screening to ascertain qualitatively the formation of complexes using only a pH meter.   An example of the pH-lowering phenomenon is shown in Fig. 8 for NTA in the presence of hard water.

The major utility of pH-lowering experiments is in the determination of complex stability constants.   Since the pH of a solution can be determined very accurately, this effect has been used by numerous investigators to develop stability constant data quite precisely.   The details of these experiments are not described in depth.   Details and discussion on these measurements are given in most of the books available on sequestering agents.

IV.   SEQUESTRATION VALUES AND STABILITY CONSTANTS

Sequestration values and stability constants are the two most common ways of reporting data on complex formation.   Sequestration values are reported (usually on a weight basis) when investigating the sequestration

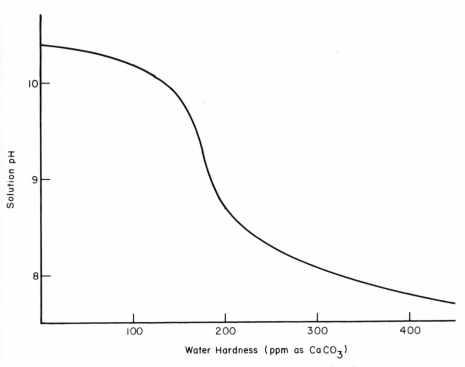

FIG. 8. pH lowering of 0.05% NTA solution due to hard-water sequestration.

phenomena in practical applications. Stability constants are favored in the more technical literature. The two can not be cross-compared to yield any meaningful conclusions. A simple way of keeping these values separate is to think of a sequestration value as a price, that is, "how much", and the stability constant as a quality, that is, "how good", or "how stable." For all practical purposes, a knowledge of the stability constant of a given sequestration reaction provides no insight into how much metal ion will be tied up in a given system. However, both values are quite meaningful when compared in the same terms, subject of course to the factors previously discussed.

Stability constants are the usual manner of expressing the thermodynamic stability of complex species. They are measures of the extent to which a particular reaction will proceed, similar to equilibrium constants. For the reaction between magnesium and pyrophosphate ligand,

$$Mg^{2+} + P_2O_7^{4-} \rightleftharpoons MgP_2O_7^{2-}$$

the stability constant would be

$$K_s = \frac{[MgP_2O_7{}^{2-}]}{[Mg^{2+}][P_2O_7{}^{4-}]} \tag{3}$$

Some authors choose to forego the general term for formation constant when the reaction is as depicted above, while others talk in terms of dissociation constants which would pertain to the reverse of the reaction shown. The term stability constant is used throughout this chapter to describe the situation. Stability constants are commonly reported as either log K or pK (negative log), with more recent authors simply reporting β, which is log K.

The stability constant, therefore, is a quantitative measure of the affinity of a sequestering agent for a specific metal ion in exactly the same manner as an acidity constant measures the affinity of a ligand for hydrogen ion. It should be evident from Eq. (3) that a large K means a high ratio of complexed to free metal ion in the system. Table 2 gives the stability constants for several metals and a selected group of sequestrants. A comprehensive survey of stability constant data was recently compiled by Sillen and Martell [27].

Valuable insight into the choice of a sequestrant for a given application can be obtained by comparing stability constants. For example, a comparison of the magnitude of the stability constants of two ligands gives an indication of how much less unsequestered metal ion may remain in one system over the other. The larger the stability constant, the smaller the amount of free ion. Stability constants provide data on which metals will be sequestered from a system containing several metal ions. In this regard, a sequestrant will react with metal ions in order of decreasing log K values (similar to oxidation potentials).

Any metal will displace from the complex a metal below it in the sequence. Hence, if the hardness ions (Ca^{2+} and Mg^{2+}) in a washing machine are tied up in a polyphosphate complex, the addition of copper or zinc ion will cause the hardness ions to be displaced back into a "free" or uncomplexed state since both the copper and zinc stability constants are sufficiently higher than calcium and magnesium for the ligands shown in Table 2.

Care must be taken when comparing stability constants to be sure the same basis is being used, particularly as to the ionic species taking part in the equilibria. In general, the stability constant of a nonprotonated ligand (K_{ML}) is greater than that of a singly (K_{MHL}) protonated ligand which is in turn more stable than a complex with a multiply protonated ligand (K_{MnHL}). The experimental conditions, such as temperature and ionic strength, must also be taken into account when comparing stability constant data.

TABLE 2

Stability Constants for Three Common Ligands [27]

Metal	Stability constants β (ML)		
	Nitrilotriacetate[a]	Tripolyphosphate[b]	EDTA[a]
Sodium(I)	2.15[c]	1.64	1.66
Calcium(II)	6.41	5.44	10.59
Magnesium(II)	5.41	5.83	8.69
Aluminum(III)	>10		16.12
Iron(III)	15.87		25.1
Copper(II)	12.96	8.70	18.79
Zinc(II)	10.67	9.7[c]	16.26

[a] In 0.1 N KCl or KNO$_3$ at 20°C.

[b] In 1.0 N Me$_4$NCl or Me$_4$NBr at 25°C.

[c] Ionic strength → 0.

The techniques used to obtain sequestration values are commonly used to determine stability constants. As previously mentioned, the pH-lowering technique has enjoyed widespread usage.

V. THE ROLE OF SEQUESTRANTS IN DETERGENT PRODUCTS

The reason(s) for incorporating sequestrants into detergent formulations is not immediately apparent to the uninitiated, hence the role of sequestrants in detergency has been the subject of numerous studies and considerable speculation. Detergency in the broad sense is the result of several processes that are often interconnected. These processes include wetting of the substrate, adsorption at solid interfaces, emulsification, and removal of dirt and its dispersion in the wash solution, to enumerate a few of the many encompassed by the word detergency. The subject is very complex and the individual functional contributions of detergent ingredients are often difficult to assess. Sequestrants obviously play a key role in the performance of detergents as cleaning efficiency is lost in their absence. Therefore, it is reasonable to suggest that sequestrants perform several important

functions in the detergency process. In the event that a particular sequestrant does not contribute all the necessary functionality, performance falls
off and the missing property must be supplied from an alternative source.
There seems to be agreement that several of the properties important to
detergent building were elucidated by Van Wazer and Tuvell [28]; these
properties are as follows:

1. Formation of soluble complexes with metal ions, including the
   calcium and magnesium ions of hard water and the sodium ions of
   the built detergent
2. pH buffering and alkalinity which involves furnishing hydroxyl ions
   to establish the initial pH in an optimum range and the ability to
   maintain pH in this range
3. Dispersion, deflocculation, and peptization of finely divided inorganic
   solids as well as organic soils
4. Electrolytic activity, including salting out and dissolubilization of
   organic substances in aqueous solution as well as the related action
   of lowering critical micelle concentration for organic actives

While this list was detailed for polyphosphates, it is believed applicable
as a checklist in determining the utility of any ingredient considered as a
builder. A detergent builder can be defined as any additive that will enhance
or extend the cleaning ability of the product. Sequestrants, therefore, would
be prime candidates to function as detergent builders.

Additional considerations which should be weighed when choosing a sequestrant for a detergent product include

5. Compatibility with other formulation ingredients or laundry additives
   such as sodium hypochlorite bleach
6. Environmental acceptability
7. Consumer safety: toxicity
8. Cost-performance
9. Processability

While the preceding listing of chemical, physical, economic, and safety
factors is not all inclusive, it does cover the major points of consideration
and serves as the basis for discussion of the various commercial and new
sequestrants.

A. Sequestration

The theoretical aspects of sequestration have been covered earlier.
This allows us to delve into the practical considerations of sequestration at
this point. The water-softening action of sequestrants has great practical
importance since the efficacy of common detergent actives is considerably
diminished by the multiply charged cations of hard water.

1. Anionic Systems

It is well known that soaps form insoluble calcium and magnesium salts, called soap curds, and that the washing ability of anionic detergent actives is diminished by increasing hardness. Several investigators have concluded that the negative effect of water hardness on detergency is a major factor. Vitale et al. [29] studied soil removal in the presence of polyphosphates and hard water. Their work included laboratory tests with artificially soiled cotton fabric and naturally soiled hand towels. The initial Launder–Ometer tests were run in distilled water and in water containing 110 and 360 ppm of hardness ions with sodium dodecylbenzenesulfonate (ABS) only at concentrations of 0.02-0.7%. A series of three approximately parallel curves was obtained as shown in Fig. 9. The detergency leveled off at about 0.1% ABS and the poorest performance was obtained in the hardest water. When the runs were repeated with excess sodium tripolyphosphate (STP) in the system, detergency was nearly constant across the ABS concentration range at slightly lower levels than those obtained in distilled water with ABS only.

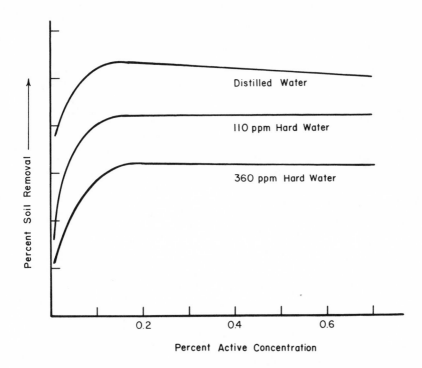

FIG. 9. Soil removal as a function of active concentration and water hardness.

In an effort to confirm these laboratory tests a practical towel test was conducted with a constant 0.1% ABS concentration and variable STP levels. As the STP concentration exceeded that necessary to sequester the hardwater ions, detergency approached the maximum value. From these studies it was concluded that (a) the primary function of STP in detergents is to suppress the large negative effect of hard water, and (b) the amount of STP required to obtain the highest possible detergency is dependent on the amount of hardness present. Additional amounts beyond that required to sequester the hardness ions did not increase detergency. A similar study, conducted more recently using oily soil on cotton cloth, produced the same results [30]. Figures 10 and 11 provide some additional data on this subject. Cotton and polyester/cotton (65/35) fabrics soiled with a synthetic sebum-airborne soil were washed in a typical anionic detergent of today, with and without the presence of 44% STP builder. With both fabrics detergency with the formulation containing STP was markedly superior to the formulation without sequestrant. The results presented in these figures also suggest that cotton fabric is more sensitive to builder sequestration action since the detergency holds up well as long as sufficient STP is present to sequester the hardness at which point it falls off. In the polyester/cotton case a gradual loss of detergency is observed across the entire hardness range studied.

Jones and Parke [31] studied the detergency efficiency of several sequestrants in hard water with an ABS active. They correlated their results with the free calcium ion concentration calculated from the respective calcium stability constants and found that it was possible to assess semiquantitatively the potential effectiveness of a builder with a knowledge of the stability constant. A portion of their data is given in Table 3. These data produce a curve similar to the one shown in Fig. 12. Detergency performance is seen to decrease nearly linearly between the breaks in the curve which occur at about 10^{-4} and 10^{-6} mole of calcium ion per liter. A reduction in calcium concentration below 10^{-6} mole/liter does not improve performance. Hence, the extra binding power of EDTA does not provide more efficient performance. The following conclusions were drawn from these studies:

1. Detergency results can be related in a semiquantitative way to the interaction between calcium ion and the sequestering builder.
2. To produce any appreciable effect on detergency, a builder must first reduce the calcium ion concentration in the wash solution to a level of about 10^{-6} mole/liter or lower, either by complex formation or formation of an insoluble salt.
3. Compounds that are capable of reducing the calcium ion concentration below about 10^{-6} mole/liter are expected to be the most effective builders.

Similar conclusions were drawn from another study wherein critical micelle concentration lowering by electrolytes was related to the function of sequestrants in "tying up" calcium [32].

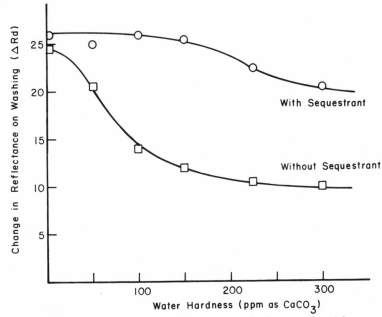

FIG. 10. The effect of complete removal of sequestrant in an anionic laundry detergent on cotton detergency.

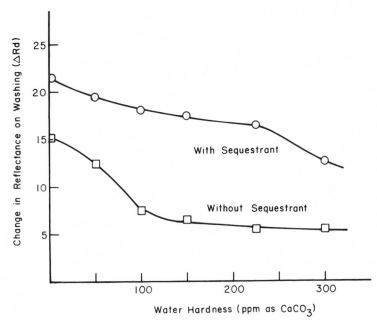

FIG. 11. The effect of complete removal of sequestrant in an anionic laundry detergent on polyester/cotton detergency.

TABLE 3

Relationship Between Detergency[a] and Calcium(II) Ion Concentration
with Various Sequestering Agents [31]

Sequestrant	Sequestrant concentration (mole/liter)	Calcium stability constant β (ML)	Calculated calcium ion concentration (mole/liter)	Detergency efficiency (%)
None			2.25×10^{-3}	7.4
Iminodiacetic acid	0.0045	3.4	3.98×10^{-4}	7.7
Taurine N,N-diacetic acid	0.0045	4.15	7.08×10^{-5}	13.1
Taurine N,N-diacetic acid	0.00675	4.15	3.54×10^{-5}	15.1
Taurine N,N-diacetic acid	0.0135	4.15	1.42×10^{-5}	20.2
Sodium pyrophosphate	0.0045	5.9	1.26×10^{-6}	24
Sodium tripolyphosphate	0.0045	6.3	5.01×10^{-7}	27
Sodium nitrilotriacetate	0.0045	6.41	3.89×10^{-7}	25.6
EDTA	0.0045	10.6	2.52×10^{-11}	26.5

[a]Conditions: 0.075% ABS, 225 ppm hardness as calcium, pH 9.5-10.2.

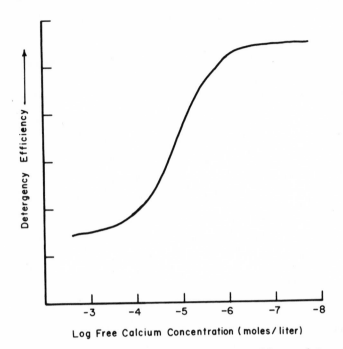

FIG. 12. Detergency efficiency as a function of free calcium concentration.

2. Nonionic Systems

A number of nonionic actives are found to be less effective in hard than in soft water. One investigation was conducted using several sequestrants and nonsequestrants with a nonylphenol 9-mole ethoxylate active in cleaning artificially soiled cotton [33]. A portion of these results is shown in Table 4. The interference from hardness is clearly shown by comparing the first two entries in the table. The improvement noted by the addition of sequestrant confirms that it is the hardness ion which causes the negative effect. These data show that all the polyphosphates bring about some improvement in detergency with the tripolyphosphate overcoming the effect of hardness most effectively.

The precipitants used in this study, that is, trisodium phosphate, sodium carbonate, and sodium metasilicate, are shown to be less efficient than STP even at the much higher (tenfold) concentrations studied with the latter two ingredients. Additionally, a portion of their efficiency is undoubtedly due to the higher pH of these systems. The equivalent performance shown for EDTA and the glassy phosphate strongly suggests that other builder attributes are required to achieve maximum detergency since EDTA is roughly a 50% better calcium sequestrant than the glassy phosphate.

TABLE 4

The Effect of Builders on the Detergency of a Nonionic
Detergent in Hard Water [33]

Builder	Builder concentration (wt %)	Water hardness (ppm $CaCO_3$)	Appearance (%)[a]
None		0	95.2
None		200	34.9
Trisodium phosphate	0.02	200	54.0
Sodium pyrophosphate	0.02	200	89.0
Sodium tripolyphosphate	0.02	200	100
Glassy sodium phosphate	0.02	200	74.6
EDTA	0.02	200	74.6
Sodium carbonate	0.10	200	28.6
Sodium carbonate	0.20	200	55.6
Sodium carbonate	0.50	200	60.3
Sodium metasilicate	0.20	200	92.1

[a] STP taken as 100%, that is, best appearance.

Sodium tripolyphosphate and EDTA were compared side by side on an
equal weight basis in this nonionic system for efficiency of whitening (detergency), redeposition, clay removal, and grease removal. The STP out-
performed EDTA by all of the measures at concentrations of 400 ppm or
less with essentially equivalent results at the higher 500–ppm level. Again,
these data imply the existence of some, as yet undefined, property posses-
sed by STP and not by EDTA.

3. Sequestrant Level in a Formulation

While the stability constants were shown to be useful in predicting
utility as a builder in detergent systems, the actual amount of calcium

"tied up" on a weight basis is required to determine the amount of sequestrant necessary to neutralize water hardness. Table 5 gives the calcium sequestration values for several commercially available sequestrants. In the polyphosphate series the pH dependence of sequestration becomes less pronounced as the phosphate chain lengthens until a nearly flat curve is obtained with the long-chain ($\bar{n}$ = 60) product. These results are not unexpected, since at pH values above 4 to 5 only the end hydrogens in a phosphate chain become hydrogen bonded. As the length of the chain increases, the percentage of end phosphorus atoms decreases. In the detergent pH range, however, STP is the most efficient calcium sequestrant of the linear polyphosphate family.

TABLE 5

Calcium Sequestration Values[a] for Various Sequestrants

| Sequestrant | g Ca(II)/100 g sequestrant at pH | | | | | |
	5	8	9	10	11	12
Tetrasodium pyrophosphate		0.4	2.4	3.7	4.0	3.6
Tetrapotassium pyrophosphate		0.2	1.9	3.0	3.2	2.7
Sodium tripolyphosphate		3.9	7.1	7.5	7.4	7.0
Sodium polyphosphate[b], $\bar{n}$ = 4	1.9	6.2	7.0	7.3	7.2	6.4
Sodium polyphosphate[b], $\bar{n}$ = 12	4.1	6.1	6.5	6.4	6.2	5.8
Sodium polyphosphate[b], $\bar{n}$ = 58	4.9	5.6	5.5	5.5	5.3	5.0
Sodium nitrilotriacetate		3.0	5.0	11.5	13.7	13.3
Tetrasodium EDTA			10.5	10.5	10.5	10.5
Sodium citrate		0.2	0.2	0.2	0.2	0.2

[a]Test conditions: 0.1% sequestrant, 0.1% sodium oxalate, temperature 25°C, 0.1 M calcium nitrate titrant.

[b]
$$(NaO)_2-\overset{\displaystyle O}{\overset{\displaystyle \|}{P}}-O-\left[\overset{\displaystyle O}{\overset{\displaystyle \|}{\underset{\displaystyle \underset{ONa}{|}}{P}}}-O\right]_{\bar{n}}-\overset{\displaystyle O}{\overset{\displaystyle \|}{P}}-(ONa)_2,\text{ where } \bar{n}\text{ is the average chain length.}$$

Sodium nitrilotriacetate is seen to be the most effective calcium seques-trant of those included in Table 5 on a weight basis. It can also be noted that this compound has a marked dependence on pH, with a large loss occur-ring between pH 9 and 10.

In addition to preventing adverse effects on surfactants from hard-water ions, sequestrants inactivate other heavy metal ions (such as iron) which can cause discoloration of fabrics or reduce the effectiveness of optical brighteners.

B. Alkalinity and Buffering

The alkalinity of a builder may be defined as the ability to provide a high concentration of hydroxide ions (high pH) in detergent solutions. Alka-linity is necessary to provide initial solution pH values in the optimum de-tergency range.

Buffering is the ability to maintain pH in a narrow region despite the addition of moderate amounts of acid or base. The buffering function is required in a detergent system to maintain the optimum pH (9-10.5) for sequestration and detergency in the presence of soil acids.

In general, the alkaline earth salts of weak acids are alkaline materials that can provide both alkalinity and buffering capacity for detergent systems. The weaker the acid, the more alkaline will be the salt. Ingredients com-monly used to provide this function include the sodium polyphosphates, so-dium silicates, and sodium carbonate. Since both sequestration and detergency are dependent on pH, the importance of the alkalinity and buffer-ing ability of detergent ingredients or formulations cannot be overlooked. Recent work has demonstrated the effect of pH on detergency and re-emphasized the necessity of providing alkalinity in the formulations [34]. The results, shown in Fig. 13 from the data listed in Table 6, were obtained using a linear alkylbenzenesulfonate (LAS)/electrolyte/sodium sulfate 20/40/40 detergent at a 0.2% concentration in 72 ppm ($CaCO_3$) hard water. The cloth was a 60/40 polyester/cotton blend that was soiled with an artifi-cial mixture having a high clay content. The pH effect on detergency is quite vivid for the nonsequestering materials. The flatter curve for the phosphate salts is undoubtedly due to sequestration by the long-chain phos-phates at low pH values. Overall, however, the need to provide alkalinity is clearly observed. Sequestrants are generally salts of weaker acids but their contribution to alkalinity is usually not sufficient to compensate for the contribution from soil acids released during the washing process.

There are two important sources of acidity in detergent systems. Per-haps the most significant of the two is the contribution from acidic soils such as fatty acids which can vary widely in the home laundry. The second source is from protons being released from, for example, STP or NTA

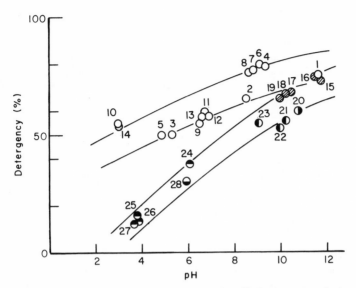

FIG. 13. The dependence of the pH of 0.20% detergent solutions with phosphates (O), silicates (⊘), carbonate (◗), borates (◐), sulfates (◓), or chloride (●) at 25°C. (The number attached to each point refers to the sample number given in Table 6.) Reprinted from Tokiwa and Imamura [34, p. 118], by courtesy of The American Oil Chemists' Society.

ligands during the sequestration process. In this latter case the formation of a chelate ring at the end of a polyphosphate chain causes the weak hydrogen atom to become strongly dissociated. In the NTA case the weak proton behaves in a similar manner as the octahedral complex with NTA is formed. Proton release by sequestration will reduce the pH of the system with increasing water hardness as shown in Fig. 14. Beyond the breaks in the curve virtually no contribution to alkalinity is obtained from either of these sequestrants.

Recall that not only must the original solution pH be in the right range but it must be held there for maximum detergency efficiency. Fig. 15 provides buffer capacity data on STP and NTA under conditions similar to those of Fig. 14. Figure 15 reveals that the relationships obtained are simply typical strong acid-weak base titration curves. Therefore, in the NTA case the curve results from the equilibrium

$$H^+ + L^{3-} \rightleftharpoons HL^{2-}$$

When the fully ionized ligand, or more correctly the starting mixture of L^{3-} and HL^{2-}, is driven completely to HL^{2-} with H^+ addition, the next small

TABLE 6

Builder Effects of Various Inorganic Electrolytes on Detergency Toward Standard Soiled Cloth at a Concentration of 0.20% Detergent[a]

Electrolytes		Sample no.	pH[b]	Detergency (%)
Polyphosphates	Na_3PO_4	1	11.6	77.3
	(Na_2HPO_4)	2	8.4	66.7
	(NaH_2PO_4)	3	5.4	50.2
	$Na_4P_2O_7$	4	9.6	79.8
	$(Na_2H_2P_2O_7)$	5	4.8	50.5
	$Na_5P_3O_{10}$	6	9.2	80.0
	$Na_6P_4O_{13}$	7	8.8	77.5
	$Na_7P_5O_{16}$	8	8.4	76.0
Metaphosphates	$Na_3P_3O_9$	9	6.6	55.6
	$(Na_2HP_3O_9)$	10	2.9	52.8
	$Na_4P_4O_{12}$	11	6.9	61.9
	$Na_5P_5O_{15}$	12	7.1	60.3
	$Na_6P_6O_{18}$	13	6.7	60.1
	$(Na_3H_3P_6O_{18})$	14	3.0	51.0
Silicates	$Na_2O \cdot 0.5SiO_2$	15	11.8	75.0
	$Na_2O \cdot 1.0SiO_2$	16	11.4	76.1
	$Na_2O \cdot 2.0SiO_2$	17	10.5	69.4
	$Na_2O \cdot 2.5SiO_2$	18	10.2	68.8
	$Na_2O \cdot 3.3SiO_2$	19	9.9	64.9
Carbonate	Na_2CO_3	20	10.8	61.9
Borates	$NaBO_2$	21	10.3	57.8
	$NaBO_3$	22	10.0	52.2
	$Na_2B_4O_7$	23	9.1	54.4
Sulfates	Na_2SO_4	24	6.2	37.5
	$Al_2(SO_4)_3$	25	3.8	14.0
	$K_2Al_2(SO_4)_4$	26	3.9	11.7
	$(NH_4)_2Al_2(SO_4)_4$	27	3.7	9.5
Chloride	$NaCl$	28	6.1	31.0

[a] Detergent formulation: Na-LAS/inorganic electrolyte/Na_2SO_4 = 20/40/40. (When Na_2SO_4 was used as an inorganic electrolyte, Na-LAS/Na_2SO_4 = 20/80.)

[b] The pH of 0.2% detergent solution before washing.

Reprinted from Tokiwa and Imamura [34, p. 118], by courtesy of The American Oil Chemists' Society.

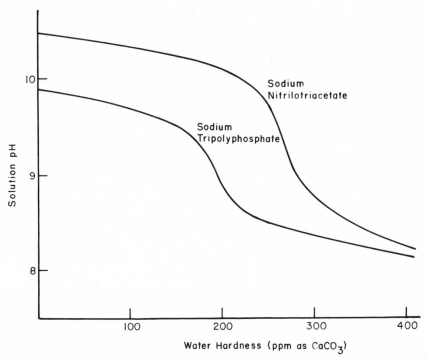

FIG. 14. Solution pH loss due to hard-water sequestration for 0.075% solutions of sodium nitrilotriacetate and sodium tripolyphosphate.

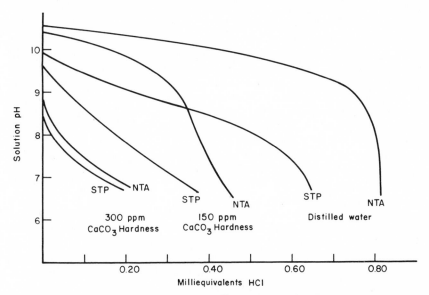

FIG. 15. Buffer capacity of 0.075% solutions of sodium nitriotriacetate and sodium tripolyphosphate with water hardness as a parameter.

485

amount of acid provides a sharp break as shown, since formation of H_2L^- does not begin until about pH 5.

The analogous situation is obtained with the STP, wherein the starting mixture is about 95% L^{5-} in solution and additions of HCl produce exclusively HL^{4-} from pH 10 to about 8, when $H_2 L^{3-}$ formation begins. Due to the formation of the H_2L^{3-} species before the HL^{4-} concentration peaks the break is shallower, as shown.

The addition of water hardness to these systems changes the equilibrium due to the presence of a calcium complex. At the pH of either builder alone in distilled water, previously reported species distributions (see Figs. 2 and 3) have shown that some quantities of the monoprotonated species must be involved in sequestration as pH lowering is observed. The titration of buffer curves obtained in the presence of various amounts of hard water is dependent then on the quantity of protons liberated from the HL^{2-} or HL^{4-} ligands participating in the sequestration reaction. These normally weak protons become strongly dissociated as the calcium complex is formed.

The various curves are therefore displaced so that less HCl is required to neutralize available sites on the ligands. A portion of the starting concentration is "used up" in the complex formation and only the remaining builder can be titrated. This suggests that complex formation is more stable or stronger than the proton addition in the pH range studied. The curves do not cross, even at low pH values where sequestration has been shown to be rather poor. It is hypothesized that they must become identical at some pH where the pK strength favors hydrogen rather than calcium. At low hardness levels (50 ppm or less), the shape of the curve is similar to that obtained in distilled water. However, at higher hardness levels (≥ 150 ppm), in addition to displacement, sharper breaks are observed starting at higher pH levels. This must be due to more involvement of the monoprotonated species in sequestration with a subsequent reduction in the number of sites available for weak proton (buffer) association. Buffer capacity is lost as a function of increasing water hardness, because of sequestration. When the builder is completely tied up, nothing remains to prevent the solution pH from falling due to soil acidity. This situation does not occur since the heavy-duty laundry detergents, and most detergent products for that matter, contain some form of silicate which has sufficient buffer capacity. Figure 16 provides a convenient way of showing the overall pH control situation in one chart. On the left side, complex formation with hardness ions causes a drop of 0.6 to 0.7 pH units depending on the builder system. The middle portion of the curve shows the amount of a given silicate type required to compensate for this pH loss. Finally, the right portion shows the effect of acid addition on a system containing 7% silicate solids. With data of this type, the amount of soil acids released from laundry loads or other factors such as silicate level or type can be estimated.

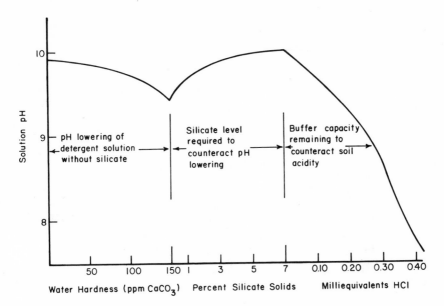

FIG. 16. pH profile of a detergent solution.

C. Dispersion, Deflocculation, and/or Peptization

Dispersion is defined by Webster as meaning "to place in a state of suspension, as finely divided particles in some other substance." Deflocculation means "to break up from a flocculant state; to convert into very fine particles," and peptization refers to an action defined as "to bring into colloidal solution, to convert into a sol." Dispersion is, therefore, a somewhat different action from the other two. It is difficult to classify the effect of sequestrants on the particulate soil in wash solutions, so the terms are used interchangeably in this discussion.

Deflocculation is a process whereby solid soil aggregates are broken up by electrostatic forces into finer particles approaching their individual particle condition. The deflocculation effect is the result of preferential sorption of ions of suspending agent which increases the charge or zeta potential of the particle. This causes the charged particles to repel each other strongly, thereby breaking down the structure responsible for the aggregation of these particles. This phenomenon results in the dispersion of finely divided soil particles in the wash solutions. It has been shown that in this dispersed state the soils do not redeposit as readily on fabric substrates as do soils in an aggregated condition. A similar situation also occurs with the fatty and oily particles in the wash solution.

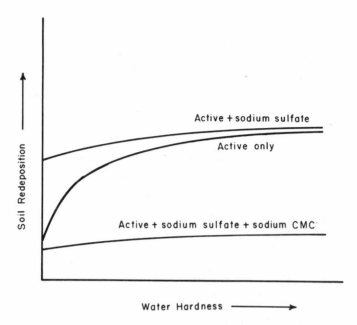

FIG. 17.   The effect of water hardness on soil redeposition.

The effect of electrolytes on soil redeposition was studied using a carbon
black soil and naturally soiled hand towels [35].   The results were similar
to those shown in Fig. 17.   The effects were straightforward, that is, active
plus sodium sulfate allowed substantial redeposition, even in distilled water,
although additional redeposition with increasing hardness was small.   Active
alone was good in distilled water, but approached the sulfate-containing case
in the presence of at least 100 ppm of hardness ions.   Practically no increase
in redeposition is observed with increased hardness when sodium carboxymethylcellulose (CMC) was present in the system.   The key point from this
work is the detrimental effect of the sodium sulfate or, more precisely,
the monovalent sodium cations and the divalent hardness ions.   The addition
of water-softening agents such as sodium tripolyphosphate reduced the
amount of redeposition in hard water although not to the level achieved with
CMC present.   Apparently, the hardness ions were removed by sequestration, but the sodium ion effect on redeposition was still present, which
agrees with the previous data.   Similar information was obtained from the
naturally soiled towel tests.   The ranking from best to poorest of the combinations tested in hard water was sequestrant/CMC/active/sodium sulfate;
sequestrant/active/sodium sulfate;   and active/sodium sulfate.   One of the
conclusions, therefore, was that any inorganic electrolyte, such as sodium
chloride, sodium sulfate, calcium or magnesium salts, or the common
alkali or phosphate builders, tends to cause deposition when used alone or

with surface-active materials. However, soil redeposition is enhanced more by the presence of hardness ions than by the relatively high concentration of sodium ions introduced from sequestrants and fillers.

A continuation of this study provided further insight into the redeposition situation [36]. The relative importance of mono-, di-, or trivalent cations on redeposition was shown to be dependent on valence state. The relative order of the effect was in agreement with the Schultz-Hardy rule, that is, the divalent ion was much worse than the monovalent ion and the trivalent ion was substantially more detrimental than the divalent species. The addition of EDTA or STP to hard-water systems improved the redeposition by complexing hardness ions. Better whiteness retention was observed up to the point where excess sequestrant was present. The breaks in the recovery curves corresponded closely to sequestrant concentration levels that could have been predicted from sequestration values. Again, while the sequestrant provided a large measure of redeposition protection, CMC is clearly shown to be a necessary ingredient for antiredeposition in a detergent formulation, particularly with cotton fabric.

A further study with carbon black as the soiling medium suggests that NTA is superior to STP in this regard [15]. This conclusion is probably based on the superior sequestration ability of NTA.

Tokiwa and Imamura [37] have studied the deflocculation or suspension stability of TiO_2 and Fe_2O_3 in the presence of various electrolytes including the polyphosphates and NTA. In general, their results show that except for an organic dispersing agent, sodium tripolyphosphate is the best deflocculating agent among the materials tested, as listed in Table 7. This comparison was done with ferric oxide in solutions containing sodium alkylbenzenesulfonate, sodium sulfate, and the electrolyte in a ratio of 20:50:30. The total additive concentration was held at 0.2% by weight. Sodium tripolyphosphate (STP) and the organic dispersing agent were very close, with the STP being just slightly inferior. After standing for 24 hr STP was considerably better than the dispersing agent and markedly better than any of the other materials tested. However, in most detergent formulations the time for a given phenomenon to take place is generally short, about 5 to 20 min, so long-term (24 hr) differences are probably not pertinent beyond their ability to reflect short-time effects.

Several studies (e.g., Porter [33]) have shown that the detersive efficiency of STP cannot be accounted for strictly on the basis of sequestration. Furthermore, the implication is usually made that some other effect, sometimes spelled out as its dispersing action on pigments and/or soil aggregates, is operating which provides the efficiency. Additionally, the referenced study suggests that soil is removed as such, that is, particulate soil (e.g., clay) is not removed preferentially by a dispersing action but rather the complex soil aggregate of pigment, oil, grease, and so on, is removed as one.

TABLE 7

Deflocculation of Ferric Oxide by Various Electrolytes
in the Presence of Sodium Alkylbenzenesulfonate [37]

	Suspension efficiency[a] (%)	
Electrolyte	2 hr	24 hr
None	52.2	13.3
Organic dispersant	100	49.0
Trisodium phosphate	41.1	20.0
Sodium tripolyphosphate	94.5	70.0
Sodium nitrilotriacetate	63.4	13.3
Sodium sulfate	44.5	22.2
Sodium silicate[b]	86.5	34.4
Sodium borate	25.6	4.5
Sodium carbonate	20.0	3.3

[a] Relative to organic dispersant at 2 hr.

[b] $Na_2O \cdot 2.5SiO_3$

D.   Electrolytic Activity

Several factors come into consideration under this category.   The first
is the ability of inorganic salts, including sequestrants, to affect the critical micelle concentration of solutions such that the surface activity characteristics of surfactants are enhanced.   This is usually a severalfold positive
effect which allows much lower usage of active in detergent formulations.
At the low concentrations employed in most detergent applications the effects
of electrolytes on surface activity properties are easily shown.

Ginn et al. [38] studied the detergent builder (sequestrants and nonsequestrants) effect on the critical micelle concentration (CMC) of surface-
active agents.   A dye solubilization technique was chosen for determination

of CMC since this method was applicable to anionic and nonionic surfactants. In distilled water solutions the addition of inorganic salts to surfactants decreased the CMC and enhanced the solubilizing activity. The anionic surfactant (sodium dodecylbenzenesulfonate) was found to be more sensitive to the salt effects than the nonionic (polyoxyethylene ether) active studied. In hard-water systems it was found that materials which form soluble salts with calcium (NaCl, Na_2SO_4, etc.) enhanced solubilization up to about 300 ppm. However, the trend reversed beyond this hardness level. Using materials that either complex or precipitate calcium the solubilization increased up to the 300-ppm value and then remained essentially constant with increasing hardness levels. It was concluded that the demonstrated superiority of certain electrolytes such as sodium tripolyphosphate could not be accounted for strictly on the basis of CMC lowering, dye solubilization, or common ion effect, but that these phenomena were indeed important in the overall detergent effectiveness.

More recent work on this same topic concentrated on the effect of hard water on the solubilizing activity of linear alkylbenzenesulfonate [39]. In this work, the role of the sequestrants, STP, NTA, and EDTA, on the CMC lowering was carefully explored using a dye solubilization technique. Several LAS materials with alkyl chain lengths from C_{10} to C_{14} were used in this study. Sodium tetradecylbenzenesulfonate was used for studying the sequestering builders because of its greater sensitivity toward water-hardness effects. The effect of NTA and EDTA on the solubilization of dye by the sodium tetradecylbenzenesulfonate was straightforward in that an increase in the concentration of either sequestrant shifted the solubilization peak to a higher level in an orderly fashion. A similar result was obtained with STP except that instead of the sharp peak obtained with no sequestrant or with the aminopolycarboxylates a broadened peak was obtained with increasing STP concentration. A correlation between the concentration of the sequestering builder and water hardness at maximum solubilization revealed a linear relationship with both NTA and EDTA. However, in the STP case, as the concentration increased, the slope of the curve increased. It was concluded from these studies that the effect of STP, NTA, and EDTA on the solubilization of LAS is mainly due to water softening. Again, STP provided improved efficiency from some unspecified mechanism which could not be accounted for from sequestration alone.

Additionally, the presence of builders brings about somewhat lower surface tensions of solutions than would result from surfactants alone. One other consideration is the effect of builders in reducing interfacial tension between detergent solutions and oils. This is undoubtedly of some importance in the removal of oily soils by emulsification.

E. Compatibility with Other Formulation Ingredients and/or Additives

Sequestrants used in detergent formulations must be compatible with the other ingredients utilized to provide the desired cleaning efficiency. Therefore, when the possibility of an undesirable reaction can occur during either processing or use, it must be investigated to determine if a real problem can exist. If so, an alternate ingredient should be employed. These considerations are more pertinent to the minor ingredients such as CMC, dyes, optical brighteners, and the like, since the major components are usually rather unreactive compounds.

STP and NTA have been shown to be compatible with a wide range of the dyes and optical brighteners frequently incorporated in heavy-duty laundry detergents. Frequently, a sequestrant tends to stabilize a minor detergent ingredient or increase its effectiveness in solution, primarily through sequestration of hard-water ions or other heavy metal ions.

Perhaps the biggest problem in the compatibility area results from the widespread use of sodium hypochlorite bleach. This usage imposes the requirement of bleach compatibility on any potential sequestrant or builder. Therefore, a sequestrant should not have reducing properties or contain chemical linkages that are susceptible to oxidative attack under the conditions of use. Loss of building efficacy, as well as reduction in bleaching performance, would result if a bleach-reactive builder was used. In general, the commonly used inorganic builders such as the polyphosphates are compatible with bleach. Organic compounds may contain linkages that are subject to oxidation by hypochlorite, and should be investigated for their stability. Nitrogen-containing sequestrants, such as NTA or EDTA, are immediately suspect since the reactive site of aminocarboxylate compounds with hypochlorite ion is the nitrogen atom.

Recent studies have shown that NTA is attacked by sodium hypochlorite with the reactivity being governed by such factors as concentration of the NTA and NaOCl, temperature, and contact time [40]. Figure 18 shows that the loss of free available chlorine in distilled water solution ranges from virtually zero when STP is the sole builder to about 20% in the presence of 0.060% NTA for a 15-min reaction time. Since the normal machine wash cycle is usually 10 to 15 min, the 15-min value is used for discussion purposes. A concentration of 0.06% NTA would be equivalent to using a formulation containing 40% NTA at a 0.15% use level. These data show that chlorine retention is a function of NTA concentration with lesser amounts being lost in the more dilute NTA solutions. The NTA loss on a percentage basis was nearly the same as that shown for the available chlorine.

However, Fig. 19 shows that the presence of water hardness effectively inhibits the NTA-OCl$^-$ reaction. In fact, if the NTA is totally involved in the sequestration process, no reaction with OCl$^-$ is observed. This point occurs at 125-150 ppm hardness with 300 ppm NTA in the system.

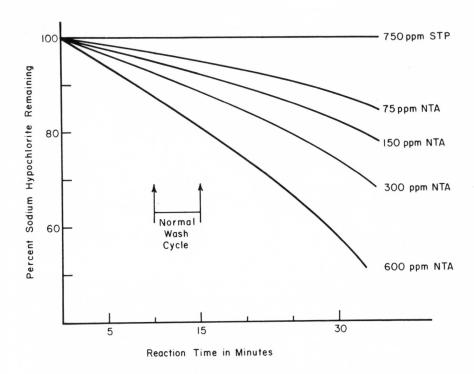

FIG. 18.   Retention of available chlorine in solutions containing NTA at 49°C.   (Initial NaOCl concentration 220 ppm.)

Carter et al. [41] show that the participation of nitrogen as a coordinating site is apparently of major importance in NTA complexes.   Therefore, since the reactive site of amines with hypochlorite is through the nitrogen, it is assumed that blocking this site by sequestration would reduce or stop the reaction.   This is consistent with the observed data.   Undoubtedly Pollard [15] was working in hard water when he found NTA was chemically stable in the presence of hot hypochlorite solutions at concentrations typical of laundry bleaching practice.   The beneficial effect of the presence of water hardness in preventing the NTA-NaOCl reaction probably contributed, also, to the efficiency obtained by Meloy [14] in his studies on the effect of NTA on fabric yellowing by hypochlorite bleach.

In general, the effectiveness of nitrogen-containing sequestrants may suffer severely in the presence of hypochlorite bleach, although the reaction in the NTA case is probably tolerable in soft water and definitely so in harder water.

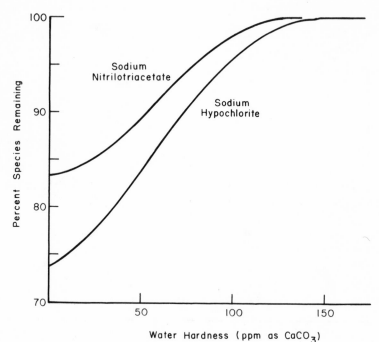

Water Hardness (ppm as CaCO₃)

FIG. 19. The retention of sodium nitrilotriacetate and sodium hypochlorite as a function of water hardness at 49°C. (Initial NTA concentration 300 ppm; initial NaOCl concentration 220 ppm; reaction time 30 min.

F. Environmental Acceptability

To be accepted by nature a product must not only be harmless to man,
it must not cause any rapid or widespread disruptions in the natural processes by which things are assimilated into the environment. This places a
new and uncommonly heavy burden upon research and development; not
only must a product function economically, it must be designed to be biolo-
gically and aesthetically compatible with the environment which will ultimately receive the material or its degradation products. Of first concern in
any product evaluation is its effect on man's health. This is usually established through toxicological studies. Second, it is highly desirable that the
product be biodegradable or at least amenable to conventional waste-treat-
ment processes since then it will not accumulate in the environment.

G. Consumer Safety: Toxicity

Any chemical substance incorporated in detergent formulations should
have a low order of toxicity and irritation to the skin and eyes. Each

chemical must be considered and tested in the specific formulation in which it is to be used. Potential problems could exist with highly alkaline ingredients, particularly when they are present at high levels in the formulation. In such cases, care should be taken to be sure that the product is labeled in compliance with the Federal Hazardous Substances Labeling Act.

H. Processability

Many nonfunctional properties of sequestrants should be considered when thinking in terms of formulating with the various candidates. Included among the more pertinent properties are bulk density, the ability to adsorb liquid actives, water-holding capacity, caking characteristics, and storage stability. Hydrolytic degration must also be considered, particularly with the polyphosphate sequestrants.

An excellent paper by Shen [42] on the properties of detergent phosphates and their effects on detergent processing has been published.

I. Cost-Performance

The last factor in the desirable characteristic list given previously is cost-performance. Due to the many different types of detergent products an economic evaluation of the many sequestrants available to the detergent formulator in each product would require a separate volume. However, this factor is certainly of major importance in choosing between several materials to perform the same or a similar function. Considerations such as those previously described, commercial availability, and competitive factors must be carefully scrutinized. In general, the choice of a sequestrant is a compromise between unit cost and unit performance and seldom does one material enjoy a dominant position like that sodium tripolyphosphate has in heavy-duty laundry products over an extended period of time.

VI. COMMERCIALLY AVAILABLE SEQUESTRANTS

A. Phosphates

At one time, the standard heavy-duty laundry detergent for household use contained between 30 and 50% sodium tripolyphosphate. The use of this material had gone from practically none 25 years ago to nearly 2.5 billion pounds in 1970. Additional amounts of sodium and potassium pyrophosphates, as well as longer-chain glossy sodium phosphates, comprised an integral part of other large-volume as well as specialty cleaning products. Since about 1971, there has been a decline in the use of phosphates in detergent products because of their suspected relation to the eutrophication problems in some surface waters in the United States and Canada (see Chapter 22, Part III). Phosphate-free detergents marketed today are based mainly on carbonate and/or sodium silicate.

Although the polyphosphates, in particular sodium tripolyphosphate, have been used as examples in much of the preceding discussion on the various builder prerequisites, a listing of the advantages and disadvantages in one place seems pertinent. On the positive side the polyphosphates

1. Are efficient sequestering agents for the common hardness ions,
2. Provide alkalinity and buffer capacity to permit operation in the proper pH range,
3. Are excellent deflocculating agents for clay as well as complex soils,
4. Contribute electrolyte activity such as lowering the critical micelle concentration,
5. Are compatible with other formulation ingredients and additives including sodium hypochlorite bleach,
6. Have not been the cause of any undue toxicity problems to the consumer,
7. Have been easily processable into various liquid and dry detergent products; sodium tripolyphosphate enjoys the unique and important advantage of tightly binding 6 moles of water per mole of STP and remaining in a free-flowing crisp state.

The disadvantage of polyphosphates most often mentioned is the tendency of this class of materials to revert, by a hydrolysis mechanism, to the monomer. Another shortcoming is the solubility characteristics of sodium tripolyphosphate, which precludes its use in some liquid products in favor of potassium pyrophosphate.

The fact that no competitive material has until recently come close to sodium tripolyphosphate effectiveness emphasizes the unequaled cost-performance provided by this product. Van Wazer [43] devotes a chapter in his two-volume work on phosphorus and its compounds to the subject of phosphates in detergents, and this reference is suggested as a source of considerable additional information on this topic.

B. Sodium Nitrilotriacetate

Although the phosphates have been the products of choice for many years, the appearance of trisodium nitrilotriacetate monohydrate (NTA) at substantially competitive pricing suggested this development would have an impact on the detergent market. NTA, however, is not being used in the United States because of the possibility that it is a carcinogen. NTA is being used in Canada. The relative merits of NTA in various detergent products are discussed in several publications [14, 15, 44]. These advantages include

1. Superior sequestration effectiveness as NTA sequesters more on a weight basis than STP in the detergent pH range
2. A greater contribution to alkalinity and buffer capacity as NTA is a somewhat weaker acid than STP

3. Critical micelle concentration-lowering capability and related electrolytic activity

4. Some deflocculation although to a lesser extent than STP and the other polyphosphates

5. Substantial reduction in the "ash content" of fabric after repeated washing and rinsing in hard water

6. Improved rinsability of detergent components from most substrates [15]

7. Stabilization of minor detergent ingredients that may be affected by trace metal contamination [15]

8. Excellent solubility to permit formulation into concentrated liquid products

9. No reversion in solution or dry storage, which makes NTA ideally suited for heavy-duty liquid products

One area in which NTA is inferior to STP lies in the processing of this material into a spray-dried detergent. NTA of commerce is the mono-hydrate, as that is the most stable form. It cannot hydrate during proces-sing and bind the water from liquid silicates, for example, into stable hydrates, as STP does. This means a product containing NTA will by ne-essity contain substantially less water and therefore require other fillers. Additionally, NTA-built products may require special packaging precautions to prevent caking on storage as NTA is hygroscopic under certain tempera-ture and humidity conditions.

The various investigators seem to be of the opinion that NTA and STP are similar in the properties pertinent to detergency, but that each has some unique properties which play lesser roles in the manufacture and use of products containing these ingredients. Detergency data from several sources indicate that maximum effectiveness is achieved when some combina-tion of the two sequestrants is employed. This result would seem to sub-stantiate that each material indeed has an attribute(s) which is unique and does participate in the detergency process.

C. Ethylenediaminetetraacetic Acid (EDTA)

Until recently, the least expensive and most versatile commercially available aminopolycarboxylate chelating agent was the sodium salt of EDTA. Although this compound has many of the characteristics desirable of a sequestering builder, cost-performance analysis shows a large gap between EDTA and the most expensive of the inorganic phosphate builders. Hence, the utility of EDTA has been limited to specialty products or to minor levels in a formulation. It is ordinarily added to provide a specific function, such as preserving solution clarity in liquid products by complex-ing heavy metals. The use of EDTA in improving the efficiency and utility of soap has been explored by Gard [45]. He concluded that soap is still a product with a wide range of utility and could compete with synthetic de-

tergents in some areas if used with EDTA. Undoubtedly, EDTA will retain
a minor position as a sequestrant in the detergent area.

VII. OTHER SEQUESTERING AGENTS OF IMPORTANCE

A. Aminopolycarboxylic Acids

Two members of this family have already been mentioned, NTA and
EDTA. A third, DTPA (diethylenetriaminepentaacetate) is also commercially available and of significance. Structures (3), (4) and (5) show the
increasing complexity of the structural configuration of this family of compounds. In general, these compounds are known for their stable alkaline
earth complexes and their very stable chelates with many transition and
heavy metal ions. In normal usage, where economics is always a big factor, a formulator usually looks first to the least expensive material. This
is normally the one with the lowest molecular weight, that is, NTA in this
family. However, if a stronger (more stable) complex is desired, or
necessary, EDTA or perhaps DTDA is utilized. The stability of a complex
comes from the number of binding sites available on the molecule. Chelate
bonds can form between both nitrogen and carboxyl groups. Therefore, by

$$N \underset{CH_2COOH}{\overset{CH_2COOH}{\underset{\displaystyle\Big\backslash}{\overset{\displaystyle\Big/}{\longleftarrow CH_2COOH}}}}$$

Nitrilotriacetic Acid (**3**)

$$\overset{HOOCCH_2}{\underset{HOOCCH_2}{\diagdown}} N - CH_2 - CH_2 - N \overset{CH_2COOH}{\underset{CH_2COOH}{\diagup}}$$

Ethylenediaminetetraacetic Acid (**4**)

$$\overset{HOOCCH_2}{\underset{HOOCCH_2}{\diagdown}} N - CH_2\ CH_2 \underset{\underset{CH_2COOH}{|}}{N} CH_2\ CH_2\ N \overset{CH_2COOH}{\underset{CH_2COOH}{\diagup}}$$

Diethylenetriaminepentaacetic Acid (**5**)

increasing the number of potential binding sites, the effectiveness of the sequestrant is improved. Structures (<u>3</u>), (<u>4</u>), and (<u>5</u>) show that NTA contains one nitrogen and three carboxyl groups, EDTA contains two nitrogens and four carboxyl groups, and DTPA contains three nitrogens and five carboxyl groups.

Another branch of the aminocarboxylate family is composed of those compounds wherein one or more of the substituent carboxyl groups are replaced with hydroxyethyl groups. Structures (<u>6</u>) and (<u>7</u>) are the two most well-known compounds of this type: DEG, dihydroxyethylglycine; and HEDTA, hydroxyethylethylenediaminetriacetic acid. The major advantage of these compounds is their superior ability to sequester iron(III), although their utility is not limited to this particular metal ion. DEG, however, has virtually no complexing ability for the common calcium(II) and magnesium-(II) hardness ions.

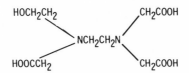

Dihydroxyethylglycine   (<u>6</u>)

HOCH₂CH₂ ... NCH₂CH₂N ... CH₂COOH / HOOCCH₂ ... CH₂COOH

Hydroxyethylethylenediaminetriacetic Acid   (<u>7</u>)

Substitution of all the carboxyl groups on NTA with hydroxyethyls would result in TEA, triethanolamine [N-(CH₂CH₂OH)₃], which is a very specific chelant for ferric iron in caustic media.

In most of the compounds that have been discussed in this section, the acids and the sodium salts are commercially available. The advantages of these chelating agents are reported to be the following [3]:

1. Thermal stability in aqueous solution.
2. Constant sequestering capacity over a wide pH range, in contrast to the behavior of the polyphosphates and the hydroxy acids.

3. The stabilities of the complexes are generally quite high, particularly
    with the transition and heavy metal ions.
4. The organic sequestering agents are potentially more compatible
    with organic systems.

Although these statements are true, in general, replacement of one sequestering agent with another is best done by experiment. For example, if
the second advantage stated above were taken as is, it would be assumed that
NTA is better than STP across the pH range. Inspection of Fig. 4, however,
shows that the sequestration curves cross and while NTA is superior above
pH 8 at 50°C, the converse is true in the pH 6-7 range. EDTA, on the other
hand, is more efficient than STP across the pH 6-12 range.

B. Hydroxycarboxylic Acids

Another family of importance as sequestering agents is comprised of the
naturally occurring hydroxy or hydroxycarboxylic acids. Structures (8)
through (11) are among the most commercially important members. None
of these compounds is as effective for the sequestration of hardness ions as
STP or EDTA at neutral or alkaline pH levels. However, there are certain

Citric Acid (8)   Tartaric Acid (9)

Gluconic Acid (10)   Saccharic Acid (11)

conditions wherein each of these materials offers unique performance. For instance, gluconate is an excellent sequestrant for calcium(II) and magnesium(II) in solutions having a pH higher than 12 or containing free sodium hydroxide. Citric acid is an excellent sequestrant for most divalent and trivalent metal ions other than the alkaline earths [46].

A good discussion of the mechanism of metal ion sequestration with hydroxy acids is given by Chaberek and Martell [3]. The utility of the hydroxycarboxylates is probably limited to specialty-detergent products as their sequestration functionality is not general.

C. Phosphorus-Based Sequestrants

The inorganic phosphates have been discussed in some depth. There are also organophosphorus compounds available which are efficient sequestrants and combine many of the desirable characteristics, such as deflocculation, of their inorganic cousins, along with the hydrolytic stability of organic sequestrants. One of these organophosphorus compounds, commercially available under the registered trademark DEQUEST, is the subject of a recent paper [47]. This product offers calcium sequestration superior to both STP and EDTA at room temperature and pH 10, as well as excellent heavy metal (iron and copper) sequestration. Detergency studies showed that this compound compared quite favorably with STP on a performance basis.

Another group of organophosphorus compounds that have been studied for use as detergent builders is comprised of the aminoalkylidenephosphonic acids [48]. The subject acids, which are reported as sequestrants with good hydrolytic stability, were compared as detergent builders to STP. Also included were NTA, nitriltris (methylene) triphosphonic acid, and hydroxyethylidenediphosphonic acid. A number of the compounds lumped under the general name of aminoalkylidenephosphonic acids were shown to possess many of the builder prerequisites, for example, sequestration, buffer capacity, and so on. The detergency results compared to STP were quite promising, being 85-95% as effective in hard water. However, all except n-monoacetyl-ADMP were shown to be quite reactive with hypochlorite. Losses of hypochlorite ion on the order of 40-95% were observed at 120°F in a 15-min period. Additionally, most of these materials are laboratory items at present. Nevertheless, the existence of such a family of compounds illustrates that many sequestrants are potentially available to replace those commonly used.

VIII. SEQUESTRANTS SELECTION

Armed with a knowledge of what chemical groups are desirable for good sequestration and a sound background in synthetic chemistry, the number of

sequestrants one could prepare is quite large. Literally hundreds of sequestrants have been prepared and have undergone at least preliminary
investigation as detergent builders, although none has achieved, as yet, the
versatility of the STP molecule. Hopefully, enough theoretical and practical
insight into this subject has been presented, along with a smattering of information on the commercially available materials, to guide the reader in
his selection of a sequestrant for detergent products.

Finally, data such as stability constants, sequestration ability, buffer
capacity, and the like should be used only as guidelines in selection of a
sequestrant for any given job. The final and definitive selection can only
be made on a cost-performance basis under the use conditions encountered
in actual practice.

REFERENCES

1. J. R. Van Wazer and D. A. Campanella, J. Amer. Chem. Soc., 72, 655 (1950).

2. L. G. Van Uitert and W. C. Fernelius, J. Amer. Chem. Soc., 76, 379 (1954).

3. S. Chaberek and A. E. Martell, Organic Sequestering Agents, Wiley, New York, 1959, p. 12.

4. R. R. Irani and C. F. Callis, J. Amer. Oil Chem. Soc., 39, No. 3, 156 (1962).

5. C. L. Mehltretter, B. H. Alexander, and C. E. Rist, Ind. Eng. Chem., 45, 2782 (1953).

6. C. L. Mehltretter and P. R. Watson, Soap Chem. Spec., 35, No. 8, 49 (1959).

7. J. R. Van Wazer and C. F. Callis, Chem. Rev., 58, 1011 (1958).

8. C. F. Callis, A. F. Kerst, and J. W. Lyons, in Coordination Chemistry, papers presented in honor of Professor J. C. Bailar, Jr. (Stanley Kirschner, ed.), Plenum Press, New York, 1969, p. 223.

9. R. R. Irani and C. F. Callis, J. Phys. Chem., 64, 1741 (1960).

10. J. I. Watters, E. D. Loughran, and S. M. Lambert, J. Amer. Chem. Soc., 78, 4855 (1956).

11. S. M. Lambert and J. I. Watters, J. Amer. Chem. Soc., 79, 4262 (1957).

12. R. R. Irani and C. F. Callis, J. Phys. Chem., 65, 934 (1961).

13. V. L. Hughes and A. E. Martell, J. Amer. Chem. Soc., 78, 1319 (1956).

14. G. K. Meloy, Paper presented before the Amer. Oil Chem. Soc. short course, "Advances in Soaps and Detergents, June 25-28, 1967," Pocono Manor, Penn.

15. R. P. Pollard, Hydrocarbon Process, 45, No. 11, 197 (1966).

16. W. W. Morgenthaler, unpublished work, 1969.

17. A. F. Kerst, unpublished work, 1968.

18. G. H. Nancollas, Quart. Rev. Chem. Soc. (London), 14, 402 (1960).

19. R. R. Irani and C. F. Callis, J. Phys. Chem., 64, 1398 (1960).

20. R. R. Irani and C. F. Callis, J. Phys. Chem., 65, 1463 (1961).

21. A. E. Martell and M. Calvin, Chemistry of the Metal Chelate Compounds, Prentice-Hall, Englewood Cliffs, N. J., 1952.

22. F. P. Dwyer and D. P. Mellor, eds., Chelating Agents and Metal Chelates, Academic Press, New York, 1964.

23. R. L. Smith, The Sequestration of Metals, Chapman and Hall, London, 1959.

24. Dow Chemical Co. Technical Bulletin, Chelating Agents, Midland, Mich., 1968.

25. E. H. Sargent Co. (Chicago), Sci. Methods, 10, No. 2, Sec. 1 (1958).

26. R. R. Irani, J. Chem. Eng. Data, 7, No. 4, 580 (1962).

27. L. G. Sillen and A. E. Martell, Stability Constants of Metal-Ion Complexes, Chem. Soc. Special Publ. No. 17, New York, 1964.

28. J. R. Van Wazer and M. E. Tuvell, J. Amer. Oil Chem. Soc., 35, 552 (1958).

29. P. T. Vitale, J. Ross, and A. M. Schwartz, Soap Chem. Spec., 32, No. 6, 41 (1956).

30. H. Arai, I. Maruta, and T. Kariyone, J. Amer. Oil Chem. Soc., 43, 315 (1966).

31. T. G. Jones and J. P. Parke, Int. Congr. Surface Activity, 3rd, 4, Sec. D/III No. 17, 178 (1960).

32. A. S. Porter, Int. Congr. Surface Activity, 4th, Sec. B/IV, Vol. 2, 593 (1964).

33. A. S. Porter, Int. Congr. Surface Activity, 4th, Sec. C/II, Vol. 3, 187 (1964).

34. F. Tokiwa and T. Imamura, J. Amer. Oil Chem. Soc., 47, No. 4, 117 (1970).

35. P. T. Vitale, J. Amer. Oil Chem. Soc., 31, No. 8, 341 (1954).

36. J. Ross, P. T. Vitale, and A. M. Schwartz, J. Amer. Oil Chem. Soc.,
     32, No. 4, 200 (1955).

37. F. Tokiwa and T. Imamura, J. Amer. Oil Chem. Soc., 46, No. 11,
     571 (1969).

38. M. E. Ginn, F. B. Kinney, and J. C. Harris, J. Amer. Oil Chem.
     Soc., 36, No. 8, 332 (1959).

39. H. Arai and K. Yoshizaki, J. Amer. Oil Chem. Soc., 46, No. 10,
     544 (1969).

40. W. W. Morgenthaler, in "Proceedings of the 57th Annual Meeting,
     Chemical Specialties Manufacturers Association, Inc.," New York,
     December 13-16, 1971, pp. 68-70.

41. R. P. Carter, M. M. Crutchfield, and R. R. Irani, Inorg. Chem.,
     6, 939 (1967).

42. C. Y. Shen, J. Amer. Oil Chem. Soc., 45, No. 7, 510 (1968).

43. J. R. Van Wazer, ed., Phosphorus and Its Compounds, Vol. II,
     Wiley-Interscience, New York, Chap. 27, 1961.

44. J. J. Singer, Jr., in "Proceedings of the 47th Mid-Year Meeting,
     Chemical Specialties Manufacturers Association, Inc.," New York,
     May 15, 1961, p. 152.

45. A. J. Gard, Soap Chem. Spec., 35, No. 3, 53 (1959).

46. T. A. Downey, Soap Chem. Spec., 42, No. 2, 52 (1966).

47. R. R. Irani and C. F. Callis, Soap Chem. Spec., 40, No. 4, 64 (1964).

48. R. W. Cummins, Deterg. Age, 5, No. 3, 22 (1968).

Chapter 12

EVALUATION OF THE RINSING PROCESS

Walter L. Marple[*]
Whirlpool Research and Engineering Center
Benton Harbor, Michigan

I. INTRODUCTION

    In the past 30 years many papers have been published on the washing
process but the rinsing process seems to have been seriously neglected.

---

[*] Now retired.

The rinsing process should be expected to effectively remove from the fabric certain specific materials: (a) water-soluble soils such as salts, sugars, etc; (b) loosely bound insoluble particulate matter such as sand, clays, carbon particles, etc; (c) fabric lint; and (d) detergents and soaps.

The rinse cycle should not be expected to effectively remove materials that remain strongly attached to the fibers and were not removed during the washing cycle. If the wash bath has failed in its major function to break the soil-fiber bonds, then the rinse bath cannot be expected to equal or exceed the effectiveness of the wash bath in removing soils.

The rinsing cycle, operating over a much shorter time interval than the wash cycle, should remove all or nearly all of the detergent materials remaining in the fabric from the wash bath. Since the commercial home laundry detergent is composed of several different chemicals, we should determine how effectively they are removed during the rinsing cycle.

The major components of the home laundry detergent are (a) surfactant (surface-active agent); (b) neutral salts, such as sodium sulfate and sodium chloride; and (c) inorganic builders, including sodium carbonate, polyphosphates, sodium hydroxide, and sodium silicates.

All of the components of the home laundry detergent must be effectively removed in the rinsing process. Although all are water soluble, several factors affect their removal efficiency. These factors are water temperature, fabric-water volume ratio, water hardness, rinsing time, degree of agitation, detergent concentration, soil concentration, and extraction speed.

TABLE 1

Detergent Compounds Removed by Rinsing

Component	In fabric after soaking (mg/g fabric)	In fabric after rinsing (mg/g fabric)	Percent removed by rinsing
Surfactant	38.8	10.60	70.1
Neutral salts	18.9	0.08	99.5
Builders	4.4	0.00	100.0

II. RINSING EXPERIMENT

In order to determine the ease of removal of the major detergent components, a controlled rinsing experiment was conducted.

Several Indian Head cotton swatches were soaked in a concentrated home laundry detergent solution for several hours, extracted, and dried. Four of the dried swatches were placed in an 8-lb load of cottons and rinsed in a top-loading automatic using 100° F tap water. The amount of each component of the household detergent removed by rinsing is shown in Table 1.

Since the surfactant is the most difficult material to remove from the fabric, a test method has been designed based on measuring the total amount of surfactant removed, during rinsing, from fabrics previously soaked in a 1% surfactant solution.

III. RINSING EFFICIENCY TEST

A. Test Procedure: Preparing the Rinsing Test Swatches

Indian Head cotton stuffers, 24 in. x 24 in. are washed in an automatic washer without soap or detergent for 10 min and rinsed for 2 min in 140° F ($\pm 5^{\circ}$) soft water. After extraction the swatches are dried in a dryer.

Several stuffers are placed in a soaking tank containing 1.0% linear alkylbenzenesulfonate (LAS) for 2 hr at ambient temperature. Allow 1 liter of the LAS solution for each swatch. A total of four swatches is sufficient for one rinsing efficiency test. At the end of the soaking period allow each swatch to drain for 10 min and tumble dry.

B. Loading Procedure: Automatic Washer (Top Loader) or Combination Washer-Dryer (Front Loader)

Divide an 8-lb load of Indian Head stuffers into four sections and add a rinsing stuffer to each section. Place the load in the washer and set the dial for the rinse cycle. Advance the timer permitting the machine to complete a normal rinse cycle for the automatic washer or rinse cycles for the combination washer-dryer. After extraction air or tumble dry the rinsing stuffers.

C. Preparing the Test Swatches for Titration

Cut a 9 in. x 9 in. swatch from each 24 in. x 24 in. stuffer. Place each swatch into a tared weighing bottle and dry in a laboratory oven for 4 hr at 105° C.

Place the weighing bottles containing the swatches in a desiccator and cool to room temperature. After cooling weigh to 0.1 mg to obtain the gross weight.

Cut each swatch in small pieces approximately 1/4 in. x 1/4 in. and place in a 500-ml Soxhlet extraction apparatus. Add 300 ml distilled or deionized water and reflux for a minimum of six extractions. Filter the solution when still hot using a Büchner funnel into a 400-ml beaker.

D. Titration Solutions

1. Methylene Blue Indicator Solution

Dissolve 0.100 g methylene blue solution in 100 ml distilled water. Transfer 30 ml of this solution to a 1-liter volumetric flask. Add 500 ml of distilled water, 6.8 ml of concentrated sulfuric acid, and 50.0 g of sodium biphosphate. Dilute to 1 liter and mix thoroughly.

2. CTAB Solution

Weigh 1.8 ± 0.001 g cetyltrimethylammonium bromide, transfer to a 1-liter volumetric flask, and add distilled water to make 1 liter.

a. Titration of extract. Pipet a 50-ml aliquot into a 100-ml graduated cylinder, add 25 ml of methylene blue indicator solution and 15 ml of chloroform. Titrate with the CTAB solution to the correct end point, shaking vigorously after each addition. The correct end point is taken at the point where the color of the two layers is equal when viewed by reflected light.

b. Titration of the CTAB solution. The CTAB solution is titrated with a solution containing a known amount of sodium alkylarylsulfonate in the same manner as the extract titration.

c. Control. Two of the unrinsed swatches serve as a control. They are extracted in the same manner and their extracts analyzed for milligrams of sodium alkylarylsulfonate per gram of fiber.

d. Calculations. The method of calculating the rinsing efficiency is outlined in Table 2.

E. Repeated Tests

In order to check the reproducibility of the method, five separate rinses were made in 100°F tap water (8 grains/gal) using four rinsing test swatches per run. The results are listed in Table 3.

TABLE 2

Calculations[a]

---

1. $\dfrac{\text{mg LAS}}{\text{ml CTAB titrated}}$ = mg LAS/ml CTAB

2. mg LAS/g fabric = $\dfrac{(\text{ml CTAB})(\text{mg LAS/ml CTAB})(6)}{\text{weight of fabric sample}}$

3. % rinsing efficiency = $\dfrac{A - B}{A}$ x 100

where A = mg LAS/g fabric (control)
B = mg LAS/g fabric (rinsed)

---

[a]LAS = linear alkylbenzenesulfonate; CTAB = cetyltrimethylammonium bromide.

TABLE 3

Surfactant Removed $100°$F Rinse

Run no.	Percent AAS removed
1	73.4
2	74.8
3	77.1
4	74.5
5	74.3
Average	74.8

F. Effect of Rinse Temperatures

Repeated runs were also made using 60 and $140°$F tap water. The results are listed in Table 4.

TABLE 4

Effect of Temperature on Rinsing

Rinse temperature ($^{\circ}$F)	Percent surfactant removed
60	62.8
100	74.8
140	82.2

IV.   SUDSING IN THE RINSE CYCLE

Some people become alarmed when they see sudsing in the rinse cycle. One should expect to see some sudsing in the rinse cycle especially with high-sudsing detergents.   The absence of suds during the rinse indicates excessive water usage.   If you continue to rinse until you no longer get any suds, then you have been wasting water.

Under abnormal conditions such as the failure of the machine to extract properly or failure to add sufficient water to the rinse bath, a buildup of detergent in the fabric is unlikely.

V.   SURFACTANT BUILDUP

An 8-lb load of clean cotton stuffers was washed repeatedly for 40 successive washings using the normal recommended amount of detergent. Several of the stuffers were then analyzed to determine the quantity of surfactant retained by the fabric.   The cottons retained 0.5 mg surfactant per gram of fabric.   This represents less than 2 g for the entire load.   About 4000 g of detergent was used for the 40 washings which represent about 800 g of surfactant.   The fabric retained less than 2 g surfactant of the 800 g available.

VI.   CONCLUSION

The rinsing cycle of the home washing machine is probably more efficient than previously believed.   Some of the washing problems that have been attributed to poor rinsing must be due to other factors that occur prior to the rinsing cycle.

Since the original study was made several years ago, a more updated procedure has been developed by the Association of Home Appliance Manufacturers based on the original procedure previously described (Household Washer Performance Evaluation Procedure, No. HLW1, Association of Home Appliance Manufacturers, Chicago, 1970).

The AHAM procedure in complete detail is listed in the Appendix. AHAM has permitted us to include the published procedure in this chapter on rinsing.

APPENDIX:
EVALUATING THE RINSING EFFECTIVENESS OF WASHERS

A. Equipment

1. Analytical balance, 1-mg graduations.
2. Gram balance, trip-type double or triple beam, 0.1-g graduations.
3. Pound scale, 0.02-lb graduations.
4. Beakers, 30 ml.
5. Beckman Model G pH meter with microelectrodes or equivalent.
6. Separatory funnels, 50 ml.
7. Volumetric flasks, 50, 1000, and 2000 ml.
8. One-centimeter closed fused silica or quartz absorption cell or test tube specified for Spectronic 20 supplied with instrument.
9. Bausch and Lomb Spectronic 20 with blue-sensitive phototube type 4409 (range 340-625 mμ). Cary recording spectrophotometer, Beckman Model DU spectrophotometer, or other equivalent.
10. Pipets, 2, 4, and 10 ml.
11. Thermometers (0-240°F range).
12. Weighing bottles, approximately 40 x 120 mm.
13. Soxhlet extraction apparatus (500-ml flat-bottomed flask, 50-mm ID extraction tube).
14. Dessicator.
15. Graduates, 10 and 25 ml.
16. Sample outline (3 in. x 3 in.), rubber stamp, ink pad, and Bates numbering ink.
17. Apparatus for checking water hardness.

B. Material

1. Appropriate AHAM standard mixed cotton test load, except on each replication substitute five new Curity diapers manufactured by the Textile Division, Kendall Company, 21 in. x 40 in. gauze diapers flat (not stretch type, prefolded, or with center panel) for one shirt and one T-shirt. Diapers should be pretreated per Sec. C. 2.
2. Quartered AHAM standard detergent.
3. Purified sodium lauryl sulfate (Sipon WD crystals manufactured by American Alcolac Corporation or equivalent is satisfactory).
4. Distilled water.
5. Hydrochloric acid, 0.1 N.
6. Methylene blue solution (Eastman P 573 or equivalent). (Prepare a solution containing 0.085 g/liter using distilled water.)

7.   Chloroform (analytical reagent grade).

8.   Liquid chlorine bleach, 5.25% sodium hypochlorite.

C. Procedure

(Caution: Validity of test depends on utmost cleanliness throughout test.)

1.   Preparation of calibration curve for sodium lauryl sulfate (SLS) for concentration of 20 ppm or less.

a.   Place approximately 2 g of SLS, item B, 3 (as received), in a weighing bottle.

b.   Place the bottle with the SLS in an oven for 2 hr at approximately 220° F with the cover removed. Replace cover and remove from oven.

c.   Allow to cool to room temperature in dessicator: weigh and record weight.

d.   Replace in oven with cover removed for 1 hr, replace cover, place in dessicator, cool to room temperature, and weigh.

e.   If this weight is the same as that found in step c, all moisture has been removed. If there is a loss of weight, repeat step d until the constant is reached.

f.   Weigh approximately 1.0 g of dried SLS and dissolve in distilled water, transfer to a 1000-ml volumetric flask with thorough rinsing, fill to mark with distilled water, and mix thoroughly. This is solution No. 1.

g.   Pipet 10 ml of solution No. 1 into a clean 1000-ml volumetric flask, fill to the mark with distilled water, and mix thoroughly. This is solution No. 2.

The concentration of SLS in solution No. 2 = dry weight of SLS (step e) divided by 100 = milligrams of SLS per millimeter of solution. Solution No. 2 will contain 0.01 mg/ml.

h.   Pipet duplicate samples of 0, 2, 4, 6, 8, 12, and 16 ml of solution No. 2 into clean 30-ml beakers and add 10 ml of distilled water to each beaker.

i.   Adjust the pH of each sample to 2.6 $\pm$ 0.2 by adding 0.1 N HCl by means of a glass stirring rod, dipping the rod in the acid then into the solution. Rinse the rod with distilled water between dips to avoid contamination. Adding acid with a dropper is permissible but solution must be stirred. These are the adjusted samples.

j.   Treat each of these adjusted samples as follows:

Add 10 ml chloroform to a 50- to 120-ml separatory funnel.

Caution: Handle chloroform with care in a well-ventilated area since effects can be cumulative.

Transfer an adjusted sample to the separatory funnel.
Rinse the beaker thoroughly with successive minimum portions of distilled water.

Add 10 ml of methylene blue solution as per Sec. B, 6 to
the separatory funnel.

Shake funnel vigorously and allow the chloroform to
separate.

Draw off the lower chloroform layer into a 50-ml volumetric flask.

Repeat this extraction twice more using 10-ml portions
of chloroform all combined with the first extraction in the
50-ml volumetric flask. Note: If during the extractions the
methylene blue in the aqueous layer is depleted, then additional blue must be added. If a fourth chloroform extraction
should become necessary and it is still not colorless, then a
dilution of the original sample is necessary.

Fill to the mark (50 ml) on the volumetric flask with
chloroform and mix thoroughly.

Transfer a portion of the blue chloroform solution from
volumetric flask to a closed fused silica or quartz absorption
cell or test tube specified for Spectronic 20 and determine
its absorbance at 650 mμ (even though Spectronic instrument
range is 340-625 mμ).

Caution: Test calls are carefully selected for uniformity
of absorbance using the recommended instrument procedure.
Be certain cells are devoid of fingermarks before insertion
into cell holder of spectrophotometer.

Before reading the absorbance (optical density) the instrument must be standardized. For a spectrophotometer with an
adjustable slit, use the medium slit.

For Spectronic instrument:

Note: When using the Spectronic 20 instrument, it may
be advantageous to use the transmission scale rather than
absorbance scale to obtain calibration curve since the transmission scale is symmetrical from 100 to 0% and, therefore,
more easily read in the low absorbance region (high transmission end). Plot the calibration curve with SLS content of
the known samples as a function of transmission on semilog
graph paper.

(1) Turn on instrument for at least 15 min prior to use.

(2) No cell in sample holder and cover closed. Set instrument at "infinity" on the absorbance scale.

(3) Place the blank calibration standard (0 ml solution
from Sec. C, 1, h after adjusting pH and preparing blue
chloroform extract as in C, 1, i and C, 1, j in the sample
holder and adjust the instrument to read "0" absorbance.

(Solutions should be stored immediately in dark place until ready for use. Use within 8 hr of preparation.)

(4) Recheck standards periodically and readjust instrument at infinity and at 0 using a freshly prepared 0 SLS calibration standard to check for drifting.

k. The sodium lauryl sulfate content of each of the samples is calculated by multiplying the number of milliliters in each sample (0, 2, 4, 6, 8, 12, and 16 ml) by the milligrams of SLS per milliliter of solution No. 2 as determined in C, 1, g.

l. Plot a calibration curve with SLS content of the known samples as a function of absorbance or optical density.

2. Test procedure.

a. Remove any finishing agents in the clothes and diapers by washing and rinsing in the machine(s) to be tested three successive times without detergent. Wash water is to be hot and wash time is to be a minimum of 10 min. The third wash period shall include 1/2 oz of liquid bleach per gallon of wash water.

b. Tumble dry and fold diapers once in middle of long axis. Stack carefully to retain flatness.

c. Using rubber stamp, item A, 16 , mark outline of the four test swatches on each of the five diapers. Label two swatches WCS (wash concentration swatches) and two swatches RCS (rinse concentration swatches).

d. Cut and remove WCS swatches.

Note: To avoid possible detergent carryover from clothes load, it is suggested that new items be used for each test run. For replications, if items are to be used which have been used in a previous run, step C, 2, a should be followed to assure minimizing the amount of residual detergent. Washer should be similarly freed of detergent carryover.

e. Preheat the test machine by filling to medium water level with 140° F water in the "rinse fill" portion of the cycle. Allow the machine to complete the rinse and spin portions of the cycle.

f. Load machine with clothes and diapers, fill and add detergent. Note that WCS swatches are not loaded into washer at this time.

g. Wash only 10 min (no sprays, etc.). Stop machine and dip the 10 WCS swatches in the wash water for 15 ± 2 sec, making sure that they are separated and completely submerged. Hang the WCS swatches with clips and allow to drip dry.

h. Restart machine and continue cycle in regular manner until completed.

i. Hang the 10 WCS swatches previously drip dried in an oven at approximately 220°F for 2 hr; then transfer them to a pre-weighed weighing bottle. Cover bottle and remove from oven.

j. Allow to cool to room temperature in desiccator; weigh and record weight.

k. Replace bottle with swatches in oven with cover removed for 1 hr. Replace cover, remove from oven, cool to room temperature in desiccator, and weigh.

l. If this weight is the same as that found in Step b above, all moisture has been removed. If there is a loss of weight, repeat step j above until constant weight of swatches is reached (weight of dried swatches is about 15-20 g). Record actual fabric weight.

m. At the completion of step h remove diapers from the load and cut the two rinse concentration swatches (RCS) from each of the five diapers.

n. Proceed as in steps i through k.

Caution: It is believed that WCS and RCS diaper samples deteriorate with time. A 24-hr limit on storage of samples is recommended. Experiments are being conducted to determine if this time limit can be extended.

o. Extract each set of 10 swatches (wash concentration and rinse concentration) in separate Soxhlet extractors with distilled water for a minimum of six extractions, being certain that the swatches are covered with water for each of the six extractions, or allow to extract overnight. The flasks and thimble must be well insulated to obtain solvent turnover. There should always be a quantity of distilled water in the bottom of the boiling flask during refluxing.

Note: Paper extraction thimbles are not necessary because of the number of swatches employed.

p. Cool the contents of the boiling flask of the extractor containing the wash concentration swatches to room temperature and transfer with rinsing to a 2000-ml flask and fill to mark with distilled water.

q. Cool the contents of the boiling flask of the extractor containing the rinse concentration swatches to room temperature and transfer with rinsing to a 1000-ml volumetric flask and fill to mark with distilled water.

r. Take three 10-ml aliquots from each of the solutions p and q and proceed to adjust pH as in C, 1, i.

s. Prepare chloroform extract from each and determine absorbance or optical density of each as in C, 1, j.

t. With measured optical density values, determine SLS content of each from calibration curve.

u. Repeat steps a through s two more times.

Note: This procedure is based on the assumption that
the efficiency of the rinsing sequence is related to the amount
of organic surfactant remaining in the fabric load after completion of the cycle as related to the amount of surfactant remaining in load at end of wash phase of cycle. The analytical
method used limits the detergent selection to those containing
anionic actives, and more specifically to those containing
SLS and/or alkali sulfates.

D.   Data Analysis

1.   Record the data. A recommended form for recording the data is
     shown in Table A-1.
2.   Calculate the percent SLS removed for each aliquot in the test
     from the following formula:

Percent SLS removed =

$$\frac{[(a/b) - (c/d)]}{[a/b]} \times 100$$

where   a = mg LAS (WCS) x 2000
        b = mg fabric (WCS) x aliquot size
        c = mg LAS (RCS) x 1000
        d = mg fabric (RCS) x aliquot size

3.   Calculate the grand average percent SLS removed.
4.   Calculate the standard deviation of percent LAS removed.
5.   Calculate the spread of percent SLS removed.
6.   Report the grand average and spread for percent SLS removed.

TABLE A-1

Data Forms and Calculations (Rinsing Effectiveness)

SUMMARY

Step No.	Description	Run 1		Run 2		Run 3	
		SLS wash	SLS rinse	SLS wash	SLS rinse	SLS wash	SLS rinse
1	Replication 1						
2	Replication 2						
3	Replication 3						
4	Total						
5	Step 4/3						
6	Multiplier	2000	1000	2000	1000	2000	1000
7	Step 5 x Step 6						
8	Fabric Weight						
9	Aliquot Size						
10	Step 8 x Step 9						
11	Step 7 ÷ Step 10	①	②	①	②	①	②
12	① - ②						
13	Step 12 ÷ ①						
14	P = Step 13 x 100	e		f		g	
15	Step 14 x Step 14	h		j		k	

G = e + f + g = _____

SS = h + j + k = _____

TABLE A-1 (continued)

ANALYSIS

Step No.	Symbol or Name	Description	Calculate	Result
1	G	Grand Total	Copy From Summary	
2	$\overline{\overline{X}}$	Grand Average	Step 1/r	
3	CT	Correction Term	(Step 1)^2/n	
4	SS	Raw Sum of Squares	Copy From Summary	
5	VGA	Variance of Grand Average	[Step 3 – (Step 1)^2]/r – 1	
6	$\overline{\overline{SX}}$	Standard Deviation of Grand Average	$\sqrt{\text{Step 4}}$	
7	σ	Standard Deviation	$\sqrt{\dfrac{\text{Step 4} - \text{Step 3}}{2}}$	

r = number of runs in the test

REPORT

Average SLS Removed % = $\overline{\overline{X}}$ = _____

Spread = $\overline{\overline{X}} \pm 3\sigma$ = _____ to _____

Chapter 13

BLEACHING AND STAIN REMOVAL

Charles P. McClain
Purex Corporation
Applications Research, Grocery Products
Carson, California

I.   INTRODUCTION

All of us in the industries related to cleaning have as our prime objective raising the standards of the homemaker to obtain the cleanest, whitest, brightest possible results, no matter what the dirty substrate may be, with a minimum amount of wear and labor. Bleaching is defined as the process of making white or more white; therefore, bleaching compounds have a role to play in achieving these goals.

There are two major classes of bleaching agents, oxidizing and reducing. The most commonly used bleaches are oxidizing and most of our discussions center around this type of bleach. Liquid sodium hypochlorite is a typical oxidizing bleach and undoubtedly the most common bleach used in household cleaning today.

II.   BLEACHING AND STAIN-REMOVING COMPOUNDS

In the light of the long history and widespread use of liquid sodium hypochlorite bleach as a laundry aid, it is interesting to note that not until 20 years ago could we have discussed many bleaches other than sodium hypochlorite. Liquid bleach, sodium hypochlorite, was the only household bleach and it has remained virtually unchanged over the years with only minor improvements in quality noted which are the result of better manufacturing techniques [1, 2].

There has been, during the last 20 years, a large amount of research data generated on bleaching and stain removal. While the preponderance of data will probably never be published and the majority of bleaching agents never reach the marketplace, we attempt herein to discuss some of the bleaches, both experimental and commercial, that have been and are now being studied. We also discuss methods used for screening, studying, and evaluating these compounds.

A.   Inorganic Chlorine Bleaches

1.   Sodium Hypochlorite

As just mentioned, the most common and widely used bleach is sodium hypochlorite [3]. It is not our intention to go into a lengthy discussion of the discovery, history, and development of sodium hypochlorite as this information can usually be obtained from any general inorganic chemistry textbook. Suffice it to say that liquid sodium hypochlorite is generally believed to have been discovered by Berthollet around 1785.

The commercial production of sodium hypochlorite is a simple, clear-cut reaction produced by reacting chlorine and aqueous sodium hydroxide. The overall main reaction proceeds as follows:

$$2NaOH + Cl_2 \rightarrow NaOCl + NaCl + H_2O \tag{1}$$

One of the tricks in manufacturing good bleach lies in the purity, that is, lack of trace metals, of the raw materials. It is important to obtain chlorine, caustic, and water relatively free of trace metals such as copper, cobalt, and nickel. These metals catalyze the decomposition of sodium hypochlorite [4] with the formation of salt and the evolution of oxygen [5]:

$$2NaOCl \rightarrow 2NaCl + O_2 \uparrow \tag{2}$$

This reaction will, of course, shorten the shelf life of the liquid bleach product.

Because hard water is generally used in the bleach-making process, a sufficient quantity of calcium carbonate and magnesium hydroxide is formed to carry down trace metals. These precipitates also function as very effective clarifying agents [1] during the final settling period of the liquid bleach product.

Although, as stated previously, bleach making is a simple operation, there are a number of pitfalls that require special attention during processing. Perhaps the most serious of these is the danger of overchlorination. This condition occurs when all the caustic has reacted with the chlorine. The further addition of chlorine causes a drop in pH so that an accelerated conversion of sodium hypochlorite to sodium chloride and sodium chlorate [6] exists. If this does occur, a bleach batch can easily be lost in a matter of minutes.

$$3NaOCl \xrightarrow{\text{pH below } 9.5} NaClO_3 + 2NaCl \tag{3}$$

Overheating (i.e., above $120°F$) is also to be avoided since there is a tendency to accelerate the decomposition of hypochlorite in a manner similar to the previous equation.

Liquid sodium hypochlorite as purchased in the grocery store ranges in guaranteed strength from 5.25 to 6.0% NaOCl by weight, is light straw in color, and has a slight chlorine odor. The pH of the bleach "as is" will range from 11.0 to 12.5, depending on the brand.

While liquid sodium hypochlorite is relatively stable under ordinary room-temperature conditions, it will lose available chlorine on prolonged storage and especially at elevated temperatures [7]. It is necessary, therefore, to manufacture the product at a higher level of sodium hypochlorite than is guaranteed to ensure that when the product reaches the consumer it is at least as its label-stated strength. The rate of available chlorine loss depends on the temperature at which the product is stored. High temperature, as already discussed, speeds up the decomposition of liquid bleach (see Fig. 1).

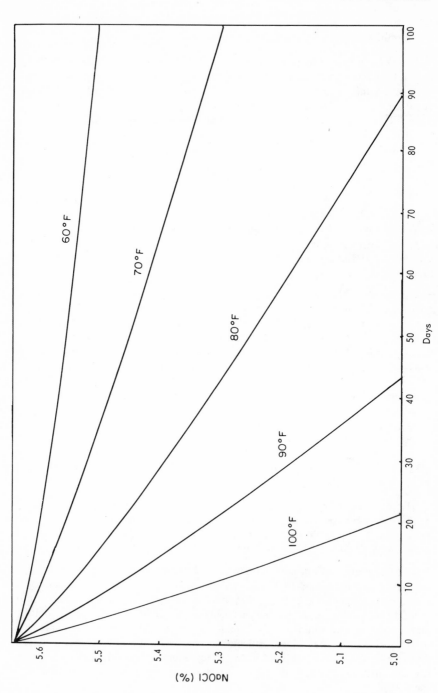

FIG. 1. Stability of 5.25% sodium hypochlorite solution.

Liquid sodium hypochlorite has some obvious disadvantages such as weight of the container, lack of safety on silk and wool, and, of course, accidental spillage usually causes immediate irreparable damage to cottons. Our studies indicate, however, that on the basis of cost and performance, liquid sodium hypochlorite is the cheapest, most effective bleaching agent available today.

2. Calcium Hypochlorite

The first chlorine dry bleach to enjoy national distribution was based on calcium hypochlorite, $Ca(OCl)_2$. This bleaching agent was also referred to as CCH (commercial calcium hypochlorite) or H.T.H. (high-test hypochlorite). Calcium hypochlorite generally has an available chlorine of 70 to 75% [8, 9] and may be prepared commercially by the (a) Mathieson Process, (b) Imperial Chemical Industries, or (c) Columbia (Columbia Alkali Division of PPG Industries).

Although calcium hypochlorite is an excellent bleach and generally considered to be equal to liquid sodium hypochlorite in its ability to remove stains, it has several undesirable characteristics. If calcium hypochlorite is not properly dissolved before coming in contact with cotton fabric, pinholing can occur. The term pinholing is a very accurate description of what can happen if small particles of the bleach fall on cotton, and depending on their degree of dissolution, may produce immediate holes or weaken the fabric to a degree that subsequent washings produce holes about the size of a pinhead. Another disadvantage of the compound is that it adds undesirable calcium ions to the wash water. The calcium ions can substantially increase the water hardness and thereby decrease the cleaning ability or efficiency of the particular detergent or soap product [10] being used.

Calcium hypochlorite is quite hygroscopic in nature, which presents a considerable problem in preparing a dry, stable product. Some success was achieved in this regard by the addition of calcium oxide to the formula for the sole purpose of absorbing excess moisture. Although calcium oxide does help, it is seriously doubted that a calcium hypochlorite dry bleach could be marketed in the common "newsboard" container used in industry today.

3. Chlorinated Trisodium Phosphate

Chlorinated trisodium phosphate has the approximate composition of $(Na_3PO_4 \cdot 12H_2O)5NaOCl$. The first reference we find regarding the commercial manufacture of this product was patented in 1925 [11]. The product of commerce is a white crystalline powder containing between 3.2 and 3.7% available chlorine with the optimum level 3.5%. This material is relatively stable if stored at room temperature in a moisture-free environment. A great deal of research time and money have been spent in an effort to develop a product of commerce [12] as well as formulations that are stable under warm, humid conditions.

In examining chlorinated TSP, it becomes obvious that because of the low available chlorine level, as compared to calcium or lithium hypochlorite, it cannot be built with water conditioners or diluted with fillers to develop a dry household laundry bleach. The main uses of chlorinated TSP as a bleaching agent then would be in the areas of household scouring or abrasive cleansers and in the formulation of automatic dishwashing detergents. It can be seen from the composition that the trisodium phosphate portion of the molecule would be a valuable addition to the bleaching agent for such cleaning jobs as a grease emulsification and water softening.

4. Lithium Hypochlorite

Lithium hypochlorite (LiOCl) is a white granular material with an available chlorine of 41.5% [13]. The granular nature of lithium hypochlorite lends ease to its ability to be dry mixed with a spray-dried base into a finished dry bleach formulation.

Although lithium hypochlorite is an excellent bleach and generally considered the equal of liquid sodium hypochlorite in its ability to remove stains [14], it has several limiting disadvantages. The price on an available chlorine basis is high compared to sodium or calcium hypochlorite. Lithium hypochlorite, as is the case with calcium hypochlorite, can produce pinholing of cotton fabrics. Lithium hypochlorite is extremely hygroscopic and unstable when formulated with the usual dry bleach builders and fillers.

B. Organic Chlorine Bleaches

During the last 15 years considerable research effort has been devoted, by both raw material suppliers and finished goods producers, to the development of dry organic chlorine bleaching compounds. We list the majority of these compounds for informational purposes; however, we concentrate more on the commercially successful and available small family of related cyclic N-chloroimides, the chlorinated isocyanurates. The bleaching agents listed include both compounds that are experimental and those that have been commercially available.

1. Chloramine T (sodium N-chloro-p-toluenesulfonamide), 25% available (Av) Cl_2
2. Chloramine B (sodium N-chlorobenzenesulfonamide), 29% Av Cl_2
3. Dichloramine T (N,N-dichloro-p-toluenesulfonamide), 59% Av Cl_2
4. Dichloramine B (N,N-dichlorobenzenesulfonamide), 62% Av Cl_2
5. Trichloromelamine (N,N',N''-trichloro-2,4,6-triamine-1,3,5-triazine), 91.6% Av Cl_2

6. Halane (1,3-dichloro-5,5-dimethylhyantoin), 71% Av Cl_2 ; BASF Wyandotte Corporation

7. Halazone (N,N-dichloro-p-carboxybenzenesulfonamide), 56% Av Cl_2

8. Metazone (N,N-dichloro-m-carboxybenzenesulfonamide), 56% Av Cl_2

9. DAC 595 (dichloroglycoluril), 67% Av Cl_2; Diamond Alkali Corporation

10. DAC 559 (tetrachloroglycoluril), 101% Av Cl_2; Diamond Alkali Corporation

11. JAT 1824 (ethylene glycol tetrachlorocarbamate), 99% Av Cl_2 ; Columbia Southern Chemical Company

12. Dow ET 202 (N,N,N',N'-tetrachlorodisulfaminotoluene), 73% Av Cl_2; Dow Chemical Company

1. Chlorinated Isocyanurates

The chlorinated isocyanurates have found acceptance in household bleaches, machine dishwashing detergents, and scouring powders [15, 16] because of a combination of desirable characteristics. They are readily soluble and give bleaching action generally comparable to liquid sodium hypochlorite. It is the latter two factors that were the primary reasons for the chlorinated isocyanurates' replacement of Halane in household products. The chlorinated isocyanurates also generally cause considerably less fabric damage than the inorganic chlorine bleaches if accidentally placed directly on fabric [17].

The chlorinated isocyanurates are made from cyanuric acid. The cyclic trimer of cyanic acid is produced by decomposing urea at high temperature [18]:

$$3H_2NCONH_2 \xrightarrow{250\text{-}300^\circ C} 3NH_3 + (HOCN)_3 \qquad (4)$$

Urea   Cyanuric acid

Cyanuric acid usually is found in the keto form, called isocyanuric acid, rather than the enol form.

Isocyanuric Acid   Cyanuric Acid   Trisodium Cyanurate

(5)

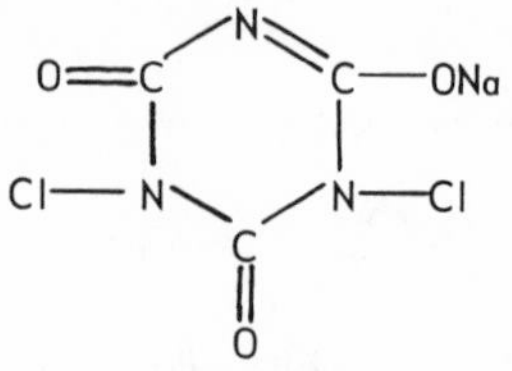

(1) 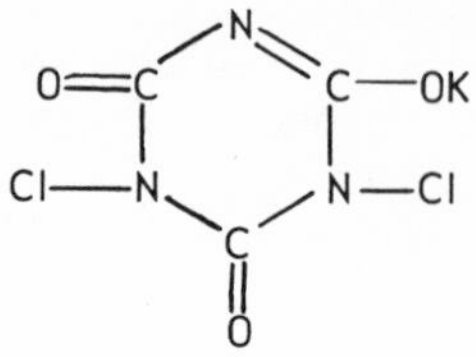　　　　　　　　　　　　　　　　　　　　(2)

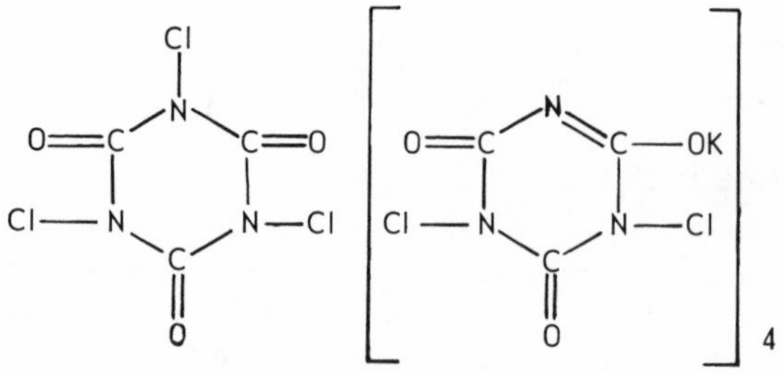

(3)

To produce trichloroisocyanuric acid trisodium cyanurate is treated with chlorine. Dichloroisocyanuric acid can be produced by the chlorination of disodium cyanurate.

To obtain the sodium (1) and potassium (2) dichloroisocyanurates the acid is neutralized with either sodium or potassium hydroxide and the salt is recovered by crystallization [19, 20].

The pentaisocyanurate (3) manufactured by Monsanto and sold as ACL-66 is described as a unique compound and not a physical mixture of trichloro-isocyanuric acid and potassium dichloroisocyanurate [21].

C. Oxygen Bleaches

Oxygen bleaches have some specific advantages over their chlorine counterparts. They can be used without seriously diminishing the effective-ness of enzyme products; they are generally safe on all fibers, fabrics, and finishes; there is no yellowing of chlorine-retentive fabrics; and there is little danger of fabric damage from accidental overuse.

For many years detergent and bleach manufacturers have looked for a bleach that is both highly effective and completely safe on all fabrics. The

$$2Na^+ \left[\begin{array}{c} HO \quad O\!-\!O \quad OH \\ B \qquad\qquad B \\ HO \quad O\!-\!O \quad OH \end{array} \right]^{2-} \cdot \ 6H_2O \qquad 2Na^+ \left[\begin{array}{c} HO \quad O\!-\!O \quad OH \\ B \qquad\qquad B \\ HO \quad O\!-\!O \quad OH \end{array} \right]^{2-}$$

(4)   (5)

ideal product will remove stains in a single wash at U.S. washing temperatures and conditions and would be completely safe on colored as well as
white fabrics. Most research efforts to develop this "miracle" bleach have
been concentrated in attempting to find an oxygen-containing compound that
would satisfy these requirements.

1. Sodium Perborate

Perhaps the most widely used oxygen compounds for dry bleach and detergent applications are the sodium perborates [22]. The two sodium perborates of commerce are the tetrahydrate (4) and monohydrate (5).

The sodium perborate tetrahydrate compound may be prepared from
borax:

$$Na_2B_4O_7 + 2NaOH + 4H_2O_2 + 11H_2O \rightarrow 4NaBO_3 \cdot 4H_2O \qquad (6)$$

The sodium perborates can, for the most part, be considered as stable,
dry, and easy to handle, and formulate bleaching compounds. In dry bleach
formulations and detergents, sodium perborate monohydrate and tetrahydrate
can be used interchangeably since their water solubility and active oxygen
release rates are both adequate under conventional washing machine conditions [23]. It should be kept in mind by the formulator that sodium perborate tetrahydrate provides a less expensive source of active oxygen and is
generally more widely used than the monohydrate.

a. Activators. We believe suppliers and formulators are generally in
agreement that sodium perborate is not an effective bleach below $160^\circ F$ at
U.S. washing cycles of 10 to 15 min [24]. Many efforts have been made to
activate sodium perborate so it may achieve its full performance potential
at low water temperatures.

These methods have included trace amounts of catalysts such as copper,
cobalt, manganese, silver, and their compounds. Colloidal silver has also
been found to be an excellent catalyst to decompose perborate rapidly [25].
Catalytic activation of perborate has met with little success because of the
probably incorrect assumption that bleaching effectiveness or stain removal
is related to the rapid release of oxygen or decomposition of the peroxide in

solution. We have developed catalyst systems that actually "fizz off" like a well-known headache remedy, but did absolutely no bleaching.

Another more productive route to perborate activation is the use of in situ conversion type of activators. The in situ theory examines activators that react with the peroxide in solution to form percompounds with higher bleaching potency. Many such activators have been and are being studied. We list only a few of these activators:

1. N,N,N',N'-Tetraacetylethylenediamine (TAED) [24]
2. Sodium p-acetoxybenzenesulfonate (SABS) [24]
3. Trisacetylcyanurate (TACA) [26]
4. N-Acetylimidazole (AID) [27]
5. N-Benzoylimidazole (BID) [27]

Thus far there have been a number of unsolved factors concerning the use of activators which have limited their use primarily to laboratory experimentation. Some of these factors are the added cost of the activators, odor development, and instability of the dry bleach formulation.

In summary, then, sodium perborates are safe bleaches, but only fair stain removers under U.S. washing conditions of low temperatures and concentrations and short wash cycles. Metal and metal/chelate catalysts, although efficient on some stains, do not appear to offer an answer. Peracids formed in situ are efficient at low temperatures but considerable work still remains to be done toward developing stable economical formulations.

2. Potassium Monopersulfate

Potassium monopersulfate or the potassium monopersulfate compound as sold commercially is a research development product of the Electro-chemicals Department of DuPont. The material of commerce is a white granular solid with a minimum available oxygen of 4.5% and a range of active oxygen of 4.5 to 5.5%. This product when first examined by the author in 1956 was known as Elchem 1384. Since that time DuPont has obtained the registered trademark name of Oxone for their monopersulfate compound.

The monopersulfate compound is a combination of from 43 to 52% of potassium monopersulfate ($KHSO_5$), also known as the potassium salt of peroxymonosulfuric acid. The remaining 48 to 57% is an approximately equal mixture of potassium bisulfate ($KHSO_4$), and potassium sulfate (K_2SO_4). Perhaps of added interest to a formulator is the bulk density, 75 to 80 lb/ft^3, and pH, 2.0-3.0 (1% solution), of the monopersulfate compound [28].

The standard electrode potential, E^o, of Oxone, is -1.44 V for the following reaction [28]:

$$HSO_4 + H_2O \rightarrow HSO_5^- + 2H^+ + 2e^- \tag{7}$$

As can be seen from the high oxidation potential of Oxone, this product is useful in a variety of home cleaners as well as many chemical reactions where a strong oxidizing agent is required.

Oxone contains on the average 4.75% available oxygen compared to 10.0% for the commercially available sodium perborate tetrahydrate. Since it is available oxygen or active oxygen that does the bleaching it would seem that on a weight-for-weight basis sodium perborate would do a better job of bleaching than the monopersulfate. Laboratory data on stain and soil removal, which is discussed later in this chapter, show the oxygen in Oxone to be more active below and at the temperatures used for laundering in the United States than is the oxygen in sodium perborate.

A very unusual property of the monopersulfate compound is its ability to oxidize chloride ions to chlorine. Combinations of monopersulfate and sodium chloride, buffered to pH 9.0 or above [28], upon dissolution produce low concentrations of available chlorine. Our studies indicate the resulting performance benefits are equal to sodium hypochlorite on an equivalent available chlorine basis.

In order for the oxidation of sodium chloride by Oxone to take place in a meaningful manner, it is necessary to have a high sodium-chloride-to-Oxone ratio. For good bleaching effectiveness in products such as laundry bleaches and abrasive cleansers the optimum ratio, on a weight basis, of sodium chloride to Oxone is 8:1 [29]. As can be seen from this ratio it is practical in the case of an abrasive cleanser which might contain 2 to 3% Oxone but impractical in a home laundry bleach with 15 to 20% Oxone. In a home laundry bleach excellent performance has been achieved with a sodium chloride-to-Oxone ratio of 3:1 [28, 29].

In formulating with Oxone a few salient points should be remembered. Oxone can be readily formulated with conventional alkaline builders and fillers into stable free-flowing products. However, Oxone is acidic and sufficient alkali must be present to maintain a pH of 9 to 10. The alkaline fillers should be anhydrous to ensure maximum stability of the finished Oxone product. The base, alkaline builders, fillers, surfactants, and so on, may be spray dried or dry mixed. However, it should be remembered that Oxone is a stronger oxidizing agent than sodium perborate and additives such as perfumes, coloring dyes, and fluorescent whitening agents which are acceptable in a sodium perborate product may be changed or destroyed in an Oxone formulation. This is especially true when formulating an activated Oxone product. sodium chloride and Oxone. The formulation should generally be treated as if you were preparing a dry chlorine bleach, that is, chlorine-stable fluorescent whitening agents and a moisture-barrier package.

$$\text{(benzene ring)}\begin{array}{c} \overset{O}{\overset{\|}{C}}-OOH \\ C-OOH \\ \overset{\|}{O} \end{array}$$

(6)

3. Diperisophthalic Acid

We shall mention just briefly other peroxygen compounds that have been studied during the last 10 years. Perhaps the most interesting of recent peroxygen candidates is diperisophthalic acid (DPI), developed by the PPG Industries. Diperisophthalic acid (6) has an available oxygen of approximately 17.0%.

DPI is a white, crystalline, odorless product which because of its instability is being formulated by the manufacturer at an active oxygen content of less than 5% [30]. Attempts have been made to encapsulate DPI with magnesium sulfate, sodium sulfate, sodium nitrate, and so on, with fair results.

Laundering and bleach studies indicate that on an active oxygen basis DPI is a significantly better bleach than hydrogen peroxide, sodium perborate, or potassium monopersulfate. This statement, of course, refers to normal washing machine concentrations of 15 to 40 ppm available oxygen and laundering temperatures of 120°F. Preliminary data indicate that at low available oxygen levels, 10 ppm available oxygen is equivalent to 45 ppm available chlorine, and the stain-removing ability of DPI approaches that of sodium hypochlorite and the chlorinated isocyanurates.

It is our opinion that the success of DPI as a bleaching compound will depend on whether or not this material can be cheaply and effectively stabilized by chemicals, agglomeration, or encapsulation.

4. Percarbonates

The percarbonates have also been studied for bleaching effectiveness, but for the most part in Europe. Sodium percarbonate, the product of commerce, is generally white, free-flowing granules corresponding to the formula $2Na_2CO_3 \cdot 3H_2O_2$ and having an available oxygen of 13.0% In solution it dissociates into sodium carbonate and hydrogen peroxide. The bleaching performance of sodium percarbonate is considered, on an equal available oxygen basis, to be similar to the sodium perborates [31].

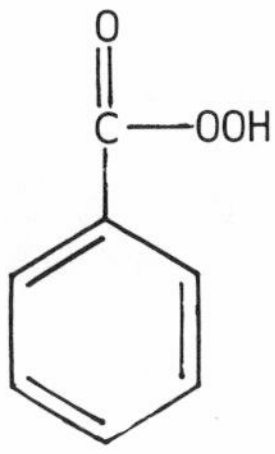

(7) 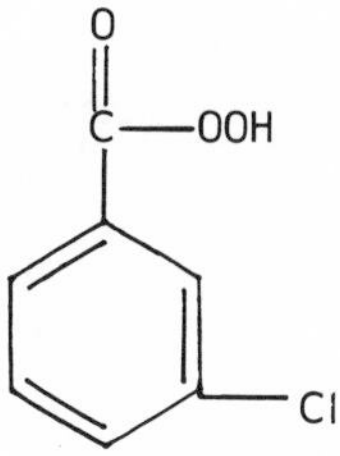   (8)

5. Peracids

Two interesting peracids developed by FMC Corporation [32, 33] are perbenzoic acid (7), 11.5% available oxygen, and m-chloroperbenzoic acid (8), 9.3% available oxygen.

Perbenzoic acid has been known and used for a number of years as an oxidizing agent. Unfortunately, it possesses poor stability, decomposing at the rate of 10% per week at room temperature [34]. FMC found that they could prepare a fairly stable 25% solution of perbenzoic acid in tertiary butanol [35].

The bleaching performance of the perbenzoic acid/tertiary butanol solution is found to be excellent for a peroxygen compound. The stain removal data obtained at washing machine concentrations of 15 and 30 ppm available oxygen indicate performance superior to that of Oxone and equal to that of diperisophthalic acid. The obvious expense involved in transporting a liquid and the poor latitude for formulation are only two of the reasons for perbenzoic acid rejection as a commercial product.

The m-chloroperbenzoic acid is, in reality, a mixture of approximately 85% m-chloroperbenzoic acid and 15% m-chlorobenzoic acid. Preliminary studies indicate that m-chlorobenzoic acid exhibits excellent bactericidal, fungicidal, and algicidal [33] properties. Bleaching studies comparing perbenzoic acid to m-chloroperbenzoic acid show that the stain-removing ability of m-chloroperbenzoic acid compares quite favorably to that of perbenzoic acid. Due to some danger in handling and processing m-chloroperbenzoic acid, it is suggested mainly as a speciality bleaching agent for treatment during processing of both natural and synthetic fibers.

D. Enzymes

Since there is a separate chapter on enzymes, we shall discuss these remarkable nonliving chemicals only briefly. We feel it is necessary to at least mention enzymes because their use in U.S. laundry products as effective stain and soil removers is a recent and explosive development. There has probably been no single development in the household cleaning field that has so thoroughly captured the imagination of both the bench chemist and the housewife as the enzyme. Although they do not replace detergents or bleaches, enzymes serve a particular function and their application both with and without bleach must certainly be at least considered in this chapter.

Enzymes are biochemical catalysts that are products of living organisms. Mutant strains of the bacteria Bacillus subtillis have been developed which are resistant to the high alkalinity and hot-water temperatures encountered in U.S. home washing conditions. With this particular type of enzyme it became possible to formulate an enzyme-active heavy-duty detergent or oxygen dry bleach that performs effectively in a 10-min wash cycle.

Once an alkaline/high-temperature-resistant enzyme was found, a variety of different enzyme types were rapidly developed. The enzymes now commercially available include those that are primarily protease (protein splitting) and those that are high in amylase (carbohydrate hydrolyzing). There are also a large number of enzymes available that have both protease and amylase activity.

Our research indicates that chlorine bleaches deactivate enzymes when used simultaneously in a wash cycle. However, an enzyme product may be used in a presoak cycle and the bleach added in the wash cycle, or in a regular wash cycle you may delay adding the chlorine bleach until the last half of the wash cycle. Bleaches based on sodium perborate are compatible with enzyme-containing laundry products.

Evaluation of enzymes presents some of the same problems encountered in bleach evaluation, that is, development of realistic soils and stains for determining their in-use effectiveness. In considering the development of soils and stains to measure enzyme activity you should examine a list of probable candidates which will be attacked by enzymes. Protease activity can be measured by blood, grass, milk, egg yolk, and other protein-containing or protein-bound materials, whereas amylase action is studied using chocolate, ice cream, starch, cocoa, or carbohydrate-containing or carbohydrate-bound substances. From this list, then, we can prepare quite a variety of soils and stains and our evaluation of these unique stain- and soil-removing chemicals is underway.

III. STAINED AND SOILED SUBSTRATES

After being in the household cleaning field for more than 20 years, the author feels he has come to at least one solid conclusion. This conclusion is that every research laboratory involved in cleaning and/or bleaching evaluations has its own set of evaluatory procedures or test methods. These methods are based on varying histories of requirements and specialized experience.

A. Preparation Methods for Fabrics

We have found through experience obtained in both cooperative and independent research programs that data obtained by laboratory 1 using its own test procedures are not necessarily the same as those gathered by another research facility using the same procedure as laboratory 1. What is even more disturbing is that not only are the data not the same, but the conclusions reached may differ widely. We, therefore, do not attempt to set ourselves up as experts in the fields of staining and soiling but rather describe some of the methods we have found satisfactory and also some of the pitfalls encountered over the years.

In this day of proliferation of fibers, fiber blends, and fabric treatment, it is absolutely essential to define, as best we can, the origin, composition, and exact nature of the fabric being tested, for example, resin-treated permanent press 65/35 Dacron/cotton blended broadcloth manufactured by X Company with a thread count of 136/68. Ideally, but very difficult to determine, are the day, month, and year of manufacture, the amount and type of resin used, the method of manufacture, age, and storage conditions of the fabric.

We never cease to be amazed at the amount of research time, money, and effort that is spent developing exotic soils and stains. When the inevitable question comes, "What fabric was used?" answers sometimes become very vague. "Cotton, I think, or a permanent press blend of some type." This information is obviously not sufficient to allow an interested party to check the test results obtained by the researchers.

From this brief discussion, it becomes obvious that the most satisfactory method would be to designate one large independent testing company to act as a fabric bank or clearinghouse for standard nontreated and resin-treated fabrics and fabric blends. In this way, and only in this way, could all laboratories at least start out with a fairly uniform piece of fabric. Perhaps all of this is only an evaluation of man's dream, but we hope someday in the near future such a bank will be available to all of us.

1. Desizing

We have found that although desized cotton may be an unrealistic substrate in today's wash, it at least does not add the variables of resins or the unknowns of a synthetic/cotton blend. The two cottons probably used most often for preparing soils and stains are bleached Indian Head 80 x 80 and Test Fabrics S/405 bleached 2.65 sheeting, 48 x 52. We have found that these fabrics may be desized quite readily using the following procedure:

1. Wash eighty 10 1/2 in. x 10 1/2 in. pieces of cotton cloth in a 3% sodium tripolyphosphate solution using an automatic upright washer.
2. Run washer through complete cycle using water of approximately 150 ppm hardness at a temperature of at least 120°F.
3. If swatches have a tendency to bunch up and become entangled during desizing, they should be separated at the end of the washing cycle. This separation reduces wrinkling of the fabric which can produce nonuniform soiling or staining.
4. Repeat complete cycle without the sodium tripolyphosphate, again using 150 ppm hard water at a temperature of at least 120°F.
5. Separate swatches and dry in automatic dryer set at hot or cotton drying temperature.

While we are certain there are many valid objections to the desizing procedure just listed, we feel it presents a cotton cloth similar to that a housewife would encounter after washing a garment a number of times. Even if the soil or stain is being applied to other fibers, natural, synthetic, or natural/synthetic blends, we believe the procedure is still applicable. In any case all fabrics should be washed and rinsed thoroughly several times. This procedure will again duplicate in-home laundering conditions which result in the removal of certain finishing oils, lubricants, and softeners used in processing the fabric. Experience dictates that thorough desizing or washing results in the preparation of more uniformly soiled or stained fabric

2. Stains/Soils

In everyday usage, the words soiling and staining are employed loosely and often interchangeably. We think the term stain implies a degree of permanency not associated with soil or dirt. While it is generally believed soil and dirt can be removed by ordinary dry cleaning or laundering, it is usually necessary to use some special means or technique to remove a stain It is undoubtedly true that a method of distinguishing between the two in technical terms would be very useful, but as yet there appears to be considerable differences of opinion among technical people in the area of defining soils and stains. For the purposes of our discussion in this chapter let us consider a soil as a material that is removed for the most part by a detergent, whereas a stain requires the use of a bleach.

The following is a listing of parameters or requirements for the acceptability of a stained or soiled test fabric for bleach evaluations:

1. The stain or soil should be deposited and removed in a uniform manner.
2. The percent SR (stain or soil removal) should not be greatly affected by changes in pH.
3. The percent SR should be uniform from batch to batch when evaluated with a standard bleach solution.

4. The test fabric's percent SR characteristics should not be greatly
    affected by aging.
5. There should be a demonstrable difference in percent SR between
    detergent alone and detergent plus a standard bleach solution.

While it is difficult to develop a stained or soiled test fabric that meets
all of the requirements just given, they should serve as guidelines and help
to determine the acceptability of any newly developed or different test fabric.

For the evaluation of bleaching compounds we have found a number of
soils and stains extremely helpful in screening possible bleach candidates.
We feel at least three of these, tea, coffee, and dry soil, are essential for
evaluations. However, it should be mentioned that the greater the variety
of soils and stains used, the more reliable are the results.

Bleaching studies indicate a specific bleach may work effectively on tea
stain, but have only medium performance on coffee, or a bleach may be very
good in removing tea and coffee stains, but show poor bleaching ability on
the difficult-to-remove dry soil.

a. Tea/coffee. Without taking up a lot of space discussing the exact
staining procedures we have found it rather easy to prepare uniform tea and
coffee stains. It is possible to use either soluble tea and coffee or regular
tea and coffee. Again a word of caution. Whatever is used as a staining
material should be defined as precisely as possible, for example, Breakfast
Club tea, orange pekoe, and pekoe cut black. An effort should also be made
to prepare as large a number of stained swatches as is practical. Our research on tea and coffee stains shows that they may be wrapped in aluminium
foil packets and stored in a dessicator under vacuum for one year without
significantly changing their reflectance or bleaching characteristics. Each
packet may be labeled with such data as original reflectance, stained reflectance, date prepared, and number and type of swatches.

Nine liters of water, approximately 150 ppm hardness, is brought to the
boil and 300 g of tea is added and boiled for 5 min. The hot tea solution is
filtered through a fritted glass funnel and the filtrate again brought to the
boil. Six hundred 2 1/4 x 3 1/4 desized Indian Head cotton swatches are
added to the filtrate and allowed to boil for 5 min. More uniform swatches
can be prepared using many small swatches rather than a few large ones.
Remove swatches, squeeze out excess water, and dry for 20 min in an automatic clothes dryer at a hot setting. Rinse swatches separately in cold tap
water and dry again. Essentially the same method can also be used for preparing coffee stains.

It may be necessary for each individual laboratory to make minor ad-
justments in the staining procedure for their particular situation. There
are, however, three critical factors that should be kept in mind:

1. The tea stains must be thoroughly heat set. A removal by detergent
   alone (0.2% concentration) of over 15% on tea and 25% on coffee indicates the stain has not been properly set.
2. The swatches should be cut to the smallest size possible which will
   still allow accurate reading for your particular reflectance-measur-
   ing instrument. As mentioned earlier smaller swatches stain more
   uniformly.
3. Care should be taken in individually rinsing each swatch to make
   certain surface stains are removed.

If these instructions are followed, we are confident that uniform, detergent-
resistant tea and coffee stains will be obtained.

   b. Dry soil. We feel that next to naturally soiled fabric "dry soil"
gives results that closely duplicate those observed by the housewife in everyday bleaching. Never have we rated a bleach a good performer on dry soil
and then found by actual panel testing, housewife evaluation, that it was
judged a poor bleaching agent. We believe this is because dry soil is a
real soil and a soil closely akin to one encountered daily by the homemaker.

   Dry soil is vacuum cleaner dirt which may be obtained from any source
that turns out a large volume of what would be normal or representative
sweepings. We recommend a large, centrally located hotel as a source of
supply. To obtain as uniform a soil as possible, collect at least 100 lb of
carpet sweepings.

   The carpet sweepings are passed through a 20-mesh screen to remove
the larger pieces of carpet lint and fiber. Generally about 50 to 70% of the
100 lb of sweepings will be removed as carpet fiber. The soil passing
through the 20-mesh screen is rescreened using an 80-mesh screen. Again
about 50% of the sweepings will be retained on the 80-mesh screen. The
material passing through the 80-mesh screen, approximately 15 to 25 lb, is
tumbled to mix thoroughly and stored in an airtight container.

   Soil 80 cotton swatches, 10 1/2 in. x 10 1/2 in., using Test Fabrics
Inc. S/405 bleached sheeting 48 x 52 or bleached Indian Head 80 x 80. The
larger size swatches are used because we are soiling, not staining. We
have found that any reasonable amount of dry soil may be used for soiling
this number of swatches. The governing factor will, of course, depend on
the desired darkness of the swatches. We think 454 g or 1 lb of dry soil
provides adequate color to obtain meaningful reflectance readings and soil-
removal data. Generally speaking, less soil will produce light-colored,
easier to remove soil, while a larger quantity gives darker, more difficult
to remove soiled swatches.

Place 2 gal of room-temperature water at 50 ppm water hardness in a 16-gal upright washing machine. Add 1 lb of dry soil to a 2 1/2 gal bucket and fill with room-temperature water of 50 ppm hardness. Stir and pour solution through a 200-mesh screen. Wash soil remaining on screen with 50 ppm water until an additional 5 1/2 gal of room-temperature water has been used. The washing machine should now contain 10 gal of soiling solution. This solution is now allowed to agitate for 5 min.

The cotton swatches to be soiled should be dried in a dryer for 15 to 20 min at a hot setting within 1 hr of the time they are to be soiled. The 80 swatches are then placed in the agitating soil solution and allowed to agitate for an additional 20 min. After the agitation period, place swatches in the 2 1/2 gal bucket. The swatches are now hand-dipped individually three times in the soil solution and run through a wringer at medium setting being careful that no creases are formed. This operation requires three people: one dipping swatches, one feeding swatches into the wringer, and the third pulling swatches out of the wringer. The total time allotted for rinsing and wringing swatches should not exceed 15 min. This time limit is critical to the ultimate uniformity of reflectance and soil removal characteristics of the finished test swatches. The 80 soiled swatches are now dried for exactly 1 hr at a hot setting in an automatic dryer. A longer drying time will result in lower soil removal, whereas a shorter drying time has the reverse effect.

We have found that the soiling procedure just described can be greatly simplified by using an Atlas Laboratory Wringer and Padder 1131D. While it may be necessary to make some modifications in the soiling procedure, we recommend this device for faster, more uniform preparation of dry soil or, for that matter, any test soil which can be padded on fabric.

c. Other soils/stains. Probably this chapter has devoted more space to the preparation of tea stain and dry soil than they warrant. The purpose is not to promote this stain and soil as much as it is to give the reader an insight into some common staining and soiling methods. Other stains that are commonly employed for bleaching evaluations are grass (chlorophyll), Merthiolate, wine, mustard, food coloring dyes, and ink. These stains for the most part are applied from an aqueous medium in a manner similar to that described for tea and coffee.

A number of the stains just mentioned have also been evaluated in aqueous solutions [36]. This provides a rapid method of determining how well and how quickly a bleach can decolorize a stain solution. We have found with liquid bleaches that the actual decoloring or bleaching of solutions of grass, tea, or coffee may be followed on a recording spectrophotometer. This method allows us to evaluate the effect of pH and level of available chlorine on the speed of color removal. While solution studies provide a rapid method for screening some bleaches, we still feel a fabric substrate is necessary for more definitive evaluations.

We do not use a great deal of space here to discuss the various greasy soiled test fabrics that are available as they are undoubtedly fully covered in other chapters. Probably more print has been expended on the development and test results obtained on greasy type of test soils than on any other single test soil or stain. A partial list of the greasy soil test fabrics that may be purchased include: Test Fabrics, Inc., American Conditioning House, Foster D. Snell, and U. S. Testing in the United States and Krefeld and EMPA fabric [37] prepared in Europe.

There are also a number of excellent test soils based on natural and synthetic sebum [38, 39]. We feel, however, that greasy soils, excluding sebum, are designed primarily to measure detergency and not bleaching. Some of the soils are sensitive to phosphates, some to anionic surfactants, and others to nonionic detergents. However, when these soils are used in bleaching evaluations only small differences are generally noted when the percent soil removal by detergent alone is compared to the percent soil removal recorded for detergent plus bleach. The performance of a bleach should, of course, be checked on several different types of greasy soils before a particular formulation is finalized. However, for screening and evaluation studies we see no great value in the routine use of greasy test soils, except for sebum perhaps, to measure bleaching.

d. Radioactive soils/stains. Since the end of World War II, a number of very good radioactive test soils have been developed and studied [40-42]. The first commercially available radioactive soils were made by Nuclear of Chicago and consisted of three separate cotton test fabrics, protein, fat, and carbohydrate, all of which contained carbon-14 and emitted relatively soft radiation. We do not argue the relative merits of the various radioactive soils, but merely point out that they were developed primarily to evaluate detergents and not bleaches. The soils for the most part are quite complicated to prepare and of course require specialized handling and measuring equipment that is not available in smaller laboratories.

Purex Corporation developed an interesting radioactive stain [43] that we feel is specific for bleaching evaluations. The stain is radioactive caramel which was chosen because bleaching studies based on reflectance measurements indicate caramel stain results closely resemble those obtained with coffee stain [43].

The subject radioactive caramel stain [43] is prepared by placing 18.8 mg of [^{14}C]glucose (2.06 mCi/mg), 919.6 mg of anhydrous glucose, and 234.6 mg of concentrated ammonium hydroxide (0.26 ml) in a piece of glass tubing

10 mm outer diameter and 5 in. long. The tube is sealed to form a capsule and this capsule is suspended below the surface of liquid pyridine which has been heated almost to the boiling point. The level of the material inside the capsule is just below the level of the pyridine. Enough heat is applied to cause the pyridine to boil and to reflux. The temperature of the boiling pyridine is 115°C. After 4 hr the capsule is removed from the pyridine and the material inside the capsule is viscous and very dark colored. The seal is broken and the contents diluted to 20 ml with warm distilled water. This dilution will produce a solution that is approximately 5.86% stain. There should be no solid material remaining in the capsule. Now 2 ml of this solution is diluted to 46.3 ml with distilled water to give a solution of about 0.25% stain. Nine circular Indian Head cotton swatches 3.0 cm in diameter are refluxed in this solution for 20 min. The stained swatches are rinsed in distilled water and then soaked in 0.25 M boric acid buffer solution at pH 9.0 for 1 hr at 120°F. The test swatches are then rinsed and dried. The reflectance and counts per minute of the swatches may now be deter-mined.

We think that the above-mentioned method is a relatively simple and clear-cut way to prepare radioactive stained fabric. We are equally certain that with a little work it can be improved upon. The results obtained with radioactive caramel stain, which are discussed later in this chapter, are meaningful and duplicate findings obtained with nonradioactive stains.

Perhaps a commercial laboratory will develop a new or adapt an exis-ting radioactive soil or stain which will be sensitive to detergents and bleaches and economically and practically feasible for small laboratories to purchase and handle. Until such a soil or stain is developed, most lab-oratories will only be able to read about radioactive soils and stains.

e. Soils/stains for enzyme products. Because there is a separate chapter devoted to enzymes, we touch only briefly on test stains and soils used to evaluate these materials. Our primary reason for mentioning enzymes is the rather strange results obtained with one of the test fabrics commonly used for enzyme evaluation.

The two most common fabrics currently being used for enzyme per-formance studies are EMPA 116 BMI (blood, milk, and ink) and CMS (cocoa, milk, and sugar) [37]. BMI test fabric is used primarily to evaluate the protease activity of an enzyme while CMS measures amylase activity.

We have found in our laboratories and it has also been noted in others that an enzyme product which also contains sodium perborate often gives low, and in some cases, negative results; that is, the test fabric is darker after bleaching and enzyme action than it was before treatment, with BMI fabric. This can be a perplexing problem when you know sodium perborate bleaches and proteolytic enzymes break down BMI soil.

We think anyone in evaluatory work trusts their analytical group when they say a product contains sodium perborate and enzyme, but we also know they like to see this information translated into percent SR (stain or soil removal). With this thought in mind, we set out to develop a soil or stain that would be detergent resistant but responsive to a product containing both perborate and enzymes.

We were quite certain that in the case of BMI the perborate was oxidizing the blood portion of the soil to a darker state thereby negating the effect of the bleach and enzymes. We therefore decided to start with stains that we knew were susceptible to enzyme action and were at the same time bleachable. After a number of false starts, including grass, eggs, tea, and so forth, we settled on a spinach stain [44].

The preparation of spinach stain consists basically of an aqueous slurry mixed in an Eppenbach Homo-mixer. Cotton strips, Test Fabrics, Inc., S/405, which have been treated with urea to fix the stain to the fabric, are placed in the slurry and evenly saturated with the spinach mixture. The stain is further set by running the stained fabric through a clothes wringer, rinsing, and drying in an automatic dryer. The spinach cloth may be stored following the regular procedure of refrigeration and protection from light.

We believe that the procedure just described provides a test fabric for measuring the protease activity of enzymatic detergents and sodium perborate-containing enzyme laundry products in the presence of sodium perborate bleach. The test fabric consists of a spinach pigment and protein complex [45] on cotton cloth and is similar to grass stain commonly encountered in the home laundry. The spinach protein is broken down by protease-containing enzymes and the chlorophyll color bodies are susceptible to the bleaching action of sodium perborates. We therefore have a stain that measured detergency, enzyme action, and bleaching.

B.   Preparation Methods for Solid Surfaces

We have generally found the staining of solid surfaces a bit more troublesome than the staining of fabric. The primary reason is that the solid surface must be prepared more carefully to uniformly receive and uniformly hold a stain. The key to good stains on a solid substrate is a clean, uniform surface. The reader should again keep in mind that the objective here is to develop only bleachable soils or stains and not material that can be cleaned by conventional detergents and cleaners.

The objective again, as was the case on fabric, is to develop a stain that is resistant to normal cleaning agents and demonstrates the action of the particular bleach being evaluated. In developing a stain for solid substrates we have the added objective, besides being detergent resistant, of good resistance to the action of abrasive materials such as feldspar and silica flour.

1. Surface Preparation

We have found good stains may be prepared by using lightly, but uniformly, sandblasted porcelainized steel. Porcelainized steel similar to that used in the manufacture of sinks, washing machines, dryers, and other home appliances may be obtained from Columware of Lynwood, California, in about any size desired; however, we found that 3 ft x 3 ft sheets with white, extra-thick porcelain on both sides of 16-gauge steel plate worked quite nicely. The best results are obtained by having the manufacturer lightly sandblast the porcelain after the sheets are prepared. In working with porcelainized steel, it becomes quickly apparent stains will not adhere to a new glasslike surface. The purpose of sandblasting then is twofold:

1. To prepare the surface so it will receive the stain
2. To duplicate the surface of an old sink where staining can and does occur

The surface may also be roughened by the use of a 48% hydrofluoric acid [46].

The 3 ft x 3 ft test sheets are now cut into 2 1/2 in. x 2 1/2 in. test pieces. The experimenter will find that a variety of stains tea, coffee, iron, and so on, can readily be applied to the previously unstained porcelainized steel test pieces. However, we, because of the expense involved, anticipated repeat usage of the test pieces. We found the following cleaning procedure absolutely necessary to remove not only the previously applied stains but also the invisible oils that had been deposited during the stain application. Just prior to staining clean plates as follows:

1. Place plates in full-strength liquid chlorine bleach for 15 min.
2. Rinse thoroughly in cold tap water.
3. Remove iron (rust) from plates by placing in a rack and immersing for 15 min in a 2% oxalic acid solution at 160°F.
4. Boil plates (in rack) for 15 min in a 1% (TSP) trisodium phosphate solution.
5. Rinse thoroughly in cold tap water.

2. Staining: Tea/Coffee

As discussed earlier, a number of oxidizable and bleachable stains may be applied to the porcelainized steel test plates. In the interest of brevity, we describe the procedure used for tea stains. It should be remembered, as was the case with stained fabric, that a specific bleach may work effectively on tea stain but show poor or medium performance on coffee stains; therefore a number of stains should be examined. Following is a general procedure for the preparation of tea-stained porcelainized steel plates:

1. Forty-five clean 2 1/2 in. x 2 1/2 in. sandblasted porcelainized steel plates are placed in a staining rack (a record rack makes an excellent staining rack).
2. Bring 8 liters of water (150 ppm hardness) to the boil in a water bath (11 in. x 13 in. x 4 1/2 in. depth).
3. Place staining rack with plates in water bath.
4. Reheat to boiling and add 250 g of tea.
5. Boil for 2 hr.
6. Remove rack and plates and allow to air dry.
7. Rinse stained plates in cold tap water and remove excess stain with soft bristled brush.
8. Dry stained plates with soft cotton towel.

With a little experimentation this procedure can also be adapted for other stains as well as other substrates such as plastic and porcelain. In the case of coffee stains, use the same procedure as tea.

The tea- or coffee-stained porcelainized steel plates, if not used immediately, should be wrapped in foil and refrigerated. The plates should not be stored longer than 30 days before use.

C. Storage of Test Substrates

It is desirable for uniformity and convenience purposes to stain a large number of test surfaces at one time. We initiated work to determine the effect of various storage conditions on test substrates. We will report the data obtained during one year's storage of tea- and coffee-stained Indian Head cotton.

1. Tea- and Coffee-Stained Cotton

Three thousand each of tea- and coffee-stained cotton swatches were prepared in the manner described earlier in this chapter. The test swatches were stored 1000 each under three different conditions. The change in reflectance and percent stain removal were determined after 1, 3, 6, and 12 months of storage as shown in Table 1.

TABLE 1

Units Change in Reflectance of Tea/Coffee-Stained Cotton

Storage condition	Storage time (months)				Type of stain
	0 to 1	0 to 3	0 to 6	0 to 12	
a	+1.8	+2.4	+3.0	+5.4	Tea
b	+0.8	+0.5	+0.4	+0.5	Tea
c	+0.7	+0.4	+0.2	+0.6	Tea
a	+1.6	+2.4	+3.8	+4.2	Coffee
b	+0.6	+0.7	+0.3	+0.4	Coffee
c	+0.5	+0.3	+0.2	+0.4	Coffee

[a] Stored in laboratory at room temperature.
[b] Stored under nitrogen atmosphere at room temperature.
[c] Stored under nitrogen atmosphere and refrigerated.

It can be seen that the tea-stained swatches stored in the laboratory were on the average 5.4 units lighter after one year of storage. Swatches stored under nitrogen at room temperature and refrigerated were 0.5 and 0.6 unit lighter, respectively, after one year of storage.

The coffee-stained swatches were 4.2 units lighter when stored in the laboratory at room temperature. Swatches stored under nitrogen at room temperature and also refrigerated were 0.4 unit lighter after one year of storage.

A bleaching evaluation was conducted using liquid sodium hypochlorite bleach at 50 and 100 ppm available chlorine in 0.15% detergent in 150 ppm water hardness for 20 min at $120^\circ F$. Generally, the data indicated that tea- and coffee-stained swatches stored in the laboratory at room temperature for one year gave slightly lower stain removal than swatches stored under nitrogen. No difference was observed between swatches stored under nitrogen at room temperature and those stored under refrigeration.

After examining both the reflectance and stain removal data we conclude that tea- and coffee-stained swatches can be prepared in amounts up to 3000 and stored for one year. Storage should be done under an atmosphere of nitrogen in the manner described earlier and no instability of the stain or its removal characteristics will be altered for at least one year.

Storage studies done with other soils and stains indicate that most of them can be satisfactorily preserved by simple refrigeration; however, to be absolutely certain we recommend storage under both refrigeration and nitrogen. If the reader is working with his own special soils and stains, we suggest he study their storage characteristics for changes in both reflectance and soil removal.

IV. STAIN REMOVAL

In evaluating stain removal we find ourselves in many of the same types of predicaments as were noted in staining fabrics. What is a standard soil, a standard temperature, a standard available chlorine, a standard fabric-to-liquor ratio, and ad infinitum? It becomes apparent from all of the variables that the serious investigator must depend on what he knows and can learn about the washing and bleaching habits of the ever-elusive "average housewife" if his studies are to be meaningful. It becomes necessary to combine a scientific approach with what is known about the actual in-use habits of the potential user of the product under study. Our experience indicates too many bleach evaluations are designed as model scientific experiments or to prove a specific point rather than in the way the bleach will ultimately be used. These approaches can and do result in misleading, and, in some cases incorrect data and conclusions.

We think it is necessary to have a number of different bleaching tests that take many variables into account. A retail product under evaluation should be examined at its recommended use or label concentration. In the case of an experimental product it should be studied versus the product against which it will compete. Because of varying habits we think it is also important to study performance at below and above recommended use levels. For illustration purposes we will choose liquid 5.25% by weight sodium hypochlorite bleach. The usual washing machine direction for this product calls for one cup per 16 gal of wash water. The available chlorine of this solution for bleach at optimum strength is approximately 200 ppm. We would therefore recommend studies be conducted at the 1/2, 1, and 1 1/2 cup levels or 100, 200, and 300 ppm available chlorine.

A factor that deserves consideration is the slope of the bleaching curve when percent SR is plotted against available chlorine concentration. We have

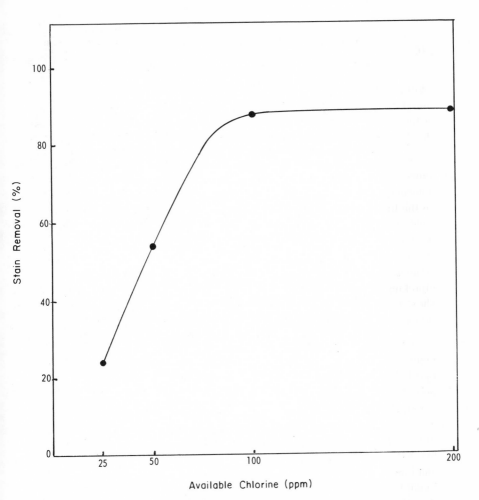

FIG. 2.   Tea stain removal by NaOCl as function of concentration.

found during standard evaluations that below 50 ppm available chlorine
percent SR decreases rapidly; however, above 100 ppm available chlorine
only small changes in percent SR are noted (see Fig. 2).

Another problem area in bleaching evaluations is the order of addition
of the detergent, bleach, and fabric. Again we do not wish to set ourselves
up as experts to determine the merit of one method over another. We believe each investigator must determine his own best method from the information he has at hand, carefully considering the factors that might influence his
particular test results. Unless specified otherwise, our standard order of

addition for bleaching evaluations will be detergent followed by bleach followed by test fabric. This procedure, although having some disadvantages, at least provides uniform distribution of the detergent and the bleach in solution before the test fabric is added.

We would like to add a brief word concerning the benefits of routinely running the pH and available chlorine or available oxygen on spent bleach solutions. We are of the opinion that valuable information may be obtained on the bleaching potential of a particular bleach or bleach composition by running these simple tests. This procedure may give you some idea of whether or not the chlorine or oxygen is available for bleaching, how effective it is bleaching, and how much is necessary to do a satisfactory job of bleaching. It may also aid in determining whether the bleaching agent is attacking the stain or the fabric. We think, considering the relatively short time involved, available chlorine or oxygen should always be determined at the end of the bleaching cycle.

Again, as was the case in staining fabrics, we are certain there will be many valid objections to our test procedures. It should be kept in mind that it is necessary to set parameters for laboratory testing. These parameters are based as closely as possible on what we know about average soil loads, types of soil encountered, soil-to-fabric ratio, and the like. We have sat on a number of committees and been in enough discussion groups to know there is considerable disagreement on what constitutes a good test method for bleach evaluation. We are not then attempting to set down hard and fast infallible test procedures, but merely methods we hope will serve to guide laboratories who have no, or only limited, experience in the evaluation of bleaching compounds.

A. Evaluation Methods: Fabric

1. Single-Bleach Method

The single-bleach method is used to evaluate the stain removal characteristics of a bleach during one stain/bleach cycle. The washing machine strength method is run at 120°F using a standard detergent at a concentration of 0.15% in 150 ppm hard water and a bleaching cycle of 15 min.

The single-bleach method at stubborn stain concentration employs a 5-min cycle for liquid bleaches and 30 min for dry bleach. The temperature for stubborn stains is 100°F for liquid bleach and 110°F for dry bleach. No detergent is used at stubborn stain concentrations. All bleach solutions will be prepared in water of 150 ppm hardness.

The test fabrics for example purposes will be tea, coffee, and dry soil cut 2 1/4 in. x 3 1/4 in. The swatches may be labeled T, C, and D, respectively. The reflectance of each swatch should be measured on a background of three similar swatches using a tristimulus green filter. Staple together two sets of swatches as follows: (a) tea-dry soil; (b) tea-coffee; and (c) coffee-dry soil.

Staple the narrow end of the swatches together so they overlap about 1/4 in. Prepare three sets of swatches from the above, (a)-(b), (a)-(c), and (b)-(c), with a rubber stopper between pairs of swatches. A rubber stopper split on both ends with a razor blade provides an excellent holder for the swatches. This procedure will provide four swatches of each of the three test soils and three containers for each test condition. If a Terg-O-Tometer is used, disregard stapling and stoppering directions, but use the same soiled swatch mix.

It is, of course, possible to use any fabric-to-solution ratio desired. The researcher may wish to change the stain and/or soil mix or he might also change the amount of soil or stain applied to the test fabric. For standard testing we prefer the previously discussed soil mix in 200 ml of test solution.

We will not go into the mechanics of a Launder-Ometer or Terg-O-Tometer as they are discussed fully in Part I, Chapter 10. At the end of the bleach cycle the excess liquid is squeezed from the test swatches into their respective jars. Available chlorine or oxygen should be run on spent solutions. The swatches are separated, rinsed three times in cold 150 ppm water hardness, and dried.

2. Multiple-Bleach Method

Multiple-bleach tests may be run in a variety of ways, again depending on what the investigator wishes to study. We mention two basic methods that employ the same conditions of temperature, time, and concentration previously discussed in our single-bleach method. The tests may be run at either or both washing machine and stubborn stain conditions.

The first method is referred to as a multiple-bleach test. Very simply this procedure measures the ability of a bleach to remove one particular soil or stain. The stained fabric is bleached a number of times to determine how many cycles are required to obtain maximum fabric whiteness.

This evaluation of the effect of multiple bleachings may also be made on unstained cloth to determine if the bleach will degrade or change the color of the fabric. This test can also be used, simultaneously with color measurements, to determine losses in tensile strength of the fabric. It is felt the procedure will help to determine a bleach's potential for stain removal, yellowing, and fabric damage.

The second method is a multiple-bleach/stain test. This test consists of staining or soiling between bleaching cycles. The stained fabric is run through a bleaching cycle, percent SR is determined, and the fabric is again soiled or stained. This procedure is repeated for as many repetitions as desired, but we recommend a minimum of 20 bleach/stain cycles.

The multiple-bleach/stain test should uncover the inability of a bleach to remove a stain completely. This weakness is indicated after each bleach/stain cycle as a lower percent SR is recorded. While two bleach candidates may appear equal after several bleach/stain repetitions, if differences are to be found, these differences in bleaching ability will be greatly magnified after 20 or 30 cycles. Again we find it very convenient to determine fabric damage simultaneously with the stain removal tests.

We suggest for screening purposes that the preceding tests be run in a Launder-O-Meter; however, a Terg-O-Tometer may be used but testing will, of course, be more time-consuming: 20 jars versus 4 cans.

Before a particular bleach or bleach formulation can be recommended to management we believe practical washing machine evaluations are necessary. Either one or both of the multiple-bleach tests may be accomplished using a dummy clothes load with the stained and soiled swatches attached. The weight of the dummy clothes load should, of course, coincide with the washing machine manufacturer's recommended fabric load. An excellent reference for determining such information as standard mixed cotton test loads, placement of test swatches, loading techniques, and so on, for washing machines is the Household Washer Performance Evaluation Procedure [47].

Multiple washing machine bleach cycles should be made using, as closely as possible the same concentrations and conditions that were used in the earlier screening studies. In this way you may then compare data obtained in the washing machine with data obtained using the Launder-Ometer or Terg-O-Tometer.

3. Weighted-Soil Method

The weighted-soil method, as the name implies, is basically a procedure that changes the soil-to-fabric ratio in an attempt to determine the full bleaching potential of a bleach. The subject method is difficult to describe, but a worthwhile tool for measuring the soil-removing capabilities of a bleach. It is relatively easy to apply a light soil which almost any bleach can remove completely. It is also possible to apply the very same soil so heavily that no bleach can remove it. What we are trying to measure is the point at which the bleaching action has become completely exhausted, either because of a heavy soil or a large amount of fabric or a combination of both heavy fabric and heavy soil load.

We again find it necessary to establish several perhaps arbitrary parameters for testing. The two parameters set down, which are based on in-home laundry studies done several years ago [48], are as follows:

1. The "average" or medium fabric load for a 16-gal washing machine is from 6 to 8 lb dry weight.

2. The particulate soil removed by a concentration of 0.2% Tide in
water of 150 ppm hardness from a 6- to 8-lb medium-soiled home
laundry load falls within the range of particulate soil removed by the
same Tide solution from 6 to 8 lb of our standard dry soil test fabric
in a 16-gal washing machine.

The particulate soil removals mentioned above are not based on reflectance values but are calculated by determining the total solids content of the
wash water and subtracting the solids contributed by fabric particles, water
hardness, and the detergent. From the data obtained, then, we define a
medium particulate soil load as 6 to 8 lb of our standard dry soil test fabric
in 16 gal of water. It should be remembered that while we found the amount
of particulate soil removed to be similar for a medium home laundry bundle
and a medium dry soil load, the reflectance of a standard dry soil load, because it is necessary to measure reflectance changes, is much darker than
a medium home laundry bundle. Using parameters 1 and 2 as guidelines,
there are a number of variations that may be used for bleaching studies:

1. Light soil load-light fabric load
2. Light soil load-medium fabric load
3. Light soil load-heavy fabric load
4. Medium soil load-light fabric load
5. Medium soil load-medium fabric load
6. Medium soil load-heavy fabric load
7. Heavy soil load-light fabric load
8. Heavy soil load-medium fabric load
9. Heavy soil load-heavy fabric load

It is possible with the preceding combinations to evaluate thoroughly the
bleaching potential of a bleach on any soil or stain.

The results indicate that even with liquid sodium hypochlorite, which
under medium soil conditions has a flat soil removal curve above 200 ppm
available chlorine, it is possible to show performance differences above
200 ppm available chlorine. The data in Table 2 are based on a medium
fabric load of 6.6 lb and a heavy soil load equivalent to the soil bodies in
9.8 lb of regular dry soil.

The data in Table 3 show under the extreme conditions of a heavy fabric
load, (9.7 lb) and heavy loading of dry soil (12.1 lb) that the entire bleaching potential of the liquid sodium hypochlorite has been exhausted.

On the other hand, a light fabric load (4.3 lb) with a light soil load
(2.2 lb) shows that the full bleaching potential of the liquid sodium hypochlorite has not even begun to be reached (see Table 4).

The experiments just described point out the value of the weighted-soil
method as well as some interesting facts:

TABLE 2

Weighted-Soil Method: Medium Fabric Load, Heavy Soil Load

Bleach	Av Cl_2 (ppm)	Percent total soil removed[a]	Av Cl_2 (ppm) after bleaching	Percent soil removed by bleach
Sodium hypochlorite	212	33.2 ± 1.5	11.1	12.2
Sodium hypochlorite	243	37.0 ± 1.5	15.7	16.0

[a]Percent soil removed by 0.2% Tide in 150 ppm water hardness is 21.0 ± 1.5.

TABLE 3

Weighted-Soil Method: Heavy Fabric Load, Heavy Soil Load

Bleach	Av Cl_2 (ppm)	Percent total soil removed[a]	Av Cl_2 (ppm) after bleaching	Percent soil removed by bleach
Sodium hypochlorite	212	32.6 ± 1.7	2.0	9.4
Sodium hypochlorite	243	33.0 ± 1.4	4.2	9.8

[a]Percent soil removed by 0.2% Tide in 150 ppm water hardness is 22.2 ± 1.4.

TABLE 4

Weighted-Soil Method: Light Fabric Load, Light Soil Load

Bleach	Av Cl_2 (ppm)	Percent total soil removed[a]	Av Cl_2 (ppm) after bleaching	Percent soil removed by bleach
Sodium hypochlorite	212	39.1 ± 1.2	108.0	17.5
Sodium hypochlorite	243	39.8 ± 1.0	129.7	18.2

[a]Percent soil removed by 0.2% Tide in 150 ppm water hardness is 21.6 ± 1.1.

1. The soil removal of the detergent remained constant with increasing soil and fabric loads.
2. The percent soil removed by liquid sodium hypochlorite can be reduced by overloading with fabric and soil.
3. The soil-removing characteristics of liquid sodium hypochlorite can be significantly changed by varying the ratio of soil and fabric to water.
4. A small increase in available chlorine can produce a significant increase in soil removal under certain conditions of soil and fabric loads.

The data in the first experiment were also calculated as K/S [49] values and treated statistically and with the aid of the "t" test was used to determine if a real difference exists. The t test compares the observed differences between averages with the inherent variability within the test to tell if the difference is significant. The t value for the first experiment is 7.099. This value tells us under the conditions of the test it is probable that a significant difference exists between the soil removal for 212 ppm available chlorine hypochlorite and the soil removal for the 243 ppm available chlorine hypochlorite more than 99.9% of the time.

Although we have used only one soil and one bleach in our experiments, it is obvious the method described is quite versatile. The weighted-soil method is applicable for evaluating the full bleaching capability of all bleaches, liquid or dry, chlorine or oxygen, on a wide variety of soils and stains.

B. Evaluation Methods: Solid Surfaces

The reader should keep in mind we are not going to discuss evaluation methods for hard surface cleaners in the classical sense of the word as this subject is covered in another chapter. The usual hard surface evaluations involve soil, wax, or grease removal from floors, walls, dishes, and so forth. Because bleaching compounds as they relate to stain removal are used primarily in abrasive cleansers or scouring powders we limit our discussion to the bleaching accomplished by these products. There is undoubtedly some overlapping into the general cleaning properties of abrasive cleansers, but we try to separate the bleaching or chemical action of cleansers from the physical or abrasive action.

1. Spot Test

The purpose of this test is to measure the rate or rapidity of bleaching as well as the amount of tea and coffee stains removed from roughened porcelain or porcelainized steel plates. We recommend using the procedure for preparing tea and coffee stains which was discussed earlier in this

552 C. P. McCLAIN

chapter; however, any bleachable stain or soil is applicable. While this test is designed primarily to measure the rate of bleaching it may also be used for longer time periods to measure the overall stain-removing ability of a bleach.

The abrasive cleanser is applied to the tea- and coffee-stained test plates in the following manner. A template is prepared using a 3 1/2 in. square plastic sheet, 1/16 in. thick or approximately the same thickness as the porcelain plates. A square is cut in the plastic sheet just slightly larger than the 2 1/2 in. x 2 1/2 in. test plates so the plastic fits snuggly around them and flush with their surface. A circle 1 7/8 in. in diameter is cut in a piece of cardboard 1/32 in. in thickness and 3 in. square. The cardboard is taped to the plastic sheet and the resulting template is then placed over the test plate and the hole in the cardboard filled with 0.70 g of cleanser. The cleanser is scraped level and the template is removed, leaving a circle of cleanser 1 7/8 in. in diameter and 1/32 in. in thickness.

A thistle tube 10-ml buret is mounted in a stand with a beaker placed underneath. The buret is filled with 150 ppm hardness water at room temperature to the top of the thistle and the stopcock opened to a position which allows eight drops, approximately 0.5 ml, of water per 6 ± 0.2 sec. Once this setting has been made, the stopcock should never be touched again during the entire run of test plates. The buret must be filled to the top at the beginning of each application of water to each stained plate.

The test plates with cleanser are placed 1/2 in. beneath the tip of the buret until the eight drops of water have been applied. After the water is added the plate is removed and held level until the desired test time of 15, 30, or 60 sec has elapsed. The plate is then flushed thoroughly with cold tap water and allowed to air dry. The reflectance of the bleached plates is measured and the percent stain removal calculated.

To illustrate the value of the spot test we prepared three typical abrasive cleanser formulations which were identical in composition and available chlorine (0.5%), with the only difference being the particle size of the bleaching agent. The bleaching ingredient was potassium dichlorotriazinetrione (KDCC), and the three different particle sizes were coarse, medium and fine. The results in Table 5 were obtained using tea-stained porcelainized steel plates.

The data demonstrates the difference in rates of solution of the three particle sizes of KDCC. The test can further show that an increase in available chlorine from 0.50 to 1.00% does not necessarily produce a corresponding increase in percent SR for a cleanser containing coarse KDCC, but it will, because of its faster rate of solution, show a substantial increase in percent SR for the fine KDCC. The subject test will also, of course, distinguish the rates of solution of different types of bleaching agents.

TABLE 5

Spot Test: Particle Size Variation

Bleaching agent	Particle size	Percent tea stain removal		
		15 sec	30 sec	60 sec
Potassium dichloro- triazinetrione	Coarse	10.6 ± 1.1	18.3 ± 1.7	22.2 ± 1.1
	Medium	16.1 ± 1.4	23.5 ± 1.3	29.8 ± 1.3
	Fine	28.2 ± 1.0	33.7 ± 1.5	40.6 ± 1.0

2. Slurry Test

The slurry test differs from the spot test primarily because we are not trying to measure the rate or speed of bleaching, but whether or not the bleach goes into solution and how good a job of bleaching it does. If there is good bleaching potential but a poor rate of solution, it may be possible to improve the rate of solution by changing the basic ingredients in the abrasive cleanser formulation. We recommend the slurry test be used as a screening tool and further testing be done using the spot test.

The slurry test evaluates the bleaching performance of abrasive cleansers on tea- and coffee-stained plates in the following manner. Each formula to be tested is run in triplicate and all water is 150 ppm hardness and at room temperature. Weigh 150 g of cleanser and place in a 400-ml beaker (three beakers are needed for each condition), add 64.5 ml of water, and mix thoroughly to form a smooth slurry. This mixture results in a 70% cleanser-30% water slurry; however, any desired cleanser-to-water ratio may be used. Place two test plates back to back, or with the sides on which reflectance has been determined facing outward, and allow to soak for 30 sec. Remove plates, rinse thoroughly in cold tap water, and allow to air dry. Repeat immersion step again but remove one plate after 30 sec and the other after 60 sec. Repeat immersion step again removing both plates after 60 sec. The reflectance of the bleached plates is determined and the percent stain removal calculated.

To illustrate the difference in the stain-removing ability of different bleaching agents we prepared four typical abrasive cleanser formulas that were identical in composition except for the bleach used. The available chlorine of all formulas was 0.70%. The data in Table 6 were obtained using coffee-stained porcelainized steel plates.

TABLE 6

Slurry Test: Bleaching Agent Variation

Bleaching agent	Cleanser-to-water ratio	Percent coffee stain removal	
		30 sec	60 sec
Chlorinated TSP	70-30	25.0 ± 1.8	35.4 ± 1.1
Trichloroisocyanuric acid	70-30	33.7 ± 0.7	43.0 ± 1.6
Tetrachloroglycoluril	70-30	18.2 ± 0.9	19.6 ± 0.7
N,N-dichloro-p-carboxy-benzenesulfonamide	70-30	25.6 ± 1.4	40.3 ± 1.8

This data show a slight superiority for trichloroisocyanuric acid and N.N-dichloro-p-carboxybenzenesulfonamide (Halazone) over chlorinated TSP; however, a very definite deficiency is noted in the bleaching action of tetrachloroglycoluril. It is our opinion that the tetrachloroglycoluril could be eliminated from further testing in this type of abrasive cleanser formulation. Further testing using the spot test would be necessary to better classify the performance of the other three bleaches.

3. Scrub Test

The scrub test measures simultaneously the bleaching and abrasive action of the cleanser. It is used primarily to determine how the individual ingredients, that is, bleach, surfactants, phosphates, abrasives, and so on, influence overall stain removal. A formulation may be prepared eliminating any one of these ingredients, and the performance evaluated against a complete or standard formulation. The stain removal data should help to determine if the ingredient being tested adds to or detracts from the stain-removing properties of the formula.

The scrub test uses the Gardner Straight Line Washability and Abrasion Tester equipped with a DuPont fine-grained photographic sponge cut 3 in. long by 1 1/2 in. wide. Porcelainized steel plates 4 in. x 4 in. are stained with tea or coffee as previously described and used as test panels. The test sponge is rinsed thoroughly with water and 15 ml of the cleanser slurry to be tested is uniformly added to the sponge. We recommend using either 70/30 or a 50/50 cleanser-to-water ratio slurry. Using the Gardner tester scrub one-half of the test plate until it appears that about one-half of the stain has been removed, counting and recording the number of strokes

required. Rinse test plate thoroughly with water. Using another sponge
wash the other half of the plate with the comparison slurry using the same
cleanser-to-water ratio and the same number of strokes as for the first
half of the plate. A set of three stained plates is scrubbed in this manner.
The reflectance of the bleached plates is determined after scrubbing and
the percent stain removal calculated.

The scrub test will show differences in the abrasiveness of silica flour
and feldspar. It will also demonstrate the beneficial effect of phosphate and
surfactants. It will show, in some cases, that the improper selection of
surfactants and phosphates can detract from the action of the bleach. The
scrub test is another tool to evaluate the bleaching and total stain-removing
properties of an abrasive cleanser formula.

C. Factors Influencing Bleaching

During the course of this chapter we have mentioned some of the factors
that influence bleaching performance, but in this section we discuss these
factors more fully. We again emphasize we are not discussing the merits
of any particular procedure or formula but trying to alert the investigator
concerning some of the factors that may substantially influence his test results. While we describe for the most part fabric evaluations, many of the
findings are also valid on solid surfaces.

Unfortunately, it is impossible for the manufacturer of a bleach to control precisely any of the conditions we discuss. It is therefore necessary
to study their effect on the performance of bleach candidates. It is equally
important, if possible, to determine which of the factors has the single
greatest effect on the stain removal characteristics of the bleach under study.
We do not attempt to analyze the data completely because an entire book
could be written on how one particular factor affects another, which in turn
affects the third, and so on. The experiments done with the weighted-soil
method in which we merely varied the soil indicate the enormity of the problem of analyzing all the factors in bleaching. We attempt here to present
meaningful data so the reader may more fully understand the mechanism of
bleaching.

1. Time, Temperature, and Concentration

Using tea-stained cotton test fabric, we examined the effect of time and
concentration on stain removal. Three chlorine bleaches: liquid sodium
hypochlorite; potassium dichlorotriazinetrione (KDCC); and 1,3-dichloro-
5,5-dimethylhyantoin (Halane), were studied (see Table 7). The dry bleaches
KDCC and Halane were tested in a typical dry bleach formulation containing
phosphate, surfactant, and salt cake. Test conditions for the experiment
were 0.15% heavy-duty detergent in 150 ppm water hardness and a 20:1
liquor-to-cloth ratio. Bleaching cycles were run at 120°F and a pH of 9.2.

TABLE 7

Effect of Time and Concentration on Tea Stain Removal
of Chlorine Bleaches

Time of wash cycle (min)	Bleaching ingredient			Av Cl_2 (ppm)
	NaOCl	KDCC	Halane	
10	20.7% SR	14.7% SR	1.2% SR	25
20	20.4	13.9	4.3	25
30	20.7	13.1	8.6	25
10	55.0	43.6	9.0	50
20	54.4	44.8	15.2	50
30	54.6	50.7	22.1	50
10	75.9	66.8	34.5	100
20	83.2	78.3	47.3	100
30	83.9	78.4	51.1	100
10	80.7	78.1	70.0	200
20	83.9	82.3	77.1	200
30	84.4	83.5	79.2	200
Percent SR by detergent (0.15%)				
10		9.2		0
20		10.2		0
30		11.1		0

The percent stain removal is the stain removed by the bleach as the percent stain removal by the detergent has been subtracted from the total stain removal.

The data in Table 7 point out quite clearly that under the parameters of our test, an increase in bleaching time from 10 to 30 min has only a small effect on the tea-stain-removing properties of sodium hypochlorite. These data were confirmed using radioactive stain [43] and it was found that most of the stain removal is accomplished in the first 5 min. The only substantial increase in stain removal due to time is in the critical concentration range of 50 to 100 ppm available chlorine. Because, as mentioned earlier in this chapter, this concentration range is on the steepest portion of the sodium hypochlorite bleaching curve, these data are not unexpected.

KDCC, which shows lower stain removal than sodium hypochlorite over the entire concentration range, is generally more susceptible to changes in bleaching time than is sodium hypochlorite. It should be noted the bleaching characteristics of KDCC are similar to sodium hypochlorite, especially at 100 ppm available chlorine, where the largest increase in stain removal produced by the factor time is also observed for KDCC.

The stain-removing ability of Halane is influenced more by changes in bleaching time than either sodium hypochlorite or KDCC. This is also as expected because in the range of 25 to 100 ppm available chlorine the stain-removing ability of Halane is considerably poorer than that of either sodium hypochlorite or KDCC; however, at 200 ppm available chlorine, Halane is rated only slightly inferior to these bleaching agents. These data indicate that Halane does have fair bleaching potential, but to realize this potential fully a higher level of available chlorine, between 100 and 200 ppm, is needed for it than for KDCC or sodium hypochlorite.

The effect of temperature on stain removal was evaluated at 75, 90, 120, and 140°F. This experiment was done using the same concentrations and conditions described in Sec. IV,C,1 in the preceding time and concentration study. The data obtained show that the temperature range of 75 to 140°F produces only a slightly larger effect on stain removal for all bleaches than did an increase in time from 10 to 30 min. Generally speaking, the same statements made for increasing time are applicable for increasing temperature. Sodium hypochlorite is rated slightly superior to KDCC in stain removal at all temperatures and both are rated more effective than Halane. The performance of Halane is improved more by temperature increases than are sodium hypochlorite or KDCC.

We evaluated the effect of time (10-30 min), temperature (75-140°F), and concentration (25-200 ppm Av chlorine) on the performance of hypochlorite, KDCC, and Halane. The single greatest factor influencing stain removal is concentration or available chlorine. A secondary factor, although not nearly as important as available chlorine, is temperature. Time is found to be the least important aspect in stain removal of the three variables we examined.

A study of the stain removal by oxygen compounds as influenced by temperature and concentration shows anomaly in the performance of sodium perborates as compared to other bleaching ingredients. It is well known that under European washing temperatures, at or near the boil, perborates show good stain-removing ability. However, at U.S. washing temperatures, their stain-removing properties in relation to chlorine bleaches are rated only fair [24].

TABLE 8

Effect of Temperature and Concentration on Tea Stain Removal
of Oxygen Bleaches

Temperature of wash cycle (^{o}F)	Bleaching ingredient		Av O$_2$ (ppm)	
	Oxone	Perborate	Oxone	Perborate
120	16.2% SR	7.0% SR	10	20
140	28.9	16.3	10	20
160	41.2	28.4	10	20
120	36.0	8.4	20	30
140	49.5	17.4	20	30
160	57.0	29.0	20	30
120	43.8	12.9	30	40
140	58.5	21.3	30	40
160	61.0	35.9	30	40
Percent SR by detergent (0.15%)				
120		9.8		0
140		15.1		0
160		20.3		0

Using tea-stained cotton fabric we studied the effect of temperature and concentration on the stain-removing ability of sodium perborate and Oxone as shown in Table 8. Sodium perborate and Oxone were tested in typical dry bleach formulations containing phosphate, surfactant, and salt cake. The test conditions for this experiment are identical to those described in Sec. IV,C,1. The bleaching cycle is 15 min and the percent stain removal is that removed by the dry bleach as the stain removal by the detergent has been subtracted from the total stain removal.

The data in Table 8 illustrate quite clearly that the performance of both Oxone and perborate is improved by increasing temperature or concentration. It also shows that the performance of Oxone is more affected by increases in concentration than in temperature, while inversely perborate is influenced more by increases in temperature than in concentration. It is interesting to note that even at what would be considered elevated temperatures for U.S.

wash cycles, 160°F, the performance of perborate is well below that of conventional chlorine bleaches. A more complete temperature versus time versus concentration study on sodium perborates has been done and prepared in a slide rule type of indicator by the FMC Corporation. The FMC evaluation uses tea stain and covers a temperature range of 120 to 200°F, bleaching intervals of 5 to 25 min, and available oxygen of 0 to 300 ppm.

2. Substrates

This section on substrates (which were briefly touched on in Sec. III, A and B) is by necessity short and incomplete. We are of the opinion the research work done on the performance of bleaches on varying substrates is quite sparse. In the case of fabric substrates the reason is quite obvious: New fibers, fiber blends, resins, and resin treatments are being developed faster than they can be evaluated. This is also true, but to a lesser degree, with solid surface substrates. It is our intention, then, to alert the researcher to some of the problems that can be encountered. Keeping in mind the rather limited experience and data in this area, we have found the following factors should be taken into consideration:

1. Define the substrate with which you are working, i.e., 100% nylon, porcelain, porcelainized steel, etc.
2. Use a mix of varying substrates in testing procedures, e.g., 100% cotton, 100% cotton permanent press, 65% polyester/35% cotton, etc.
3. Define the porosity of your substrate, i.e., is fabric tight or close weave versus loose weave, in porcelain glaze versus unglazed, etc.
4. Define the condition of substrate to be used, i.e., new, laboratory aged substrates washed and worn under in-home conditions have different staining and stain removal characteristics than laboratory-aged substrates.
5. State accurately the amount and type of a particular stain as well as the particular substrate to which it is applied.

Obviously some laboratories cannot justify the time necessary to conduct all the above-mentioned studies. These laboratories can make up this deficiency with thorough literature searches and good industry contacts. The information gained from these sources may provide answers that will shorten a planned bleaching evaluation.

In our bleaching evaluation we have found standard stains such as tea and coffee are readily removed from cotton, more difficult to remove from permanent press cotton, and very difficult to remove from nylon. A fabric composed of 65% polyester and 35% cotton permanent press has stain removal properties somewhere between cotton permanent press and 100% polyester.

TABLE 9

Tea Stain Removal by Sodium Hypochlorite from Cotton and Nylon Fabric

Type of fabric	Av Cl_2 (ppm)	Percent tea stain removal
Cotton (new and desized)	200	82.8
Cotton (new permanent press)	200	69.4
Nylon (new tricot)	200	38.7

We examined the ability of liquid sodium hypochlorite to remove tea stain from desized cotton, new permanent press cotton, and nylon tricot (see Table 9). Test conditions for the experiment were 0.15% heavy-duty detergent in 150 ppm water hardness and a 20:1 liquor-to-cloth ratio. Bleaching cycles were 15 min at 120°F. The percent stain removal is the stain removed by the bleach as the percent stain removed by the detergent has been subtracted from the total stain removal.

The data in Table 9 are but one simple example of how bleaches perform on varying substrates. In the marketplace of today, where changes in fibers, fiber blends, and permanent press resins are occurring almost daily, it is vitally important to know how bleaches perform on these new substrates.

3. pH, Surfactants, and Builders

In any discussion of bleaching and stain removal considerable thought should be given to the roles of pH, surfactants, and builders. Although bleaches are generally used in a well-buffered system, that is, in conjunction with phosphates or a heavy-duty detergent that contains its own builders and surfactants, it is still necessary to determine what effect, if any, these factors have on the stain removal, fabric damage, and stability properties of a particular bleach or bleaching ingredient. It is quite possible to develop a bleach with excellent stain-removing characteristics which has unsatisfactory fabric damage and/or storage stability properties.

In an effort to determine the effect of pH, surfactants, and builders on bleaching performance we must again set down arbitrary guidelines and definitions. We define improved bleaching performance as "improvement in the bleaching action of the bleaching ingredient only, not of the entire formulation." This means the stain removal of the experimental or improved formula must be determined both with and without bleaching agent and should be compared simultaneously to a basic bleach formula with and without the same bleaching ingredient being studied in the experimental formulas. The soil removal properties of all four formulas can then be compared and it should be possible to say if any improvement in bleaching performance, as compared to an overall performance improvement, occasioned by a better surfactant, or more efficient water softener, and so forth, has taken place.

A basic bleach formula in the case of liquid sodium hypochlorite is obvious and changes in pH and the addition of surfactants, builders, and so on, can be studied rather easily. In the case of dry bleach we should consider a basic formula as sodium sulfate and the bleaching agent whereas an abrasive cleanser is silica flour and bleaching agent. It is quite obvious that builders and surfactants should be added to improve the overall performance of the product but what we are also interested in finding out is do they actually improve the performance of the bleaching agent. For the purpose of our discussion, let us define a dry bleach and abrasive cleanser formula as follows:

Dry bleach	Abrasive cleanser
3% Linear alkylbenzenesulfonate	3% Linear alkylbenzenesulfonate
25% Sodium tripolyphosphate	5% Sodium tripolyphosphate
q.s. Sodium sulfate	q.s. Silica flour

In an effort to determine the effect of pH on bleaching performance, we consider several bleaching systems, liquid and dry, with the dry including abrasive cleansers. Most commercially available liquid sodium hypochlorite bleaches are manufactured in a pH range of 11.4 to 12.5 on an as-is basis. We believe the majority of dry bleach formulas in a 1.0% solution are in the pH range of 8.5 to 9.5. Therefore, we refer to a low-alkalinity bleach as a formulation having a pH below 8.5 and a high-alkalinity bleach as having a pH above 9.5. In the case of abrasive cleansers they generally have a 1.0 solution pH ranging from 10.5 to 11.0. As with dry bleaches, products below and above these limits are considered low- and high-alkalinity abrasive cleansers.

  a. Liquid sodium hypochlorite. In the preparation of liquid sodium hypochlorite it is possible to chlorinate the bleach to a desired pH [50] and it is also possible to chlorinate fully at a low pH and adjust to the desired pH with sodium hydroxide. For experimental purposes we prepared liquid bleach, 5.25% sodium hypochlorite, using both the preceding methods, at pH levels of 10.8, 11.4, 12.0, and 12.4.

Bleaching studies were conducted with these bleaches using a washing machine concentration of 200 ppm available chlorine in water of 150 ppm

TABLE 10

Dry Soil Removal from Cotton by Sodium Hypochlorite
at Varying pH: Weighted-Soil Method[a]

Liquid NaOCl prepared by	pH	Av Cl_2 (ppm)	Percent soil removed[b] by bleach
Fully chlorinating to	10.8	200	12.6
Fully chlorinating to	11.4	200	12.1
Fully chlorinating to	12.0	200	12.9
Fully chlorinating to	12.4	200	12.7
Adjusting with NaOH to	10.8	200	12.1
Adjusting with NaOH to	11.4	200	12.4
Adjusting with NaOH to	12.0	200	12.2
Adjusting with NaOH to	12.4	200	12.7

[a]Fabric load 7.1 lb; soil load 10.0 lb.

[b]Percent soil removed by 0.2% Tide in 150 ppm water hardness is
21.1 ± 1.2.

hardness with no detergent and the usual bleaching time and temperature of
15 min at 120°F. Bleaching effectiveness was determined on tea, coffee,
and dry soil, weighted soil, cotton swatches. The data indicate that in the
absence of a heavy-duty detergent the lower the pH, the better is the bleaching action. Similar studies shown in Table 10 made in the presence of Tide
at 0.20% concentration showed no significant differences in the performance
of the bleaches at varying pH.

We conclude from this study that low-pH sodium hypochlorite is probably
more effective under stubborn stain usage and for hard surface cleaning
where no detergent buffering action is encountered. However, for normal
washing machine usage the initial pH of the bleach appears to have no effect
on overall stain- or soil-removing efficiency.

Liquid sodium hypochlorite storage studies show that the method of preparation, chlorination to a specific pH or chlorination to a low pH and

adjusting to the desired pH with sodium hydroxide, has no effect on the
finished product's stability. The pH of liquid sodium hypochlorite must,
however, be 11.3 or greater to have acceptable storage stability [51]. Because pH does affect stability [52] and pH 11.0 is in the critical area for
liquid sodium hypochlorite, we recommend a minimum pH of 11.3 to ensure
good product stability.

The addition of certain surfactants, Dowfax 2A1 [53] and cetyl betaine
which are themselves stable in, and do not affect the stability of, liquid
hypochlorite, does improve performance. This is also true for builders
such as tetrasodium and tetrapotassium pyrophosphate when added in quantities of 10% or more. Again, however, we find the improvement in bleaching disappears when the bleach is used in conjunction with a good heavy-duty
detergent. This is not to say the addition of surfactants and builders to
liquid hypochlorite is not somewhat beneficial in removing soil and stains,
but we do not believe they significantly improve the soil- and stain-removing
properties of the bleach.

b. Halane. Although we have made only a slight mention of Halane,
1,3-dichloro-5,5-dimethylhydantoin [54], we briefly discuss this bleaching
agent here because its performance does appear to be influenced by changes
in pH. While doing some routine bleaching and pH studies with Halane, we
first noted great losses in available chlorine at pH 9.0. A more thorough
examination of this phenomenon [55] showed that at pH 9.0 Halane decomposes
rapidly to 1-chloro-5,5-dimethylhydantoin, N-chloroisopropylamine, chloride ion, nitrogen, and carbon dioxide. Although we believe a pH above
10.0 is not practical for washing machine conditions, other investigators
found the reflectance of unbleached muslin is significantly increased by
aqueous solutions of Halane in the pH range of 12 to 14 [56]. It is our opinion that this finding is more applicable to scouring cleansers than it is to
dry bleaches.

c. Chlorinated isocyanurates. The family of chlorinated isocyanurates
shows an anomaly of bleaching properties at varying pH levels. Our data
indicate the solubility of trichloroisocyanuric acid (TCCA) is both greater
and faster at pH levels above 10.0 The stain removal both on fabric and
solid surfaces of TCCA is also enhanced at a pH of above 10.0 We find
generally that dichloroisocyanuric acid (DCCA) is less affected than TCCA,
but a slight improvement in performance is also noted on fabric and solid
surfaces at a pH above 10.0. The sodium and potassium salts of dichloroisocyanuric acid do not respond to changes in pH within the ranges previously
discussed for dry bleaches. Again we want to emphasize the point that the
addition of surfactants, builders, fluorescent whitening agents, and so on,
does improve the overall performance of the formula but not the bleaching
activity of potassium or sodium dichloroisocyanurate.

d. Perborates. Considerable work has been done using changes in pH
and builder systems to activate or improve the bleaching performance of

perborate compounds. Small improvements in bleaching activity have been
noted for high-alkalinity formulations containing large amounts of sodium
silicate. It is our opinion, however, the slight improvement in bleaching
performance would be more than offset by reduced product stability and increased fabric damage. Considering bleaching performance, product stability, and fabric damage, we believe the optimum pH for perborate bleaches
is between 8.5 and 9.5.

    e. Potassium monopersulfate. Potassium monopersulfate (Oxone) is
quite different in respect to changes in pH than are the other bleaches we
have discussed. In a pH study Oxone was added to a typical linear alkylbenzenesulfonate-based heavy-duty detergent at a level that would produce
12 ppm available oxygen in the wash water. Because Oxone is quite acid
the pH of the detergent-Oxone solution is 8.4. All other pH variations were
made by adding sodium hydroxide to the wash water. The pH of the heavy-
duty detergent at 0.2% concentration in 150 ppm water hardness is 9.3. The
detergent alone was run as a control at its normal pH of 9.3 and adjusted
with sodium hydroxide to pH levels of 9.7, 10.0, 10.4, and 10.8. Test
conditions for the experiment in addition to a heavy-duty detergent at 0.2%
concentration in 150 ppm water hardness are a 20:1 liquor-to-cloth ratio
and a bleaching cycle of 20 min at 120°F. Shown in Table 11 are the results
obtained using Oxone over a pH range.

    The data indicate that the percent tea stain removal by the detergent
alone is almost doubled by raising the pH from 9.3 to 10.8. Over the same
pH range the percent stain removal by Oxone alone is almost trebled. The
same evaluation was repeated at 24 ppm available oxygen and results were
similar, except the big jump in stain removal was between pH 9.7 and 10.0
rather than 10.4 and 10.8, as was the case at 12 ppm available oxygen.

    As mentioned earlier, we have not attempted to cover the obvious func-
tions of pH, surfactants, and builders which include water softening, grease
emulsification, soil suspension, wetting, and the like. We are certain
these areas are covered fully in other chapters of this book. Anyone with
a knowledge of detergents is cognizant of the role these compounds play in
overall cleaning performance. We have also purposely neglected to mention
fluorescent whitening agents for the same reasons.

    In the case of builders and surfactants it becomes a job of selecting or
balancing economics versus performance, that is, the most economical and
effective surfactants and builders for the bleaching agent of choice. What
we have tried to convey is that it is necessary to evaluate these factors on
new bleaching agents for they can, and in some cases do, substantially affect the bleaching performance and/or stability of the bleaching agent.

TABLE 11

Tea Stain Removal from Cotton by Oxone at Varying pH

Bleaching agent	pH[a] Before	After	Av O_2 (ppm)	Percent tea stain removal By detergent	By bleach	Total
Oxone	8.4	8.0	12	Not determined	Not determined	20.7
Oxone	9.3	9.0	12	10.7	13.4	24.1
Oxone	9.7	9.4	12	12.0	14.3	26.3
Oxone	10.0	9.6	12	13.2	16.3	29.5
Oxone	10.4	10.1	12	17.6	22.6	40.2
Oxone	10.8	10.5	12	20.1	39.0	59.1

[a]Before and after bleaching cycle.

D. Measurements

It is not our intention in this section, which is devoted to color measurements, to in any way misrepresent ourselves as experts in this field. For the novice interested in the fundamentals of color and color measurements, we would refer him to Hunter [57], Judd [58], Hardy [59], and Judd and Wyszecki [60]. Here we give a brief description of some of the less expensive instruments currently available for measuring and observing color as it pertains to bleaching.

In 1931 the International Commission on Illumination (ICI), later renamed Commission Internationale de l'Eclairage (CIE), recommended all color data be expressed using the "tristimulus system." The idea behind tristimulus values is quite simple and based on the fact that the tristimulus values of each pure spectral color have been determined. The tristimulus values were determined by what is defined as the "standard observer." The standard observer actually consisted of a group of 17 normal observers whose results were averaged. The results of the standard observer were adopted in 1931 by the CIE as the fundamental data on which modern colorimetry is based.

At the time the standard observer was set up by the CIE they also recommend three standard illuminants as well as angular conditions and a
reflectance standard. The standard illuminants are the following:

1. Illuminant A, which represents a gas-filled incandescent lamp oper-
    ated at a color temperature of $2854^{\circ}K$.
2. Illuminant B, which is operated at a color temperature of $4870^{\circ}K$,
    represents noon sunlight.
3. Illuminant C, which is operated at a color temperature of $6770^{\circ}K$,
    represents average daylight on a completely overcast day.

The angular specifications recommended for measuring opaque specimens
are that the light will strike the specimen at 45° and that specimen will be
viewed along the perpendicular of its surface or 0°, The reflectance standard for opaque specimens is a white surface prepared by collecting magnesium oxide on a suitable surface. It is, of course, possible to prepare
more durable secondary standards by calibrating them against freshly prepared magnesium oxide.

The primary colors chosen by CIE, of course, do not exist, but are
defined mathematically and are designated X, Y, and Z. Hunter designed
three filters, A, amber or red, G, green, and B, blue, to duplicate X, Y,
and Z and found the approximate tristimulus values relative to a magnesium
oxide surface to be

$$X = 0.80A + 0.18B$$
$$Y = 1.00G$$
$$Z = 1.18B$$

Hunter simultaneously adjusted a projection lamp to approximate illuminant C

In the preceding several paragraphs we have tried to give a thumbnail
description of the reasoning and developmental work which led to photoelectric tristimulus colorimetry. Most of the instruments that are used to
measure detergency, whiteness retention, bleaching, and so on, are based
on tristimulus values obtained with illuminant C, 45° 0° geometry, and a
magnesium oxide standard. The tristimulus values for X, Y, and Z may be
treated mathematically a number of different ways, depending on the instrument used; however, the fact remains these values are still the basis for
calculating yellowness, whiteness, color difference between two surfaces,
and soil and stain removal.

1. Instrumental

There are many manufacturers and types of recording spectrophotometers, abridged spectrophotometers, and filter photometers or colori-
meters. The author has found that the medium-size laboratory can do very

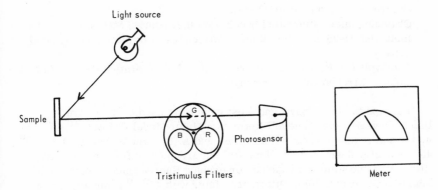

FIG. 3. Optical system for filter photometer.

nicely using a filter photometer; however, we briefly mention the other two types.

Of the recording spectrophotometers the General Electric (Hardy) instrument has achieved the reputation of the standard of accuracy for color measurement. This instrument is quite expensive and we believe not necessary in bleaching and detergency work.

The abridged spectrophotometers are usually less expensive and simpler to operate than a recording spectrophotometer. Some of the abridged spectrophotometers available are the Martin & Sweets, Institute of Paper Chemistry; Color-Eye from Kollmorgen Corporation; Zeiss Elrepho from West Germany; and the Colorcord Unit from Loebl Ltd., made in the United Kingdom.

As mentioned earlier, we believe a filter photometer will do an adequate job and is applicable for bleaching studies. The optical system for a typical filter photometer is shown in Fig. 3.

It is most important to remember that the instrument shown filters the light after it has reflected from the sample and it will, therefore, measure fluorescence. A filter photometer that filters the light before it has impinged on the sample will not measure fluorescence.

Some of the more common commercially available filter photometers are

Color-Eye: Kollmorgen Corporation (United States)
Colorcord: Loebl Ltd. (United Kingdom)
Color Difference Meter: Gardner Laboratories (United States)
Colormaster: Manufacturers Engineering and Equipment Company (United States)

Colormate: Neotec (United States)
Chromatronic: Automated Specialties Inc. (United States)
Hunterlab D-25 and -40: Hunter Associates Laboratory Inc. (United States)
Photovolt 610 Reflection Meter: Photovolt Corporation (United States)
Zeiss: Elrepho (West Germany)

Perhaps the best known and most commonly used of the instruments listed above are the Photovolt Reflection Meter Model 610 with 0° 45° geometry and readings recorded as G, B, and A (R); Hunterlab D-40 with 0° 45° geometry described as a blue (B) and green (G) reflectometer with a filter available which will include or exclude fluorescence effect; Hunterlab D-25 Color and Color Difference Meter with 45° 0° geometry which measures color in terms of L, a, and b values; Gardner AC-3 and C-4 Automatic Color Difference Meters with the AC-3 having a geometry of 45° 0° and the C-4 0° 45°. Gardner meters have three readout options: L, a_L, b_L; R_D, a_{Rd}, b_{Rd}; and R, G, B; Colormaster has 45° 0° geometry and gives values as R, G, and B.

Regardless of the instrument used, there are a number of basic factors that should be considered and followed when selecting an instrument for measuring color. Some of the factors that should influence your particular selection are as follows:

1. Does the instrument measure the effect of FWAs (fluorescent whitening agents) on fabric?
2. What is the most rapid and accurate machine for your application?
3. What is the size and physical nature of the test fabric to be studied?
4. How often is the instrument to be used, i.e., cost versus usage?
5. Do you want and need tristimulus values or are you interested only in the trigreen function?

The following color measurements are applicable for judging various aspects of bleaching performance and can be determined with a filter photometer:

1. Lightness or degree from white to black only. Use G, Y, Rd, or L scales.
2. Yellowness or yellowness index used to measure fabric degradation, chlorine-retentive resins, etc., on white and near-white surfaces. Use green and blue filters or green, blue, and amber (red) filters.
3. Blue reflectance measures yellow and blue and is especially useful in color pickup studies as well as bleaching studies using artificial soils. Use B, Z, and b filters.
4. Amber or red reflectance measures red and green. Use A or R, X, and a filters.

5. Whiteness, i.e., whiteness of fabric. Use green and blue filters.
6. "NBS" unit of color difference: the amount of color difference between two surfaces.

Now that we have explained a little about color, selection of an instrument, and calculations that are applicable for bleaching studies we are ready to make color measurements. The following are some of the factors that can and do affect reflectance and color measurements:

1. Some instruments do not compensate for gloss, and readings may be high on glossy surfaces.
2. Use a working standard that is spectrally similar to the sample being measured.
3. Make certain fabric is flat and free of wrinkles.
4. Read fabric in both warp and fill directions, 90°.
5. Use a fabric backing the same as, or similar to, the fabric being measured.
6. Measure all fabrics under the same tension or pressure.
7. Determine if color bodies, i.e., soil or stain, are uniform throughout the fabric.

We think the preceding suggestions, used in conjunction with those made earlier in this section and some common color sense, will allow the investigator to obtain accurate and meaningful instrumental color measurements.

2. Visual

We believe the more color factors measured the better the chance of developing a bleach product that will be successful in the marketplace. As discussed earlier, such aspects as stain removal, color change, color pickup, and so on, should be measured instrumentally. We are also of the opinion that they should be examined visually. Regardless of the sensitivity and expense of the instrument it is always necessary to verify instrumental data with that extra-sensitive apparatus known as the human eye.

Because this chapter is concerned with bleaching and stain removal, we do not attempt to delve into the role of fluorescent whitening agents (FWA) as they pertain to visual whiteness. It goes without saying, however, the interaction of bleaches and FWAs must be considered in any visual evaluation. What we attempt to do here is give the reader some simple facts about making observations that pertain to evaluating the visual effects of bleaches on fabric.

There are several factors that must be kept in mind while making visual observations. The first and foremost of these is what does "Mrs. Average Housewife" prefer? The information we have obtained indicates the U.S. housewife, while inspecting her laundry, prefers white clothes with a slightly

violet cast. The reason for her selection of violet-whites has not been defined, but is probably related to psychological factors.

Another factor to be considered is that the human eye can detect, under
ideal conditions, a reflectance difference of 1.00%. The eye is four times
as critical of yellowness, G-B, as compared to white G alone [61]. This
means that in yellowness reflectance the eye can detect a difference of
0.25%, which is an important number to remember in studying bleaches.

We know that an object such as fabric is visible because it reflects light.
The color of the fabric is dependent on the color of the light reflected by the
fabric to the observer's eye. It becomes apparent, then, that color is not
a characteristic of the fabric alone, but also of the illuminating source.

a. Daylight. In the days before clothes dryers, and even to a large
extent today, the light source most readily available was natural daylight of
one type or another. Traditionally, people in businesses involving color
have preferred the light from the north window, or as it is referred to sci-
entifically, north sky daylight. The reason north sky daylight is preferred
is because it is the least variable type of natural daylight. It is further
noted that the variables can be reduced even more by using a slightly overcast north daylight.

We are well aware of the variabilities of north daylight but still believe
a large number of housewives view their clothes under natural daylight.
We are of the opinion it is good practice to view test fabrics under north
daylight. It is a relatively simple task to set up a small panel to rate colors
and color changes of fabric caused by bleach candidates. In this day of
numerous resins, fabric blends, and fabrics, we think viewing in north daylight is another way of ensuring the eventual success of your bleach product.

b. Artificial light sources. As mentioned earlier, north sky daylight
and natural daylight vary considerably in quantity and color composition. It
also becomes obvious that standard daylight is at times unavailable. The
investigator may also find if a large number of samples are being studied
over an extended time period, it is somewhat of a task to make many trips
to the window or sidewalk to make color evaluations. Because of these
factors there have been attempts to develop electric lights, filters, and
combinations of lights and filters that will produce a constant light source
which simulates daylight or north daylight. We discuss two of these artificial light sources briefly; if the reader is interested, he may investigate
this type of lighting further on his own.

The Examolite, manufactured by the Macbeth Daylighting Corporation of
Newburgh, New York, produces a light that is a combination blend of precision color-connected fluorescent and incandescent light sources simulating
north daylight at 7400°K [62]. Their colorimetric data show x = 0.302 and
y = 0.312. They also manufacture Macbeth filtered incandescent high-fidelity

daylight lamps which are said to duplicate natural daylight closely. We
discuss the Examolite, which simulates north daylight, as our experience
is with this fixture and we have found it to be reliable and fairly constant in
intensity and color illumination.

The Examolite may be installed as a suspended fixture or it can be
mounted flush in the ceiling. Information on the electrical features and the
various combinations of incandescent bulbs, filters, and fluorescent tubes
available can be obtained from the manufacturer. Suffice it to say, there
are many different combinations and arrangements that can be made, depending on your specific requirements.

For our particular application, we have hung the Examolite 6 ft over
the working area. We prepared gray cotton draw curtains that completely
enclose the viewing area and exclude extraneous light. We feel this supplies
us with an ideal neutral gray background. Using our particular arrangement,
a large number of test swatches may be studied simultaneously by one or two
viewers. A good duplication of results using the Examolite and comparisons
obtained in north daylight has been observed.

Another good source of artificial light are the Ultra-Lux fluorescent
lamps manufactured by the Nu-Lite Division of El-tronics, Inc., of Newark,
New Jersey. The Ultra-Lux can be used in practically every type of fluorescent fixture and supplies a spectral distribution curve very similar to
that of the ideal slightly overcast north daylight [63]. So that the reflectance
of the fluorescent ficture does not change or distort the color of Ultra-Lux,
an internal reflector is built into the lamp itself. A viewing room, therefore, can be built quite easily, using existing fixtures and the Ultra-Lux
fluorescent lamps.

For our particular situation, we equipped an entire small room with
Ultra-Lux lamps. We had the walls and viewing surface painted a neutral
gray and were in business in short order. Our room allows many people,
including interested top management personnel, to view the test swatches
all at one time. We found an excellent duplication of results using Ultra-
Lux lamps when compared to actual north daylight observations.

Before we conclude this section we would briefly like to mention the use
of an ultraviolet or black light source. We believe every bleach laboratory
should have a black light if just to make a visual comparison of fluorescent
whitening agent destruction or buildup produced by various dry bleaches.
It is also handy for quick determination or demonstration as to whether a
particular product contains an FWA. A black light can also be used to determine if fabric damage has taken place. We discuss this latter use in
the section devoted to fabric damage.

E. Calculation of Test Results

The final step in any test of bleaching performance is of necessity that of computing the results. In nearly all cases, one must reduce the raw data to a form that can be compared to the results of other tests as well as communicated to others. This requires that we develop some numbers which convey the relative bleaching efficiency of the samples tested. The specific equations employed in the reduction of experimental data must be selected in view of the type of measurement employed.

1. Visual Data

The lack of an expensive reflectometer need not prevent one from making exact measurements of bleaching effects. The human eye is a very precise instrument capable of yielding accurate data when properly employed. While the eye will not, of course, yield direct percentage measurements as does a reflectometer, it can quite exactly detect equivalence when two samples are directly compared. Moreover, the eye can reliably detect if a given object is lighter or darker than another similar object. Such visual evaluations of bleaching performance can give no better than ordinal measures. Statistical treatment of these data requires use of nonparametric statistical tests. A nonparametric test is one that does not depend on the validity of the usual assumptions about the parameters of the population from which the test samples are drawn. In particular, it is not required that the variables being tested have been measured on an interval or ratio scale. These nonparametric tests do not depend on arithmetic manipulation of test data, since the common operations of adding, dividing, averaging, and the like are invalid for both nominal and ordinal data.

a. Paired comparisons. Let us consider an example that shows how the "plus, equal, or minus" system of the human eye may be made to yield results of a high confidence level:

We wish to compare bleach A to bleach B. We bleach a number of test swatches with bleach A and a like number of test swatches with bleach B, taking both sets from the same group of stained swatches and carefully using the same method and conditions for each set. After bleaching, we arrange the swatches in pairs, one swatch bleached with A paired with each bleached with B. We cover or turn under the identification marks and visually examine each pair of swatches, deciding which is the lighter. For each pair in which we feel A is the lighter, we record an "A." For each pair in which swatch B is lighter, we record a "B." If we absolutely cannot decide which swatch is lighter, we can record a "0," but each such decision weakens the power of the test. It is better to guess in these cases and arbitrarily select a winner. We compute the results by the following steps:

1. Count the number of As recorded.
2. Count the number of Bs recorded.
3. Calculate D by subtracting the smaller count from the larger.
4. Calculate N by totaling the number of As and the number of Bs.

Now if more As than Bs were recorded, we guess that A is the better bleach. If the value of D from step 3 is greater than $1.6\sqrt{N}$, we can be 90% confident that our guess is correct. If D is greater than $2\sqrt{N}$, our confidence level increases to 95%, whereas if D exceeds $2.6\sqrt{N}$, we can be 99% confident that A is the better bleach.

The statistical test we have just applied is known as the "sign test" from the fact that it depends only on plus or minus relationships rather than exactly measured quantitative data [64, 65]. The test is more powerful as N increases in size. The smaller the difference we wish to detect with certainty, the larger the number of sample pairs we must judge.

Suppose that in the previous example, we scored eight As and four Bs, having run 12 pairs of swatches, with no ties. Now D = 4, which is less than $1.6\sqrt{12}$, or about 5.5, and we are therefore less than 90% confident that A is a better bleach. However, if we obtained the same result each time, we would consider a ratio of 8:4 a <u>commercially</u> significant superiority for bleach A. We can compute the total number of pairs we must judge in order to demonstrate that a given ratio of superiority is statistically significant at any desired confidence level:

$$N'_{0.90} = \left(\frac{1.6N}{D} \right)^2 \tag{8}$$

$$N'_{0.95} = \left(\frac{2N}{D} \right)^2 \tag{9}$$

$$N'_{0.99} = \left(\frac{2.6N}{D} \right)^2 \tag{10}$$

N' values thus obtained, taking N = 12 and D = 4, are the sample sizes needed to demonstrate statistical significance for an 8:4 ratio at the indicated confidence levels. For the example just considered we find that at least 23 pairs of swatches must exhibit an 8:4 ratio of superiority for the difference to be significant at a 90% confidence level. For 95% confidence 36 pairs will be required and for 99% confidence we must examine at least 61 pairs.

Now let us consider briefly the practical application of the aforementioned "confidence levels." This term is frequently employed in a misleading manner and we wish to define the sense in which we have used it. All statistical tests normally test the null hypothesis that the observed difference is not real but occurred through chance. We calculate the <u>probability</u> that

the null hypothesis is true: that is, the probability that the observed difference occurred through chance alone. If we calculate a probability of
0.05, we are saying that a difference as large as the one in question might
occur through chance as often as 5% of the time. We commonly express
this as "95% confidence," or say "the difference is statistically significant
at the 95% confidence level." Modern industrial research practice usually
interprets a 95% confidence level as adequate statistical support for a commercial decision. A 90% confidence level is usually taken as indication of
an encouraging trend which might be developed and optimized to yield a 95%
level.

Anything less than a 90% confidence level is ordinarily dismissed as
lacking in importance. A 99% confidence level is usually taken as incontro-
vertible proof!

Several variations are possible on the basic scheme of paired comparisons without making the statistics invalid. Visual matching of many pairs
of swatches can be a tedious chore and fatigue may influence results when
many pairs must be matched. The matching chore can be divided among
several individuals and the combined scores treated as one without invalida-
ting the statistical test. Several individuals may be used to grade the same
set of swatches in cases where there is doubt as to which of two different
shades is the lighter. Again, the scores should be pooled when testing for
significance.

b. Ranking techniques. If the individual swatches in a group can be
visually ranked in order of increasing lightness, one can apply even more
powerful nonparametric statistical tests in detecting significant differences.

When each group numbers roughly 8 to 16 in size the "outside count
test" can be used [65]. This test uses the degree of overlap between two
groups to determine the extent of the similarity between them. It requires
that neither group completely overlap the other in range. The two groups
need not be of equal size as long as the smaller is at least 75% of the larger
in number. We apply the outside count test to visual measurement of
bleaching as follows:

1. Select the lightest and the darkest swatch in each group of bleached
   swatches.
2. Compare the lightest swatch of group A to the lightest swatch of
   group B.
3. Compare the darkest swatch of Group A to the darkest swatch of
   group B.
4. Examine the results of steps 2 and 3 to ensure that neither group
   contains both the lightest and the darkest swatch of all.
5. Determine how many swatches in the group having the lightest swatch
   of both groups are lighter than the lightest swatch in the other group
   and note this number.

6. Determine how many swatches in the group containing the darkest swatch of both groups are darker than the darkest swatch in the other group and note this number.

7. Add the numbers noted in steps 5 and 6 to determine the total outside count.

If the total outside count is 10 or more, we conclude the two groups are different at a 99% confidence level. If the count is seven or more we have a 95% confidence level; and if four or more, we have a 90% confidence level that the observed difference is real.

For visually comparing groups of eight or fewer swatches, the most powerful test is the Mann-Whitney U test [64, 66]. It does not require that the two groups in question be of equal size. It is applicable to larger groups, but the problem of visually ranking larger numbers of swatches is very difficult and often yields data of questionable validity. The procedure for this test follows:

1. Pool the two groups of swatches and arrange them in order of increasing lightness. Each swatch must retain its identity, but the markings should, of course, be obscured to the person performing the ranking.

2. Compute the statistic U:
   a. For each B swatch count the number of A swatches ranked below it.
   b. Add together the individual scores for each of the B group swatches to obtain the B group score.
   c. Compute the A group score by

$$A \text{ score} = (\text{number of A swatches})(\text{number of B swatches}) - B \text{ score} \qquad (11)$$

   d. The smaller of the two scores thus obtained is U.

3. Consult the appropriate table to determine the probability of a value of U as small as the one obtained by chance above [64, 66].

An abridged table valid for comparing two groups of equal size is shown in Table 12. We conclude a real difference exists, with the indicated confidence, whenever the determined value of U is equal to, or less than, the tabular value.

2. Conventional Percent Stain Removal (Percent SR)

When a single instrumental value is recorded to express the reflectance of each swatch, the simplest and perhaps the most common treatment of the data is to calculate "percent stain removal" directly:

TABLE 12

Critical Values of Mann-Whitney U for Various
Percent Confidence Levels When Groups Are Equal Size

Group size	90%	95%	99%
8	19	15	10
7	13	11	6
6	9	7	3
5	5	4	1
4	3	1	
3	1		

$$\% \text{ SR} = \frac{R_b - R_s}{R_o - R_s} \times 100 \tag{12}$$

where R_o = reflectance of the original, unstained fabric
R_s = reflectance of the stained swatch before bleaching
R_b = reflectance of the stained swatch after bleaching

We assume here that each reflectance measurement is taken relative to the same standard and with the same instrument.

If subsequent statistical treatments are to be applied to the data, one must calculate the percent SR for each individual swatch. If no such treatment is planned, computational effort may be reduced by determining an average percent SR, based on the average of reflectance readings for the entire group of swatches representing a single treatment or run.

Each stained swatch from a given batch can usually be assumed to have an R_o equal to the average R_o determined for the unstained fabric before staining. When the swatch-to-swatch differences in the reflectance of a batch of stained swatches are sufficiently small, or when the stained swatches are selected for a test so as to be fairly uniform in stained reflectance, it is possible to eliminate the computation of percent SR and obtain the result directly. This is accomplished by setting the reflectometer so that a reading of 100% corresponds to R_o and a reading of 0% corresponds to R_s. We now have an instrument scale of 0 to 100 corresponding to the denominator in Eq. (12) and the reflectance reading obtained for each bleached swatch will exactly correspond to the percent SR for that swatch. An instrument must have a "zero suppression" adjustment or the like to permit setting it up in this fashion. A variable scale ruler such as the Gerber variable scale may be used to obtain percent SR to the nearest whole percent directly from the reflectance readings when the two ends of the variable scale are set to R_O and R_S.

3. Percent SR by Kubelka-Munk

A fundamental shortcoming of conventional percent SR computations is that percent reflectance is not, as these equations assume, linearly related to the amount of stain present. For measurements made of rough surfaces of a fabric, light scattering plays an important role in the observed response.

Consider a surface composed entirely of perfectly white, completely reflecting spheres, being illuminated and viewed so that a fixed portion of the diffusely reflected light is detected by our instrument. We say the reflectance of this surface is 100. Consider also a second surface just like the first except that it consists only of perfectly black, completely absorbing spheres. The reflectance of this surface is, by definition, zero. Now if we consider a third surface composed of equal numbers of the white spheres and the black spheres, uniformly mixed or distributed, our instrument will register a reflectance of only about 27 when we might have expected a reading of 50. We see that the black spheres have a greater influence on the observed reflectance than do the white ones. This is easily understood when one considers that a single ray of light striking a white particle may be scattered to a second particle or even to a third, or fourth, or more, before ultimately being reflected back away from the surface. The presence of a single black sphere can negate the reflection power of more than one white sphere because any time a ray of light hits a black sphere it is absorbed. This is true of light reflected off from neighboring white spheres in addition to all of the light rays falling directly on the black sphere.

The complexities of a system of partly absorbing, partly reflecting particles in a translucent layer have been dealt with by a variety of workers. The most successful treatment is that of Kubelka and Munk [49] as further amplified by Kubelka [67, 68] and by Park and Stearns [69]. A detailed discussion is presented by Judd and Wyszecki in Color In Business, Science, and Industry [60].

Kubelka-Munk postulated a general expression for reflectance, R, of a partly absorbing, partly reflecting, light-scattering surface which depended on reflectivity, $R\infty$, of the observed surface. They further defined this term as depending on the ratio of the absorption coefficient K and the scattering coefficient S:

$$\frac{K}{S} = \frac{(1 - R\infty)^2}{2R\infty} \tag{13}$$

Now, in our idealized surfaces previously considered, K/S turns out to be the relative concentration of black/white spheres. We now see that for such a surface, Eq. (13) permits conversion of an observed reflectance measurement to a fairly exact estimate of the percentage of black spheres mixed in with the white ones. Further, to the extent that a stain of interest approximates a perfectly absorbing (black) particle and the white fabric substrate approximates a perfectly reflecting surface, Eq. (13) allows us to compute the ratio of stained to unstained surface. We now have a measurement more linearly related to concentration of stain on a surface and directly related, rather than inversely as with R_∞.

K/S can be used to compute percent SR (K/S):

$$\% \ SR \left(\frac{K}{S} \right) = \frac{[\ (1 - R_s)^2 \ / \ 2R_s] - [\ (1 - R_b)^2 \ / \ 2R_b]}{[\ (1 - R_s)^2 \ / \ 2R_s] - [\ (1 - R_0)^2 \ / \ 2R_0]} \ 100 \tag{14}$$

where R_s = reflectance of the stained swatch before bleaching
         R_b = reflectance of the stained swatch after bleaching
         R_0 = reflectance of the original fabric before staining

It is more convenient to convert individual reflectance values to K/S by Eq. (13) or from published tables [60], and then use Eq. (15):

$$\% \ SR \left(\frac{K}{S} \right) = \frac{K/S_s - K/S_b}{K/S_s - K/S_0} \ 100 \tag{15}$$

Applications of the Kubelka-Munk equations to bleach testing data will never change the order of ranking of various bleaches or treatments. That is, it cannot transform a loser into a winner. The foremost advantage of using K/S values is that it permits more accurate judgments as to the relative spacing between bleaches that are very good and between those that are comparatively poor. It also permits more direct comparison between data obtained with dark stains and those obtained with lighter stains.

Another advantage of K/S values lies in the ability to correct for extraneous effects which may at times obscure the bleaching action one wishes to measure. Should thermal or chemical discoloration of the substrate or redeposition of soil affect the reflectance readings in addition to bleaching changes in the test stain, one can correct with fairly good validity. All that is required is a reflectance reading on an unstained portion of the test fabric both before and after the bleaching treatment. We may then compute a corrected, "absolute percent stain removal" as follows:

$$\% \text{ SR}_{\text{ABS}} = \frac{(K/S_s - K/S_b) + (K/S_a - K/S_0)}{K/S_s - K/S_0} \, 100 \tag{16}$$

where K/S_s = K/S value for stained swatch before bleaching
K/S_b = K/S value for stained swatch after bleaching
K/S_0 = K/S value for unstained swatch before bleaching
K/S_a = K/S value for unstained swatch after bleaching

Equation (16) may be rearranged to

$$\% \text{ SR}_{\text{ABS}} = \frac{(K/S_s - K/S_0) - (K/S_b - K/S_a)}{K/S_s - K/S_0} \, 100 \tag{17}$$

which may be reduced to

$$\% \text{ SR}_{\text{ABS}} = \left(1 - \frac{K/S_b - K/S_a}{K/S_s - K/S_0} \right) 100 \tag{18}$$

As was the case when dealing with conventional percent SR, computations of percent SR (K/S) or percent SR_{ABS} may be made less tedious with very little loss in precision if we first compute average reflectance values determined in each group of swatches before and after bleaching and proceed with the conversion to K/S values from the averages. If the observed values for R_s and R_b and R_a are reasonably free of excessive variation, the use of average values will not yield misleading results. Of course, preliminary averaging makes most later statistical analysis impossible.

4. Multistimulus Reflectance Values

Data obtained with multistimulus reflectometers are widely used in a wide variety of equations representing various attempts to quantitate color differences with respect to some approximation of a perceptually uniform scale. Each of these systems has its own merits and shortcomings which deserve serious study when applied to color specification, color matching, or color acceptance problems. For detailed discussions of this subject, the reader is referred to Judd [60], MacKinney and Little [70], and Billmeyer and Saltzman [71] among the many excellent publications on the subject.

For use in evaluation of bleaching performance on a practical basis, we need not be overly preoccupied with selection of the "best" or "most accurate" color difference formula. The "best" for these purposes is better determined on the basis of the scale our particular instrument uses and which equation is most easily applied. When concerned with fabric discoloration, usually yellowing, one should use an equation designed to express whiteness or yellowness.

If our instruments read in A, B, G terms, we may compute yellowness index (YI)

$$YI = \frac{100(A - B)}{G} \tag{19}$$

If the instrument has R, B, G scales, we use

$$YI = \frac{100(R - B)}{G} \tag{20}$$

Equations (19) and (20) are identical since A (amber) and R (red) are two designations for the same function. For yellow specimens between Munsell 2.5Y and 2.5GY, ASTM [72] prefers a restated form where

$$YI = \frac{100(1 - B)}{G} \tag{21}$$

For an instrument reading in CIE coordinates,

$$YI = \frac{128X - 106Z}{Y} \tag{22}$$

In Hunter's L, a, b system, yellowness is read directly as +b.

Deviations from white are not always in the yellow direction and then a more general expression is useful. Many of those that have been used take the form of expressing whiteness (W). None of the calculations of whiteness is recommended unless the specimens in question are nearly white. One equation commonly used is

$$W = 1 - \left\{ [30(\alpha^2 + \beta^2)^{1/2}]^2 + \left(\frac{100 - Y}{200}\right)^2 \right\}^{1/2} \tag{23}$$

where

$$\alpha = \frac{2.4266x - 1.3631y - 0.3214}{x + 2.2633y + 1.1054} \tag{24}$$

$$\beta = 0.5710x + 1.2447y - 0.5708$$

In Hunter's L, a, b system, Eq. (23) becomes

$$W = 100 - [(100 - L)^2 + (a^2 + b^2)]^{1/2} \tag{25}$$

An increasingly popular measure closely related to whiteness is appearance value (AV) [73]:

$$AV = R_d + 3_a - 3_b \tag{26}$$

A preferred form is

$$W = L + 3_a - 3_b \tag{27}$$

where R_d is Hunter's value related to L as follows:

$$R_d = (0.01)L^2 \tag{28}$$

The a, b of the R_d scale are slightly different from the a, b of the L scale, but for near-white specimens no practical difference exists.

Hunter's D-40 whiteness meter uses only the B and G values, similar to b and R_d, to compute whiteness. For samples that are not whitened by the presence of fluorescent whitening agents:

$$W = 100 - \left\{ \left[\frac{220(G - B)}{G + 0.242B} \right]^2 + \left(\frac{100 - G}{2} \right)^2 \right\}^{1/2} \tag{29}$$

Where fluorescent whitening is a factor, Hunter used

$$W = 4B - 3G \tag{30}$$

Equation (30) has also been adopted by the ASTM for expressing whiteness in terms of instrumental readings for yellowness index [74].

5. Computational Mechanics

On a practical basis, as much consideration needs to be given the problem of computing the results of instrumental measurements as must be used in selecting the measuring instrument. Given unlimited funds, it is possible to provide interfaces between a measuring instrument, a computer, and a data printer or plotter so that computation and statistical analysis of results happen nearly immediately and automatically as samples are measured. Short of this sort of ultimate situation, each laboratory must consider how to gain maximum computational efficiency with the resources available. Volume of work and frequency of repetition of a given calculation are also influencing factors.

A small desk-top computer is a very satisfactory solution to all of the computational demands of an extensive bleach evaluation program. Most of these use a keyboard language so that anyone understanding the mathematics of a problem can easily program its solution. For example, rapid computation of percent SR (K/S) by Eq. (14) directly from reflectance values is easily handled by these small units. Programs allowing for simultaneous calculation of percent SR, average percent SR, and variance of percent SR are also possible.

Next most desirable are the modern electronic calculators with one or more memory banks. Several of the older electromechanical calculators also have such memory capacities but production of these has been largely replaced by all-electronic versions. The availability of some memory capacity greatly simplifies most of the more complicated calculations, particularly those of statistical analysis.

As we progress downward toward the basic pad and pencil, much can be gained in computing efficiency through the use of special aids. If no more than an adding machine is available, the auxiliary use of a slide rule can greatly facilitate the determination of percent SR, whiteness, and other such values. Even the variable scale rule is capable of making many computations nearly automatically, as mentioned earlier.

Nomographs are another often overlooked computational aid. A particularly useful one was devised for obtaining percent SR_{ABS} directly from reflectance values [see Eqs. (13) and (18)]. This nomograph was constructed with the help of several texts on the subject [75, 76] and is faster to use than any method other than a computer.

One can construct a nomograph leading to the solution of just about any relation that can be expressed by a mathematical equation. A nomograph's precision is easily improved by increasing its size. A set of excellent nomographs was prepared by the Polychemistry Department of the Research Division of E. I. DuPont De Nemours for converting between Hunter Rd, a, b values and ICI X, Y, Z. The larger of these nomographs measures 22 in. x 28 in. and can be read to the nearest 0.005 on the ICI X and Z scales.

V. FABRIC DAMAGE

It becomes fairly obvious in a study of bleaches that fabric damage is a prime factor for consideration. It is also apparent one must be able to separate chemical damage produced by bleaches from the physical damage occasioned by washing, drying, and wearing a garment. It is also of interest to know if the item is chemically damaged or has been accidently ripped or torn.

Because all bleaches by their very nature produce fabric damage to varying degrees, it is necessary to study and understand this subject area. Since there are numerous types and degrees of fabric damage it is essential to become familiar with the fabric damage characteristics of bleaches in general and especially the particular bleach in which there is an interest.

Needless to say, there are many simple as well as sophisticated tests and methods for the study of fabric damage. We discuss some of these tests and methods in this section. We also attempt to profile the fabric damage properties of both chlorine and oxygen-releasing bleaches.

A. Test Procedures

1. Visual

A visual study of fabric damage is particularly useful in handling customer complaints and questions about bleach damage. Visual examination is also important to determine whether the damage is general or localized in nature. This can be done by simply feeling and pulling the fabric to find areas of possible weakness. If holes or rips are present, it is best to work around these areas. It should become apparent rather quickly if general or local deterioration has taken place.

If general deterioration has occurred, there is a good chance the bleach was added directly to the fabric. It is also possible some other chemical has come in contact with the fabric or that the well-known acid chloride reaction [77] has taken place. We find a large number of general fabric tenderization problems are due to the addition either knowingly or unknowingly of chemicals other than bleach. We put the acid chloride reaction in this last category.

Acid reactions are almost always general and severe, especially for cellulosics and cellulosic blends. The acid reaction is usually formed in one of two ways. The first, and by far the most common, is a coin-operated or "do it yourself" dry cleaning unit that uses chlorinated solvents and is adjacent to or near the clothes dryers in a laundromat. The second is rare, but has happened. It is a leaking in home refrigeration unit emitting Freon which is in the same proximity as the clothes dryer. It is, of course, also possible for Freons used in some aerosol containers to be drawn into the dryer. In both cases, the halogen is drawn into the dryer and in this hot, humid atmosphere is eventually converted to either hydrochloric, in the case of dry cleaning, or hydrofluoric, leaking fluorine, acid. Because of the humidity, heat, and tumbling action of the dryer, the damage is always severe and general.

Usually, but not always, the acid chloride or fluoride reaction can be determined by measuring the pH of the fabric. The pH of the fabric instead of being neutral or slightly alkaline will be in the range of 2 to 5. If the fabric is washed subsequent to the acid reaction, the fabric pH will probably be normal.

Localized fabric damage can be observed rather easily and is characterized by pinholing or larger holes where the fabric is completely destroyed. This localized damage may in the case of dry bleaches be due to incomplete dissolution of the bleach, for example, bleach that has been caught in a pocket or some other portion of the garment and has been in direct contact with the fabric. With liquid bleaches localized damage is almost always produced by accidental spillage, improper dilution, or a bleach dispenser which, for one reason or another, is not functioning properly.

In any visual examination of fabric damage, ultraviolet or black light should be used. If the fabric has not been rewashed several times since the damage occurred, ultraviolet light can show the pattern of damage. In the case of the acid chloride reaction a deadening or destruction of the fluorescent whitening agent is noted. In the case of localized fabric deterioration, the remainder of the garment will appear normal or white under ultraviolet light while the damaged area can be seen as dark purple splotches because the fluorescent whitening agent has been destroyed. The ultraviolet light study is particularly valuable when liquid bleach has been accidentally spilled on the fabric because the damage pattern becomes readily apparent.

2. Chemical Tests

Chemical tests may be used to determine if chemical or physical damage has taken place. If chemical tests such as Fehling's solution [78] and Turnbull's blue test [79] are negative, the damage is physical and was probably produced by abrasion, wear, or a sharp object. The fluidity test, on the other hand, is used to determine the degree of fabric damage; however, it does not distinguish well between chemical and physical damage.

a. Fehling's solution. Fehling's test may be used to determine chemical damage of cotton because both hydrocellulose and oxycellulose contain aldehyde groups. These aldehyde groups cause a reduction of alkaline copper salts to insoluble red cuprous oxide. The Fehling test is done in the following manner: Ten milliliters of solution A is mixed with 10 ml of solution B and the resultant mixture heated to boiling. The fabric under test is added and boiled for several minutes. The test fabric is then removed and rinsed well in running water. The formation of red or pink spots shows the presence of hydrocellulose or oxycellulose which are indicators of chemical damage.

Fehling's solution A: 69.28 g of copper sulfate per liter of water

Fehling's solution B: 346 g of sodium potassium tartrate and 100 g of sodium hydroxide per liter of water

b. Turnbull's blue. Turnbull's blue test may also be used to determine chemical damage to cotton because oxycellulose contains carboxyl groups. The carboxyl groups will form a ferrous salt that cannot be washed out of the fabric while hydrocellulose and cellulose do not have carboxyl groups and therefore cannot hold the ferrous salt. Turnbull's blue test is done in the following manner: Place the test fabric in a 1% solution of ferrous sulfate and hold at room temperature for 10 min. Then rinse the sample thoroughly in running water after which the test swatch is placed in a 1% solution of potassium ferricyanide for 5 min at room temperature. The swatch is then rinsed thoroughly again in running water. Cellulose gives a very faint blue color, hydrocellulose is even more faintly blue, while oxycellulose yields a deep blue, Turnbull's blue, color.

In either Fehling's or Turnbull's test, if the test sample is dyed, it will of course be necessary to strip the color. The reader is probably familiar with several methods of color stripping. We have found that a hot solution of sodium hydrosulfite usually does a good job.

c. Fluidity. The chain length of cellulose molecules is decreased by the action of alkali, acids, reducing, or oxidizing agents. The severity of the treatment determines the extent of the shortening of the cellulose chain and the fluidity [80]. The fluidity of a dispersion of bleached cellulose in cupriethylenediamine or cuprammonium hydroxide solvent is a measure of the degradation, and indirectly, the tensile strength of the cloth. These facts make the fluidity test useful in determining the fabric damage produced by bleach.

We do not describe the fluidity method here, however, a standard test 82-1961 may be found in the Technical Manual of the American Association of Textile Chemists and Colorists [81]. This test is a sensitive, but somewhat time-consuming method. Fluidity, which is the reciprocal of viscosity, is reported in rhes. It should be kept in mind that the higher the rhes number, the lower is the viscosity or the greater the fluidity of the test solution, and therefore, the higher the degree of fabric damage. We would like to add one word of caution. If the reader is interested in running fluidity tests, a careful study of the literature could save considerable time. The use of copper-amine disperse solutions of cellulose has received extensive study because this has been one of the methods used for making rayon.

3. Physical Tests

As everyone knows who has run fabric damage studies, there is considerable variation in the strength of any bolt of cloth. It is very easy to compound this variation by using faulty or improper testing equipment and/or techniques. Therefore, no matter how exact and careful fabric damage studies are, if the equipment used is not applicable, accurate, and functioning properly, very little will be accomplished. We hope in this section on physical testing to explore some of the test devices that are used to measure loss in fabric strength and fabric damage. We do not attempt to make specific recommendations on what testing machines should be used, but mention those available for different types of testing.

a. Breaking or tensile strength. Breaking or tensile strength measurements are probably the most common method of evaluating fabric damage. The tensile strength of fabric may be defined as the actual resistance in pounds that a fabric will give to a breaking or tensile strength apparatus, before the sample is broken. Tensile strength is usually reported in pounds per square inch while loss in tensile strength may be recorded as loss in pounds per square inch or percent loss based on the loss and the original fabric strength.

There are a number of testers and accessories manufactured to measure the tensile strength of fabric and, of course, there is a wide range in prices to also be considered. We believe that in the selection of a fabric-testing instrument prime consideration should be given to the machine's versatility. The question of price is important, but the buyer should also evaluate how many applications the machine has in his company and how often it will be used.

There are three basic, but different, types of machines for measuring breaking or tensile strength. The machines may be classified as operating on one or more of the following three principles: (a) constant rate of traverse, (b) constant rate of specimen extension, and (c) constant rate of load.

A constant rate of traverse testing machine is one in which the pulling clamp moves at a uniform rate and the load is applied through the other clamp which moves appreciably to acutate a load-measuring mechanism. The constant rate of specimen extension is one in which the rate of increase of specimen length is uniform with time, and the load-measuring device moves a negligible distance with increasing load. The machine for measuring constant rate of load is one in which the rate of increase of the load is uniform with time and the specimen is free to elongate. The elongation is dependent on the extension characteristics of the specimen at any applied load value [82].

Probably the most widely used tensile strength machines are of the constant rate of traverse design and are commonly referred to as the pendulum type [83]. Information can be obtained on this type of machine from Scott Testers, Inc., Providence, Rhode Island; Thwing-Albert Instrument Company, Philadelphia, Pennsylvania; or Testing Machines, Inc., Mineola, New York.

The constant rate of extension testing machines are also widely used, but are generally more expensive than the pendulum type. The same manufacturers as are listed above should be contacted as well as the Instron Corporation of Canton, Massachusetts.

The constant rate of load machine is based on the inclined plane principle and is not as popular in fabric testing as the two previously described machines. If the reader is interested in this type of machine, the same manufacturers as are listed above should be contacted. Instron, for instance, makes an accessory that allows conversion of their constant rate of extension machine to a constant rate of load device.

There are two common methods for measuring the tensile strength of cloth. The first is the "grab method" [84] which uses a cloth sample 6 in. long by 4 in. wide. The fabric is gripped by two jaws and pulled until it is broken. The second method is called the strip or raveled strip test [85].

The fabric samples are cut into strips 6 in. long and 1 1/2 in. wide. Rav-
elings are done by removing fibers until the fabric is exactly 1 in. in width.
The fabric is then placed in the machine jaws and pulled until it ruptures.

In making tensile strength measurements, regardless of the equipment
used or the method chosen, there are several basic rules that should be
followed to obtain meaningful results.

1. Tensile strength measurements should be made on both the warp and
    filling fibers.
2. Fabric samples that break at the jaws should not be recorded as the
    true breaking strength has not been determined.
3. All samples should be conditioned to constant temperature and
    humidity prior to testing.

b. Bursting strength. The Mullen Tester manufactured by the B. F.
Perkins Company, Inc., of Holyoke, Massachusetts is used to measure the
bursting strength of fabric. In fabric testing it is used primarily for measuring the bursting strength of knitted fabrics. However, it may be used on
woven fabrics as well. The Mullen Tester makes use of a hydraulic system
with the pressure exerted on the sample by a rubber diaphragm. The tester consists of a set of ring clamps to hold the fabric which is placed over a
well of glycerine that is covered by a rubber diaphragm. Several different
sizes of Mullen Testers are available.

When the Mullen Tester is activated, pressure is built up under the diaphragm and it distends or expands into a dome shape and forces its way
through the test fabric. Bursting strength readings are recorded as pounds
per square inch. A correction factor should be applied for the amount of
pressure necessary to distend the diaphragm by itself. Care should be
exercised so as not to break the rubber diaphragm.

c. Tear strength. Tear strength is another way of measuring damage
to woven fabrics. One of the advantages of this test is that it can be run on
both treated and untreated fabrics, including those that are coated or heavily
sized. Basically, the method involves a fabric sample that has been precut
a measured distance and the force required to complete the tear is determined. The work force required to continue the precut tear is measured and
the data obtained can be used to calculate both tear force and tear energy.
The tear force or tear strength of the fabric is reported in grams or pounds,
while tear energy is the energy in inch-pounds per inch or gram-centimeters
per centimeter of torn fabric.

There are several machines available for measuring the tear strength of
fabric. There are also many methods of adapting as well as accessories
available which will allow conversion of a conventional tensile strength tester to a tear testing device. The Instron Tensile Testing Instrument, just
to name one, can easily be adapted to measure tear strength.

Perhaps the best known apparatus for determining tear strength is the Elmendorf Tearing Tester manufactured by Thwing-Albert Instrument Company. The Elmendorf Tearing Tester is referred to as a falling pendulum type of apparatus [86]. Due to the simplicity of its design, many modificiations and attachments have been made to the basic unit. The instrument has a heavy sector-shaped pendulum with a scale reading from 0 to 100. The sector has a moving clamp which is in alignment with a nonmovable or fixed clamp. On the same axis as the pendulum, a pointer is mounted which has just enough constant friction to make it stop at the highest point reached by the swing of the sector. The test sample is fastened in the clamps and a tear is started by a slit cut in the fabric. The weighted sector swings down, falling pendulum, and tears the sample as the moving jaw moves away from the fixed one. The amount of swing at its maximum point is recorded by the pointer. Calculations may then be made to determine tear energy and tear force. Tear strength measurements should be made on both the warp and filling fibers.

We have attempted to give a brief description of some of the equipment and test methods used for determining fabric damage. We urge the reader to contact the manufacturers of the test equipment in which he might be interested for complete details. We also think reading of the ASTM and TAPPI manuals of standard test procedures and Chapter 14, Part II, will be of help in understanding the physical methods employed for determining fabric strength.

B. Effect of Bleaches

Fabric damage is of obvious concern to people in the bleach industry. It is quite apparent that no matter how efficient a bleach is, if it is capable of producing fabric damage, and they all are, then this becomes a problem area for study. In this section, which is devoted to the effect of bleaches on fabric damage, we examine liquid sodium hypochlorite as well as several dry chlorine and oxygen bleaches. We intend to examine both laboratory and in-home test results obtained on both natural and synthetic fibers. We evaluate data gathered when bleach is used at label recommended concentrations and also when bleach is used under conditions other than ideal. This latter study includes full-strength usage simulating what might occur from accidental spillage or an improperly functioning bleach dispenser, or, in the case of dry bleaches, what might happen if it becomes trapped in the folds or pocket of a garment.

There are so many factors that can and do influence fabric damage it becomes a difficult task to classify them all. For the purpose of this discussion, let us use two general classifications, "physical" and "chemical" contributors to fabric damage. We know that in the reader's mind, as well as in ours, there is some overlapping of the physical and chemical categories, but let us consider them in the following manner. Physical factors will include washing machines with chipped tubs and chipped or broken agitators; different drying conditions; flexing and abrasion of fabric produced by normal wear and use; the time and temperatures of the washing and drying cycles; and completeness of rinsing action. Under the chemical category we will place bleach concentration, mineral content of the water and clothes, especially iron, type of soil, and pH of the washing solution.

A great deal of research has been done on the physical and chemical causes of fabric damage by appliance manufacturers, textile producers, the U.S. Department of Agriculture, and the bleach industry. The following is a list of some of their results:

1. It has been noted many times by people in the appliance business that even a small chip in the porcelain basket of a washing machine can contribute significantly to fabric damage.
2. We have found, as have others [87], that of the four common drying methods (indoor rack, outdoors, electric dryer, and gas dryer) cotton fabrics dried outdoors suffered more fabric damage than cotton items dried using the other three methods.
3. Studies done in our laboratory and again substantiated by others [87, 88] show that normal wear accounts for 50% of the total damage to cottons produced by chemicals used under average washing conditions.
4. Increasing the temperature of the washing and drying cycles will degrade fabric and, of course, increases in time result in more flexing and abrasion of the fabric.

Under the chemical category we defer our discussion of bleach concentration until later. Results obtained by Thomas and Mack [89] indicate that the type of soil present can play a role in the fabric damage produced by some bleaches. It is also obvious that acid-type soils such as citric acid will contribute to fabric degradation.

Mineral contamination of the clothes and water has been shown to be a contributing factor to fabric damage [89, 90]. This is accomplished by the fact that fabric can entrap particles of iron and this iron serves as a catalyst in the presence of chlorine bleach, speeding up its decomposition to the extent that cellulose fibers are tendered and the fabric strength is reduced.

1. Liquid Chlorine

When all of the preceding physical and chemical factors are considered, we believe the three which affect the fabric damage characteristics of liquid chlorine bleach per se are concentration, temperature, and time. In our evaluations of chlorine liquid bleach and fabric damage based on U.S. washing temperatures and time, we are of the opinion the greatest single effect is produced by concentration, with time being rated second and

TABLE 13

The Effect of Full-Strength 5.25% NaOCl on the Tensile
Strength of Cotton at 100°F

Type of bleach	Tensile strength (psi) after contact times of				
	0[a]	2 min	5 min	10 min	20 min
5.25% NaOCl (by weight)	64.5	52.3[b]	37.5[b]	31.4[b]	13.9[b]

[a]Original fabric strength.

[b]All numbers are averages of eight tensile strength determinations, four warp and four filling tests averaged.

TABLE 14

The Effect of Full-Strength 5.25% NaOCl on the Tensile
Strength of Cotton at Various Temperatures

Type of bleach	Tensile strength (psi) after 5 min contact[a] at various temperatures			
	100°F	120°F	140°F	160°F
5.25% NaOCl (by weight)	37.5[b]	33.2[b]	25.1[b]	15.1[b]

[a]Original fabric strength 64.5 psi.

[b]All numbers are averages of eight tensile strength determinations, four warp and four filling tests averaged.

temperature least important. Perhaps it is not possible to separate the three as they are closely interrelated, but we are making an effort to do it so the reader might more clearly understand and study the problem . The results in Table 13 were noted in our laboratory at a temperature of 100°F, no detergent, and using full-strength 5.25% by weight sodium hypochlorite on white desized Indian Head cotton of the same type described in this chapter.

The data in Table 13 show a percent loss in tensile strength of almost 20% in the first 2 min and 40% in 5 min, however, it takes another 15 min to show a further 40% loss in tensile strength. These data, although obtained on full-strength bleach, tend to substantiate stain removal data that show most of the bleaching action occurs in the first 5 min.

We next studied variations in temperature using the same fabric and full-strength 5.25% hypochlorite used in the first experiment (see Table 14).

Although at 100°F after 5 min contact the fabric has already been seriously damaged, 40% loss in tensile strength, it should be noted that an increase in temperature produces further fabric deterioration. A loss of about 33% of the remaining fabric strength is produced by going from 100° to 140°F; however, a further increase to 160°F rapidly increases this figure to a 60% loss in remaining strength.

Tables 13 and 14 show quite clearly that full-strength sodium hypochlorite bleach can produce serious fabric damage, losses up to 50% of the original fabric strength, on new cotton fabric in as little time as 5 min at a temperature of 120°F. It is easy to see from these data that a garment which is already badly worn can be completely destroyed in a matter of minutes under normal washing machine temperatures. This is, we feel, the basis for many customer complaints concerning fabric damage when, unknown to the customer, full-strength liquid bleach comes in contact with the fabric and severe fabric tendering takes place.

We next measured the fabric damage produced by liquid hypochlorite at a stubborn stain concentration of 1000 ppm available chlorine on cotton sheets (Harmony House 6682) that had previously been washed in a Sears Kenmore washing machine 40 times in a 0.10% concentration of a typical sodium alkylbenzenesulfonate-based dry detergent. All evaluations done in the washing machine were in water of 150 ppm hardness at 120°F. The sheets were dried 30 min at a hot setting in a gas-fired Sears dryer after each wash cycle.

The actual stubborn stain studies, 1000 ppm Av Cl_2, were done using a Launder-Ometer and a 10-min bleaching cycle in water of 150 ppm hardness at 100°F with no detergent and a 2-min rinse in cold water of 150 ppm hardness. The cotton sheets were cut into 4 in. x 6 in. swatches and bleached an additional 45 cycles using the drying conditions just described after each cycle. Tensile strength measurements were made after 5, 10, 15, 20, 30, and 45 cycles. The data obtained are shown in Table 15.

The data in Table 15 show the loss produced by water alone is negligible, approximately 6%, and this figure may be slightly high due to the variability of the fabric and fabric-testing apparatus. The damage produced by liquid hypochlorite is six times this amount, 36% or slightly more than one-third of the strength of the fabric at the beginning of the test.

TABLE 15

The Effect of 5.25% NaOCl at Stubborn Stain Concentration
on the Tensile Strength of Cotton

	Tensile strength (psi)	
Number of cycles	5.25% NaOCl at 1000 ppm Av Cl_2	Water at 150 ppm hardness
0 (original)[a]	45.6 ± 1.3[b]	45.6 ± 1.3[b]
5	42.8 ± 0.8	43.2 ± 1.1
10	40.2 ± 0.6	42.9 ± 0.8
15	37.9 ± 1.0	42.7 ± 1.1
20	35.2 ± 1.4	43.1 ± 1.0
30	33.6 ± 0.5	43.0 ± 1.7
45	29.1 ± 0.9	42.8 ± 0.8

[a]Fabric cut from sheets previously washed 40 times.

[b]All numbers are averages of eight tensile strength determinations,
four warp and four filling tests averaged.

We repeated the preceding experiment exactly, using new cotton sheeting of the same brand and tensile strength and purchased at the same time
and place as in the first test. The loss in tensile strength after 45 cycles
for fabric treated with water is only 4% while liquid sodium hypochlorite at
1000 ppm available chlorine reduced fabric strength by 26%. We know, of
course, that in new fabric the sizing will help protect the fibers from bleach
attack but these data, in our opinion, lend credence to the theory that liquid
bleach will attack already weakened fibers more readily than new material.

We wanted also to determine if the addition of a stain to cotton fabric
has an effect on the fabric damage characteristics of liquid hypochlorite.
In the instant study we used the identical fabric that was evaluated in the
first stubborn stain experiment, cotton sheeting that had been washed 40
times in a 0.10% concentration of a typical anionic-based detergent. We
carefully duplicated the first Launder-Ometer experiment for a total of 30
cycles, keeping all conditions the same except one. We stained the test
fabric with tea after each bleaching cycle following our test procedure for
preparing tea-stained cotton as described earlier in this chapter. Because
tensile strength measurements were to be made, we changed the swatch

TABLE 16

The Effect of 5.25% NaOCl at Stubborn Stain Concentration
on the Tensile Strength and Staining Properties of Cotton

Number of cycles	1000 ppm Av chlorine		Water at 150 ppm hardness	
	Tensile strength (psi)	Percent stain removal	Tensile strength (psi)	Percent stain removal
0 (original)[a]	45.6 ± 1.3[b]	Not run	45.6 ± 1.3[b]	Not run
5	40.3 ± 1.5	89.0	45.0 ± 0.6	2.6
10	38.4 ± 1.0	84.4	43.2 ± 1.2	0.3
15	36.8 ± 0.8	82.4	44.3 ± 1.2	0.7
20	35.4 ± 1.0	80.3	43.0 ± 0.7	0.5
25	34.6 ± 1.1	79.9	43.0 ± 0.8	0.1
30	31.7 ± 1.4	74.0	42.8 ± 1.3	0.0

[a]Fabric cut from sheets previously washed 40 times.

[b]All numbers are averages of eight tensile strength determinations, four warp and four filling tests averaged.

size from 2 1/4 in. x 3 1/4 in. to 4 in. x 6 in. The usual tensile strength measurements were made and we also calculated the percent tea stain removal using the conventional stain removal equation (see Table 16).

We believe the work shown in Table 16 shows a good correlation with the first Launder-Ometer study made on clean cotton sheets. It will be noted in the first test that after 30 cycles the percent loss in tensile strength from 5.25% sodium hypochlorite is about 26.5% while in the tea stain study it is 29%. The loss in fabric strength by 150 ppm hard water is 6% in both experiments. After viewing all the data in both tests we are of the opinion that the action of liquid hypochlorite on tea stain may increase fabric damage marginally, but it is a negligible amount and would be completely lost among the other more important factors contributing to fabric deterioration.

The stain removal data in Table 16 are of more than slight interest because even under these high-use levels, 1000 ppm Av Cl_2, it demonstrates liquid bleach is not 100% effective. It can readily be seen that there is a gradual buildup of tea stain. This tea stain buildup gives the investigator

TABLE 17

The Effect of 5.25% NaOCl at Stubborn Stain Concentration on the
Tensile Strength of Nylon, Rayon Acetate, and Polyester

Type of bleach	Number of cycles	Tensile strength (psi)		
		Nylon (sharkskin)	Rayon acetate	Polyester
5.25%	0 (original)	141.1 ± 2.6[a]	47.0 ± 0.6[a]	44.6 ± 1.1[a]
NaOCl	5	138.9 ± 2.1	45.9 ± 1.0	43.1 ± 0.8
(by weight)	10	137.1 ± 1.9	45.0 ± 0.8	42.0 ± 1.2
Water	0	141.1 ± 2.6	47.0 ± 0.6	44.6 ± 1.1
of 150 ppm	5	139.7 ± 2.0	46.7 ± 0.5	45.0 ± 1.8
hardness	10	138.5 ± 1.7	46.1 ± 0.6	43.8 ± 1.5

[a]All numbers are averages of eight tensile strength determinations, four
warp and four filling tests averaged.

an opportunity to compare any bleach with the accepted standard for good
stain removal, liquid sodium hypochlorite.

We next evaluated the effect of liquid hypochlorite on new nylon, rayon
acetate, and polyester fabrics. Ten-cycle Launder-Ometer studies were
made at 1000 ppm available chlorine in 150 ppm water hardness at 100°F
and no detergent; the data are shown in Table 17. All test fabrics were
dried at a warm setting for 20 min after each cycle.

Although only a 10-cycle evaluation was made the data in Table 17 indicate that at stubborn stain concentration, 1000 ppm Av Cl_2, liquid hypochlorite does not produce a great deal more damage on sharkskin nylon and
rayon acetate than water alone. On polyester material liquid bleach appears
slightly more damaging than water alone. The point we would like to make
here is that the data show liquid sodium hypochlorite is considerably less
damaging to the synthetic fibers nylon, rayon acetate, and polyester than it
is to cotton. The data show liquid bleach produces a loss in tensile strength
of 6% on polyester after 10 cycles. The earlier data on cotton showed twice
as much damage or a loss in tensile strength of 12% after 10 bleaching
cycles. Further evaluations using full-strength 5.25% sodium hypochlorite
on nylon, rayon acetate, and polyester showed liquid bleach produced significantly less damage to these fibers than was reported earlier in this section
for cotton.

TABLE 18

The Effect of Low Levels of NaOCl on Cotton Sheets and Pillowcases

	Tensile strength (psi)	
Number of cycles	Sheets (Harmony House 6682)	Pillowcases (Harmony House 7240)
0 (original)	53.3 ± 1.8[a]	63.7 ± 1.7[a]
10	51.9 ± 1.1	60.5 ± 3.5
20	50.5 ± 1.5	56.8 ± 1.3
30	50.8 ± 1.2	55.7 ± 0.7
40	47.8 ± 1.4	Not run
50	46.7 ± 0.7	Not run
60	45.1 ± 1.2	54.2 ± 1.0
70	45.5 ± 1.6	52.2 ± 0.8

[a]All numbers are averages of eight tensile strength determinations, four warp and four filling tests averaged.

In contrast to the preceding data we have shown liquid chlorine bleach can be used at a low level of 1/4 cup/16 gal washing machine 50 ppm Av Cl_2, and negligible fabric damage is observed. We demonstrated this with washing machine studies using a Sears Kenmore and new cotton sheets and pillowcases. A load equivalent to 8 lb was simultaneously washed and bleached for 15 min in 0.1% Tide and liquid sodium hypochlorite at 50 ppm available chlorine using water of 200 ppm hardness at a temperature of 120°F. All fabrics were dried in a Sears gas-fired dryer at a hot setting for 30 min. The data obtained are summarized in Table 18.

The data show that after 70 wash/bleach and dry cycles the sheets lost 15% of their original strength and the pillowcases lost approximately 18%. Unfortunately a control of water alone was not run in this evaluation, but other data obtained with the same washing machines and dryers show a total loss of 5 and 6%, respectively, for sheets and pillowcases due to the combined action of washing and drying. This, then, would leave a loss of 10 and 12% produced by the action of the bleach and detergent. We believe that if bleach is used in an in-home test, this small amount of fabric damage would be overshadowed by the damage produced by normal flexing, abrasion, handling, and sleeping on the sheets.

TABLE 19

Clothes Items Used in Kendall Home Laundry Project

Item	Fabric and identification
Men's shirts	White 100% cotton resin treated (Arrow brand)
Children's underpants	Pink, flower print, and white, 100% cotton (Carter brand)
Blouses	White 100% Dacron (Pilot brand)
Petty skirts (slips)	White 100% nylon (Vanity Fair brand)

Mrs. Helen Kendall, former director of the Good Housekeeping Institute, did a home laundry project for us which included the soiling and washing of clothes under normal use conditions [91]. A total of 20 wash/wear cycles were carried out. The items of clothing used in this study are shown in Table 19. The washing conditions under which the tests were conducted are as follows:

Shirts wash time: 12 min at $130^{o}F$ initial temperature
Cotton underpants wash time: 12 min at $130^{o}F$ initial temperature
Dacron blouses wash time: 10 min at $130^{o}F$ initial temperature
Nylon slips wash time: 10 min at $130^{o}F$ initial temperature

All fabrics were washed in a Maytag automatic washing machine and dried in a Maytag gas-fired dryer. The water hardness for all washing studies ran between 52 and 56 ppm. The following products were evaluated:

1. A typical sodium perborate bleach used at a level equivalent to 30 ppm Av O_2 plus 3/4 cup of All detergent
2. A typical potassium monopersulfate bleach used at a level equivalent to 15 ppm Av O_2 plus 3/4 cup of All detergent
3. A liquid sodium hypochlorite (5.25%) bleach used at a level equivalent to 200 ppm Av Cl_2 plus 3/4 cup of All detergent
4. Detergent only: 3/4 cup of All detergent

After 20 wash/wear cycles the garments were forwarded to our research laboratory for additional testing. Samples of the original garments purchased, not washed or worn, were tested to determine the original tensile and bursting strength. We report here only the results observed with the

TABLE 20

Fabric Damage by NaOCl in Kendall Home Laundry Project

Garment	Product used	Tensile strength	Bursting strength
Shirts	None (original)	41.3 ± 1.8[a]	104.4 ± 2.7[b]
100% cotton	Detergent	36.8 ± 1.7	105.2 ± 2.8
(resin)	5.25% NaOCl	37.1 ± 2.6	103.2 ± 2.4
Blouses	None	45.6 ± 0.6	144.4 ± 2.9
100%	Detergent	41.3 ± 2.6	142.0 ± 2.4
Dacron	5.25% NaOCl	39.4 ± 2.4	142.2 ± 2.3
Slips	None	50.8 ± 1.5	155.2 ± 2.0
100%	Detergent	52.3 ± 2.6	153.8 ± 1.8
Nylon	5.25% NaOCl	50.7 ± 2.6	149.2 ± 2.6
Underpants	None	56.6 ± 2.7	147.5 ± 2.3
white	Detergent	57.0 ± 2.5	146.7 ± 1.9
cotton	5.25% NaOCl	50.5 ± 2.8	132.5 ± 2.7
Underpants	None	24.1 ± 1.4	112.0 ± 2.0
pink	Detergent	23.0 ± 1.1	111.5 ± 1.5
cotton	5.25% NaOCl	20.1 ± 1.6	100.5 ± 2.5
Underpants	None	24.7 ± 1.4	110.5 ± 1.4
print	Detergent	23.5 ± 1.6	110.5 ± 2.2
cotton	5.25% NaOCl	20.7 ± 1.6	98.8 ± 2.3

[a]All numbers are averages of eight tensile strength determinations, four warp and four filling tests averaged.

[b]Average of six bursting strength determinations.

liquid chlorine bleach. The data obtained with sodium perborate and potassium monpersulfate are discussed in the section devoted to oxygen bleaches. Summarized in Table 20 are the data obtained from Helen Kendall's home laundry project of 20 wash/wear cycles.

After examing the data obtained from both tensile and bursting strength measurements it becomes obvious that on the resin-treated cotton shirts, Dacron blouses, and nylon slips, the damage noted for the detergent alone is generally as large as that noted for the detergent plus bleach. We must conclude then that this damage is produced by the combination of wearing, washing, and drying the garments rather than by liquid chlorine bleach. Because we have shown that liquid hypochlorite will damage cotton we must also assume the resin on the shirt acted to protect the cotton from bleach damage. The damage to the cotton underpants is more pronounced than that noted for the shirts, blouses, and slips. The loss in bursting strength produced by liquid hypochlorite on all underpants, white, pink, and printed, is approximately 10%. The loss in tensile strength on the white underpants is also 10% while that noted on the weaker pink and print underpants is 17%.

Based on the data obtained in this particular study we can state that the damage to resin-treated cotton shirts, Dacron blouses, and nylon slips produced by washing and wearing for 20 cycles is generally less than 5% of the original fabric strength. The fabric damage caused by liquid 5.25% sodium hypochlorite at 200 ppm available chlorine to the garments just mentioned under the conditions tested is negligible. The damage produced by liquid bleach at 200 ppm available chlorine on untreated cotton fabric after 20 wash/wear cycles is 10 to 15% of the original fabric strength. We must also note, however, that in the instant study the factor of wear is not yet apparent after 20 wash/wear cycles.

2. Dry Chlorine

We have shown that full-strength 5.25% liquid hypochlorite can produce serious deterioration of cotton goods. We believe the housewife is well aware of this problem and treats liquid bleaches with a great deal of respect. But how about a dry bleach with which she is less familiar? Earlier in this section we mentioned some of the factors that can influence the fabric damage characteristics of liquid bleaches. We would now like to point out that with a dry product these same factors, time, temperature, and concentration, are still important, but we also have additional elements that contribute to bleach damage which must be considered. In the case of a dry product, we must consider particle size, rate of solution, and the possibility of the product being trapped or confined in the folds or pocket of a garment.

We have found the entrapment of dry bleach in garments during the washing cycle happens more frequently than we had expected. We have observed, as have others [92], the particle size and rate of solution play an important role when dry bleaches and especially dry chlorine bleaches come in contact with fabric during the wash cycle. In an effort to evaluate the effect of particle size, rate of solution, and the entrapment of dry bleach on fabric damage we developed a confined sample or bag test. This test may be run by placing the dry bleach samples in the pockets of garments, sewing the pockets shut, and running the garments through a normal washing cycle in a washing machine. A more rapid method that may be used for screening dry bleach candidates or the bleaching ingredient itself is the confined sample test.

a. Confined sample test. The cloth swatches in this test may be of any fabric but 100% cotton is usually studied first. We find it is good practice to run this test on both white Indian Head cotton and navy-blue Fruit of the Loom cotton percale. The navy-blue cotton, upon completion of the test, may be opened and examined for fading and/or localized discoloration or speckling.

Place 5 g of the dry bleach sample in the center of a 6 in. x 6 in. cloth swatch. Fold the swatch to form a bag with the bleach sample confined to a small lump in the center of the swatch. Wrap a rubber band tightly around the swatch to hold the bleach sample in a small, confined area. Place 2 liters of water of 150 ppm hardness at $120^{\circ}F$ in a 4-liter beaker. Attach the rubber band to a glass rod, 3/8 in. in diameter by 6 in. long, and drop the rod into the beaker. Start the timer and after the allotted time (samples are to be tested for 1, 3, 5, and 10 min), remove the bag from the water. Rapidly cut and remove the rubber band and rinse the bleach off the cloth in cold running tap water. Rinse the test swatches thoroughly in cold water and then dry. Examine the dried swatches under a long-wavelength (3650 Å) ultraviolet lamp. Record the size and location of dark areas, if any. If no holes have appeared, measure the bursting strength of the area where the dry bleach is placed or cut a 1 1/2 in. strip through the area of bleach contact parallel to the warp threads. The 1 1/2 in. strip may be used to measure the breaking or tensile strength of the test fabric.

The results in Table 21 were obtained using the confined sample test on Indian Head cotton and with the bleaches evaluated at full strength.

The data in Table 21 show that chlorine dry bleaches fall into three distinct classifications as to the amount of fabric damage they produce. The inorganic chlorine bleaches, as represented by calcium and lithium hypochlorite, the cyanurate family, and Halane. The inorganic chlorine bleaches have a very rapid rate of solution and can produce serious damage when coming in contact with cotton even for short time periods. The second classification, cyanurates, can reduce the tensile strength of cotton by 25% in 10 min contact time. It is interesting to note that although there is considerable range in the available chlorine of the cyanurates, large differences in fabric damage are not observed when these bleaching ingredients are tested "as is." We believe this is due to the slower rate of solution noted for TCCA and DCCA in comparison to the more rapidly soluble, but lower available chlorine, sodium and potassium salts. Halane, on the other hand, which has both a slow rate of solution and a limited solubility, causes a reduction in tensile strength about one-third of that noted for the cyanurates.

We have been unable, by either formulation or granulation procedures, to change the fabric damage characteristics significantly, that is, pinholing produced by either calcium or lithium hypochlorite. We also found the relatively mild action of Halane on fabric could not be dramatically changed by differences in granulation, but it can be altered by formulation [56]. However, with the cyanurates, and especially TCCA, we are able to change the fabric damage properties by modifying either the granulation or formulation.

TABLE 21

The Effect of Various Chlorine Bleaches on the Tensile Strength
of Cotton: Confined Sample Test

Type of bleach	Tensile strength[a] (psi)				
	Original	1 min	3 min	5 min	10 min
CCH[b]	56.4 ± 2.7	13.6 ± 1.5	4-5 pinholes	Large holes	Large holes
LiOCl[c]	56.4 ± 2.7	18.1 ± 1.9	8-10 pinholes	Large holes	Large holes
TCCA[d]	56.4 ± 2.7	44.9 ± 1.0	45.8 ± 1.8	46.5 ± 1.6	42.9 ± 1.1
DCCA[e]	56.4 ± 2.7	48.7 ± 1.0	49.0 ± 1.6	46.1 ± 1.6	45.8 ± 1.7
NaDCC[f]	56.4 ± 2.7	45.6 ± 1.4	46.0 ± 1.9	44.4 ± 1.3	42.8 ± 2.1
KDCC[g]	56.4 ± 2.7	47.2 ± 2.1	45.6 ± 1.5	44.8 ± 0.9	42.5 ± 1.5
Halane[h]	56.4 ± 2.7	54.0 ± 1.2	53.8 ± 1.0	51.5 ± 1.1	52.3 ± 1.1

[a]All data are the average of six tensile strength determinations.

[b]Calcium hypochlorite 70.1% Av Cl_2.

[c]Lithium hypochlorite 34.8% Av Cl_2.

[d]Trichloroisocyanuric acid 85.8% Av Cl_2.

[e]Dichloroisocyanuric acid 69.6% Av Cl_2.

[f]Sodium dichloroisocyanurate 57.6% Av Cl_2.

[g]Potassium dichloroisocyanurate 59.0% Av Cl_2.

[h]1,3-Dichloro-5,5-dimethylhydantoin 69.1% Av Cl_2.

The data in Table 22 indicate that when a coarse mesh size TCCA is
used in conjunction with a base containing sodium metasilicate, the TCCA
can produce holes in cotton fabric. The data also show that a low-silicate
TCCA product, formula II, produces about one-half the damage of the same
type of dry bleach with increased silicate, formula III. We repeated these
experiments with DCCA and found it reacts in much the same way as TCCA,
but to a lesser degree. A DCCA formulation with high-silicate base produced more damage than the same formula with low silicate, but both the
high- and low-silicate DCCA dry bleaches caused less fabric damage than
the corresponding TCCA dry bleaches. Further experiments made with

TABLE 22

Fabric Damage Produced by Various TCCA Formulations on Cotton

Type of bleach formula[b]	Mesh size (USS) of TCCA	Original	Tensile strength[a] (psi) after			
			1 min	3 min	5 min	10 min
TCCA I	-10 + 20	71.1 ± 2.1	40.8 ± 1.2	29.7 ± 1.0	15.1 ± 1.8	Small holes
TCCA I	-30 + 140	71.1 ± 2.1	52.0 ± 1.6	38.2 ± 1.2	35.7 ± 1.9	31.9 ± 0.9
TCCA II	-30 + 140	71.1 ± 2.1	50.9 ± 1.9	40.7 ± 1.5	41.0 ± 1.1	38.7 ± 2.0
TCCA III	-30 + 140	71.1 ± 2.1	43.1 ± 2.0	40.2 ± 1.3	36.2 ± 1.1	21.3 ± 0.8

[a] All numbers are averages of six tensile strength determinations.

[b] TCCA I, II, and III all contain 8.0% TCCA (85.8% Av Cl_2), 2.8% sodium alkylbenzenesulfonate, but varying levels of sodium metasilicate. Sodium sulfate is added in quantity sufficient to make each formula up to 100%. The primary difference in the three TCCA formulas is that I contains 5.5% sodium metasilicate, II has 3.7%, and formula III contains 8.5%.

sodium metasilicate show the addition of this material does not significantly influence fabric damage properties of the sodium or potassium salts of dichloroisocyanurate.

b. Multiple wash. We also examined the fabric-tendering properties of TCCA and Halane using some of the same multiple-wash tests discussed earlier in this section. Both TCCA and Halane, at levels of 12 and 15%, respectively, were formulated into typical dry bleach products which also contained 3% sodium alkylbenzenesulfonate, 15% tripolyphosphate, and the remainder sodium sulfate. The tests in which TCCA and Halane were run in conjunction with liquid sodium hypochlorite are as follows:

1. Launder-Ometer stubborn stain concentration of 1000 ppm available chlorine in 150 ppm water hardness and no detergent at 100°F for a total of 45 10-min cycles using cotton sheets that had previously been washed 40 times.
2. The same as 1 except the test fabric is stained with tea, standard tea stain procedure, after each bleaching cycle and only 30 cycles are run.
3. Washing machine studies done at 50 ppm available chlorine with 0.1% Tide in 200 ppm water hardness at 120°F for 15 min with new sheets and pillowcases for a total of 70 complete cycles.

It will be recalled that in the stubborn stain studies with used white sheets liquid chlorine bleach reduced the tensile strength 36% after 45 cycles. The data show the TCCA dry bleach reduced the tensile strength of these same sheets after 45 cycles 37% while Halane caused a reduction of only 19% or about one-half that of liquid chlorine bleach and TCCA dry bleach.

The stubborn stain tests made with tea-stained fabric show a loss in tensile strength after 30 cycles of 29% for both liquid bleach and TCCA dry bleach while Halane dry bleach produces a 15% loss or, again, about one-half that noted for liquid bleach and TCCA. The tea stain removal for liquid sodium hypochlorite after 30 cycles of staining and bleaching is recorded as 74%. Simultaneous studies done with TCCA and Halane dry bleaches show stain removals of 73 and 67%, respectively, after 30 cycles.

The washing machine tests run at 50 ppm available chlorine present results similar to those noted at a stubborn stain concentration of 1000 ppm available chlorine. Liquid chlorine bleach caused losses of 15% on sheets and 18% on pillowcases after 70 cycles. On the same fabrics TCCA dry bleach showed losses of 14 and 16% after 70 cycles. Halane dry bleach again produced the least damage, recording an 8% loss on sheets and 10% on pillowcases after 70 cycles.

The preceding data indicate to us that on an equal available chlorine basis Halane dry bleach is less damaging to cotton than is liquid chlorine bleach

TABLE 23

Fabric Damage Produced by Chlorine Bleaches on Cotton:
Multiple Wash

Type of bleach	Tensile strength (psi) after 20 cycles[a]
Liquid 5.25% NaOCl (by weight)	42.3 ± 2.6[b]
KDCC (dry bleach)	42.6 ± 1.4
NaDCC (dry bleach)	41.9 ± 2.1
0.2% Tide	46.8 ± 2.0

[a] Original tensile strength of fabric is 47.5 ± 2.9 psi.

[b] All numbers are averages of eight tensile strength determinations, four warp and four filling tests averaged.

bleach or TCCA dry bleach. Halane, as would be expected, is less effective in removing tea stain than the other two bleaches in this study. We believe at the particular concentrations and conditions evaluated the fabric damage and tea stain removal properties of TCCA dry bleach and liquid chlorine bleach are similar on cotton. There is slight, but we do not believe significant, from an in-use standpoint, evidence that TCCA produces less fabric damage and tea stain removal than liquid hypochlorite bleach.

As demonstrated earlier, it is possible to change the fabric damage properties of some cyanurate bleaches; however, when the cyanurates, TCCA, DCCA, NaDCC, and KDCC, are properly formulated, we believe their fabric damage and stain-removing characteristics are similar. NaDCC and KDCC were formulated at levels of 7.8% into typical dry bleaches which also contained 3.0% sodium alkylbenzenesulfonate, 15% sodium tripolyphosphate, with the remainder being sodium sulfate. These two dry bleaches and liquid chlorine bleach were studied for fabric damage in the Launder-Ometer at 100 ppm available chlorine on white desized Indian Head cotton with 0.2% Tide in 150 ppm water hardness at 120°F for 15 min. The test fabrics are rinsed thoroughly in water of 150 ppm hardness and dried in a gas-fired dryer for 30 min at a hot setting after each bleaching cycle. The results obtained after 20 complete cycles are summarized in Table 23.

The preceding data further substantiates our opinion that when properly formulated there is a similarity in the fabric damage properties of the cyanurate dry bleaches. The data also substantiate earlier findings that the bleach damage produced by cyanurates on cotton is similar to that noted for a liquid chlorine bleach. We would once again, however, like to emphasize there are a number of factors such as high pH or high available chlorine and those already mentioned, granulation and sodium metasilicate, which do increase the fabric damage produced by the cyanurates. It is always necessary to study carefully the fabric damage characteristics of the particular bleach in which the investigator is interested and also any contemplated changes in bleaching ingredient or product formulation.

3. Oxygen

This section is devoted to the fabric damage properties of sodium perborate tetrahydrate which we will refer to as perborate and DuPont's potassium monopersulfate compound Oxone. The housewife believes these are safe all-fabric bleaches which produce no fabric damage. This assumption is generally true and considerable research has been done in Europe and the United States [93, 94] to show that perborates produce very little damage to cotton fabric. Because perborate and Oxone bleaches are considered to be safe, the user may not exercise as much care with these bleaches as with the chlorine type. This attitude can result in the oxygen bleaches being added directly on fabrics which have dyes that are susceptible to oxygen attack, that is, fading. We do not dwell on this point, but bring it up as a warning to the bleach formulator. It is our opinion, based on marketing experience, that any oxygen bleach candidate should be thoroughly screened at full strength to determine its effect on as many different fabric dyes and dyeing methods as possible.

With perborate and Oxone bleaches the amount of fabric damage is, as was the case with Halane, dependent for the most part on the factors of temperature, time, and concentration. It is well known that temperature plays an important role in the stain-removing ability of perborates. Research done with perborates shows some increase in dabric damage, but not a dramatic one, at high temperatures. Because U.S. washing temperatures rarely get above 140°F and also because we do not believe it is an important factor, we do not discuss the effect of temperature on the fabric damage properties of oxygen bleaches.

Changes in pH, granulation, or formulation can affect the fabric damage characteristics of perborate and Oxone dry bleaches, but here again we believe the effects are for the most part academic and not significant to the ultimate user of the bleach. There are two notable exceptions to the preceding statement and these are the addition of activators to perborate and sodium chloride to Oxone. We have already discussed some of the many perborate activators and do not think they are currently pertinent because they are impractical either from a cost or stability standpoint and, to our knowledge, are not being used at the present time. The addition of sodium chloride to Oxone converts Oxone to a chlorine bleach. The severity of

TABLE 24

Fabric Damage Produced by Halane, Oxone, and Perborate on Cotton

Type of dry bleach	Tensile strength (psi) after[a]				
	Original	1 min	3 min	5 min	10 min
Halane[b]	70.6 ± 2.9	69.1 ± 2.0	68.7 ± 1.7	66.3 ± 2.1	65.0 ± 1.5
Oxone[c]	70.6 ± 2.9	69.8 ± 1.1	69.5 ± 1.9	68.1 ± 1.9	68.0 ± 1.3
Perborate[d]	70.6 ± 2.9	70.8 ± 1.5	70.1 ± 1.6	69.3 ± 2.0	69.0 ± 1.0

[a] All data are the average of six tensile strength determinations.

[b] Contains 10.0% Halane (68.7% Av Cl_2), 2.7% sodium alkylbenzenesulfonate, 20.0% sodium tripolyphosphate, and the remainder sodium sulfate.

[c] Contains 33.0% Oxone (4.85% Av O_2), 1.8% sodium alkylbenzenesulfonate, 18.0% sodium tripolyphosphate, 5.0% sodium metasilicate, and the remainder sodium sulfate.

[d] Contains 25.0% sodium perborate tetrahydrate (10.5% Av O_2), 2.0% sodium alkylbenzenesulfonate, 35.0% sodium tripolyphosphate, and the remainder sodium sulfate.

fabric damage produced by this combination depends on the pH of the formula and the amount of sodium chloride present. The amount of fabric deterioration produced can range from that noted for a liquid sodium hypochlorite at full strength to that observed for a cyanurate bleach. We do not present data on the combination of sodium chloride and Oxone because it is not a factor in the bleach market today.

It should be remembered that oxygen-releasing dry bleaches have the same tendency to be trapped or confined in the pockets and folds of garments as chlorine dry bleaches. Oxone, because of its acid pH, by itself produces more damage to cotton than perborate used at full strength. Because Oxone does not bleach at its natural pH, this fabric damage comparison is not valid and of no particular consequence. When properly formulated, we have found Oxone and perborate bleaches produce very little deterioration of cotton fabric. To give a yardstick of comparison, we conducted a confined sample test using typical dry bleaches containing Halane, perborate, and Oxone. The instant study was made with desized Indian Head cotton and the results are summarized in Table 24.

TABLE 25

Fabric Damage Produced by Perborate and Oxone in
Kendall Home Laundry Project

Garment	Product used	Tensile strength (psi)	Bursting strength (psi)
Shirts, 100% cotton	None (original)	41.3 ± 1.8[a]	104.4 ± 2.7[b]
(resin treated)	Detergent	36.8 ± 1.7	105.2 ± 2.8
	Perborate	36.1 ± 1.8	105.7 ± 2.3
	Oxone	36.0 ± 2.0	103.6 ± 2.5
Blouses, 100%	None	45.6 ± 0.6	144.4 ± 2.9
Dacron	Detergent	41.3 ± 2.6	142.0 ± 2.4
	Perborate	41.7 ± 0.9	142.2 ± 2.1
	Oxone	41.0 ± 1.1	142.0 ± 2.1
Slips, 100% nylon	None	50.8 ± 1.5	155.2 ± 2.0
	Detergent	52.3 ± 2.6	153.8 ± 1.8
	Perborate	51.1 ± 2.0	152.6 ± 1.3
	Oxone	50.9 ± 0.5	153.4 ± 1.7
Underpants, white,	None	56.6 ± 2.7	147.5 ± 2.3
100% cotton	Detergent	57.0 ± 2.5	146.7 ± 1.9
	Perborate	57.1 ± 2.0	147.1 ± 2.0
	Oxone	56.3 ± 2.2	141.5 ± 2.5
Underpants, pink,	None	24.1 ± 1.4	112.0 ± 2.0
100% cotton	Detergent	23.0 ± 1.1	111.5 ± 1.5
	Perborate	25.1 ± 1.6	108.8 ± 0.9
	Oxone	22.4 ± 0.8	111.6 ± 2.1
Underpants, print,	None	24.7 ± 1.4	110.5 ± 1.4
100% cotton	Detergent	23.5 ± 1.6	110.5 ± 2.2
	Perborate	25.1 ± 1.7	109.5 ± 0.8
	Oxone	23.7 ± 0.8	106.0 ± 2.0

[a]All numbers are the averages of eight tensile strength determinations,
four warp and four filling tests averaged.

[b]Average of six bursting strength determinations.

The data in Table 24 show that neither Oxone nor perborate bleaches, when placed directly on cotton, attack it as readily as the mildest chlorine bleach Halane. The data also demonstrate that a perborate formulation with an available oxygen of 2.5% appears slightly less damaging than an Oxone bleach with 1.6% available oxygen. We consider the damage produced by perborate and Oxone bleaches when added directly to cotton fabric as a real, but, when viewed in the overall life of a cotton garment which will also be subjected to wearing, washing, and drying, negligible factor.

As we discussed earlier in this section, Helen Kendall did a laundry project which studied the fabric damage properties of liquid sodium hypochlorite bleach, and perborate and Oxone dry bleaches. The oxygen bleach formulations used are the same ones shown in the confined sample test comparing Halane, perborate, and Oxone (see Table 24). Both oxygen bleaches were used in conjunction with 3/4 cup of All detergent. The perborate bleach was used at a level which resulted in 30 ppm available oxygen in the washing machine while Oxone was used at a concentration equivalent to 15 ppm available oxygen. A total of 20 wash/wear cycles were carried out and the data obtained are summarized in Table 25.

Upon examining the data in Table 25 from both tensile and bursting strength measurements, it becomes apparent that Oxone and perborate dry bleaches produce no more fabric damage on resin-treated cotton shirts, Dacron blouses, and nylon slips than is noted for the detergent alone. The damage to cotton underpants, white, pink, and printed, is also negligible for the perborate and Oxone bleaches. There appears to be slight evidence that Oxone bleach is more damaging to cottons than is perborate; however, there is not sufficient evidence to firmly substantiate this as fact.

Based on the data obtained from the Kendall study and other fabric damage evaluations [28, 95] we can state that Oxone and perborate dry bleaches, when properly formulated, produce no more damage to cotton, nylon, and Dacron garments after 20 wash/wear cycles than the detergent. It will be noted in the instant study the factor of wear has not yet become apparent. Although the wear factor might slightly alter the results obtained, we are still of the opinion that the fabric damage produced by perborate or Oxone bleaches when used at their recommended concentrations is indeed small.

ACKNOWLEDGMENT

The author would like to acknowledge the fine help of John H. Barrett and especially his contribution in preparing the section on calculation of test results (Sec. IV, E).

REFERENCES

1. J. O. Hinshaw (to Purex Corp.), U.S. Pat. 2,610,905 (1950).

2. L. J. Barton (to The Clorox Co.), U.S. Pat. 2,918,351 (1956).

3. J. Burtis, Deterg. Age, 1, 22 (1965).

4. M. W. Lister, Can. J. Chem., 34, 479 (1956).

5. M. W. Lister and R. C. Petterson, Can. J. Chem., 40, 729 (1962).

6. M. W. Lister, Can. J. Chem., 34, 465 (1956).

7. R. M. Chapin, J. Amer. Chem. Soc., 56, 2211 (1934).

8. H. L. Robson and G. A. Petroe (to The Mathieson Alkali Works), U.S. Pat. 2, 195,755 (1940).

9. I. E. Muskat (to Pittsburgh Plate Glass Co.), U.S. Pat. 2,225,923 (1940).

10. M. A. Lesser, Soap Sanit. Chem., 24, 37 (1948).

11. L. D. Mathias (to Victor Chemical Works), U.S. Pat. 1,555,474 (1925).

12. H. Adler (to Victor Chemical Works), U.S. Pat. 1,965,304 (1934).

13. Allied Chemical and Dye Corp., Product Development Booklet LH-1 (1947).

14. R. B. Ellestad, Soap Chem. Spec., 37, 77 (1961).

15. Anonymous, Chem. Week, March 2, 63 (1963).

16. J. S. Thompson, Soap Chem. Spec., 40, 45 (1964).

17. B. M. Milwidsky, Mfg. Chem., 34, 302 (1963).

18. R. L. Formaini (to Allied Chemical Corp.), U.S. Pat. 3,093,641 (1963).

19. W. F. Symes and N. S. Hadzekriakides (to Monsanto Chemical Co.), U.S. Pat. 3,035,054 (1962).

20. W. F. Symes (to Monsanto Chemical Co.), U.S. Pat. 3,035,056 (1962).

21. W. F. Symes (to Monsanto Chemical Co.), U.S. Pat. 3,150,132 (1964).

22. M. A. Lesser, Soap Sanit. Chem., 29, 154 (1953).

23. FMC Corp., Technical Bulletin, FMC Sodium Perborate.

24. A. H. Gilbert, Deterg. Age, 4, 18 (1967).

25. C. P. McClain, unpublished work, 1955.

26. B. L. Davis, Deterg. Age, 2, 20 (1965).

27. American Cyanamid, Technical Report (1969).

28. E. I. DuPont de Nemours Co., Technical Bulletin, Oxone Monopersulfate Compound (1964).

29. C. P. McClain, unpublished work, 1957.

30. Pittsburgh Plate Glass Co., Technical Bulletin, CPA-2 (1964).

31. Nippon Peroxide Co. Ltd., Technical Bulletin, Sodium Percarbonate.

32. FMC Corp., Technical Bulletin, Perbenzoic Acid (1964).

33. FMC Corp., Technical Bulletin, m-Chloroperbenzoic Acid (1963).

34. P. Brocklehurst and P. Pengilly (to the Procter and Gamble Co.), U.S. Pat. 3,075,921 (1963).

35. J. H. Blumbergs and H. K. Latourette (to FMC Corp.), U.S. Pat. 3,130,169 (1964).

36. R. L. Liss and T. B. Hilton, in "Proceedings of the 47th Annual Meeting Chemical Specialties Manufacturers Association, Inc.," New York, 1960.

37. G. Weder, Amer. Dyest. Rep., 51, 23 (1962).

38. W. G. Spangler, H. D. Cross, and B. R. Schaafsma, J. Amer. Oil Chem. Soc., 42, 723 (1965).

39. B. Rutowski, J. Amer. Oil Chem. Soc., 44, 103 (1967).

40. J. W. Hensley and C. G. Inks, ASTM Special Technical Publication, No. 268, 27 (1959).

41. B. E. Gordon, J. Roddewig, and W. T. Shebs, J. Amer. Oil Chem. Soc., 44, 289 (1967).

42. B. E. Gordon and W. T. Shebs, J. Amer. Oil Chem. Soc., 46, 537 (1969).

43. R. P. Allard, unpublished work, Purex Research Fellowship, 1957-1960.

44. T. H. Hogan, unpublished work, 1969.

45. E. I. Rabinowitch, Photosynthesis and Related Processes, Vol. 1, Wiley-Interscience, New York, 1945, p. 371.

46. Proposed Interim Federal Specification, Scouring Cleansers, P-S-00311E, dated Jan. 22, 1971.

47. Association of Home Appliance Manufacturers, Household Washer Performance Evaluation Procedure, Standard No. HLW-1, Association of Home Appliance Manufacturers, 1970.

48. W. J. Park, unpublished work, 1964.

49. P. Kubelka and F. Munk, Z. Tech. Phys., 12, 593 (1931).

50. M. J. Engberg (to Maurice Preston Corp.), U.S. Pat. 1,883,649 (1932).

51. R. A. Robinson, unpublished work, 1966.

52. K. W. Young and J. A. Allmand, Can. J. Res., 27, 318 (1949).

53. A. F. Steinhauer and J. C. Valenta (to Dow Chemical Co.), U.S. Pat. 3, 172, 861 (1965).

54. P. L. Magill (to E. I. DuPont de Nemours and Co.), U.S. Pat. 2,430,233 (1947).

55. R. C. Petterson and U. Grzeskowiak, J. Org. Chem., 24, 1414 (1959).

56. R. A. Blomfield (to Wyandotte Chemicals Corp.), U.S. Pat. 2,938,764 (1960).

57. R. S. Hunter, Circular of the National Bureau of Standards C429, United States Government Printing Office, Washington, D.C., 1942.

58. D. B. Judd, Circular of the National Bureau of Standards C-478, United States Government Printing Office, Washington, D.C., 1950.

59. A. C. Hardy, Handbook of Colorimetry, The Technology Press, Cambridge, Mass., 1936.

60. D. B. Judd and G. Wyszecki, Color in Business, Science, and Industry, 2nd ed., Wiley, New York, 1963.

61. R. T. Hunter, J. Amer. Oil Chem. Soc., 45, 362 (1968).

62. Macbeth Daylighting Corp., Technical Bulletin No. 252 (1953).

63. Nu-Lite Division of El-tronics Inc., Data Bulletin No. UL-10A (1961).

64. S. Siegel, Nonparametric Statistics for the Behavioral Sciences, McGraw-Hill, New York, 1956, p. 116.

65. B. S. Brown, Chem. Eng., 68, 137 (1961).

66. H. B. Mann and D. R. Whitney, Ann. Math. Stat., 18, 50 (1947).

67. P. Kubelka, J. Opt. Soc. Amer., 38, 448 (1948).

68. P. Kubelka, J. Opt. Soc. Amer., 44, 330 (1954).

69. R. H. Park and E. I. Stearns, J. Opt. Soc. Amer., 34, 112 (1944).

70. G. Mackinney and A. C. Little, Color of Foods, A.V.I. , Westport, Conn., 1962.

71. F. W. Billmeyer and M. Saltzman, Principles of Color Technology, Wiley-Interscience, New York, 1966.

72. Amer. Soc. Testing Mater., ASTM Standard D 1925-70, Part 27, 1970, p. 598.

73. P. Stensby, Soap Chem. Spec., 43, 80 (1967).

74. Amer. Soc. Testing Mater., ASTM Standard E313-67, Part 30, 1970, p. 981.

75. A. S. Levans, Graphical Methods in Research, Wiley, New York, 1965.

76. D. S. Davis, ed., Chemical Processing Nomographs, Chem. Publ., New York, 1960.

77. Amer. Inst. of Laundering, Service Bulletin 484-B, 1955, p. 1.

78. J. H. Skinkle, Textile Testing, 2nd ed., Chemical Publ., New York, 1949, p. 266.

79. J. H. Skinkle, Textile Testing, 2nd ed., Chemical Publ., New York, 1949, p. 267.

80. F. L. Fennell, Amer. Dyest. Rep., 30, 481 (1941).

81. Amer. Ass. of Text. Chem. and Color., AATCC Technical Manual, 40, Part II, 1964, B-44.

82. Amer. Soc. Testing Mater., ASTM Standard D76-67, Part 24, 1970, p. 1.

83. J. H. Skinkle, Textile Testing, 2nd ed., Chemical Publ., New York, 1949, p. 149.

84. G. E. Linton, Applied Basic Textiles, 1st ed., Duell, Sloan and Pearce, New York, 1966, p. 320.

85. G. E. Linton, Applied Basic Textiles, 2st ed., Duell, Sloan and Pearce, New York, 1966, p. 322.

86. Amer. Soc. Testing Mater., ASTM Standard D1424-63, Part 24, 1970, p. 323.

87. M. S. Furry, P. L. Bensing, R. K. Taube, N. D. Poole, and E. S. Ross, Amer. Dyest. Rep., 48, 67 (1959).

88. V. I. McLendon and S. Davison, USDA Tech. Bull. No. 1103 (1955).

89. L. B. Thomas and P. B. Mack, Linen Supply News, Sept., 54 (1966).

90. P. E. Smith and P. B. Mack, Linen Supply News, Jan., 27 (1964).

91. H. Kendall, unpublished work, 1964.

92. R. R. Keast and E. S. Roth, Soap Chem. Spec., 44, 129 (1968).

93. A. H. Gilbert, Deterg. Age, 4, 26 (1967).

94. M. S. Furry, P. L. Bensing, and J. L. Kirkley, Amer. Dyest. Rep., 48, 59 (1959).

95. M. Lapitsky, C. Kyes, and M. B. Brown, Research Circular 112, Ohio Agricultural Experiment Station (1962).

Chapter 14

ASSESSMENT OF PHYSICAL DAMAGE TO A TEXTILE SUBSTRATE
DURING LAUNDERING AND DRY CLEANING

J. A. Dayvault
Celanese Fibers Marketing Company
Charlotte, North Carolina

I. INTRODUCTION

For the purpose of this chapter a textile substrate is taken to be either
a woven or a knitted fabric manufactured from the typical man-made or

natural fibers or blends of these fibers. Physical damage can be judged to
be any detrimental change in the utility or aesthetics of a fabric caused by
the physical as opposed to chemical actions of laundering and dry cleaning.
However, this chapter is concerned only with the assessment of laundering-
induced losses of the following fabric properties: strength, abrasion resistance, appearance, and some special properties, namely flame resistance
and water repellency. In addition, the measurement of abrasion, shrinkage,
and delamination of bonded fabrics occurring during laundering are discussed.

A. Tensile Strength

A direct loss of tensile strength can be caused either by chemical degradation of the fibers, which was discussed in more detail in a previous
chapter, or by the abrasive loss of fibers from the fabric. The usual techniques for measuring strength loss are grab or strip tensile tests, tear
tests, and bursting strength tests.

B. Abrasion Resistance

Direct abrasion can occur during the cleaning process and if excessive,
results in fabric breaks or holes. Laundering abrasion can also be a source
of color change at sharp edges and creases in some permanent-press-finished
blended fabrics. The loss of fiber lubricants or softeners during cleaning
can significantly reduce the abrasion resistance of garments during subsequent wearing.

Laundering abrasion resistance is measured by repetition of the laundry
cycle and loss of abrasion resistance to wear measured on specially developed rubbing and flex abrasion testers used on laundered fabrics.

C. Appearance

The advent of durable press finishing has increased the requirement for
a smooth ironed appearance in fabrics after laundering. In addition to the
mechanical laundering variables which affect laundered appearance, acid
hydrolysis of the cross-linking resin finish during laundering can reduce the
dry wrinkle resistance of a fabric. Testing of appearance usually involves
the difficult step of subjective assessment of degree of retained appearance.

D. Shrinkage

Shrinkage of a garment during cleaning is a perennial textile problem
that reduces the usefulness of a product for the consumer. Ester et al. [1]
found that detergents can affect shrinkage significantly.

E. Miscellaneous Special Properties

More specialized products have particular features which are affected
by laundering and dry cleaning and this chapter considers the assessment

of the following: (a) delamination of bonded fabrics, (b) changes in flammability, and (c) loss of water repellency. Loss of dyestuff and the consequent change in color is a typical cleaning problem that is not considered in this chapter since this problem is usually directly associated with the dye rather than the substrate. It is recognized that the relative fastness of a dyestuff varies considerably with the substrate and any major detergent evaluation must consider the effect on colorfastness. The various colorfastness procedures listed in the AATCC yearbook serve as an excellent base for comparing detergents for their effect on colorfastness.

Of the properties considered in this chapter most of them change as a result of either the detergent used in the system or an additive involved. Frequently no direct damage can be observed due to the cleaning process itself, but the process can render the fabrics susceptible to damage by reducing its resistance to abrasion, wrinkling, and so on. It has also been found [2] that abrasion during laundering can accelerate the soiling of a garment during actual wear.

In evaluating the selected properties and their reaction to different detergent systems, it is important to know the limitations of the test procedures in terms of their reproducibility and the statistical significance of any data being compared. Even more important from a consumer's standpoint is the correlation of test data to end-use wear results. Many fiber producers, retail chains, and major mills run extensive and continuing wear trials to ensure the reliability of their testing and the acceptability of their products.

II. STRENGTH RETENTION

Damage from retained chlorine is the most common laundering problem involving strength loss. Some detergents can also cause strength loss due to chemical damage, particularly when the fabrics that are being tested are alkali sensitive. More subtle reasons for strength loss during cleaning are removal of lubricants and resultant abrasive loss of fibers. Usually the fabrics are tested as received by an appropriate strength test and then retested after multiple cleanings in sufficient steps to determine the rate of loss due to cleaning. Some knowledge of the expected wear life of the fabric and the normal number of cleaning cycles is needed. An excellent guide to expected wear life of dry-cleanable garments has been published by the National Institute of Dry Cleaners [3].

ASTM Standards, Parts 32 and 33, give detailed instructions on how to conduct the strength tests discussed below. Any deviations from the standard methods should be carefully considered since many years of laboratory and ASTM committee experience have established the accuracy and precision of the tests when performed as specified.

A. Tensile Strength

The grab method (ASTM-D-1682) is commonly used for predicting end-use performance of fabrics. This test requires more fabric and gives a wider spread of data than the strip test, but the samples can be prepared faster and the test is easier to conduct. The raveled strip (ASTM-D-1682) method is more accurate and reproducible and for these reasons, is the more desirable test in laboratory comparisons where the amount of damage may be small and difficult to detect.

With either the grab or strip test, it is important to take into account any shrinkage that occurred during cleaning. Both tests measure the breaking strength of a 1-in. section of yarns in a fabric and more yarns must be broken when significant shrinkage has occurred. Most testing equipment in use today, whether constant rate of loading or constant rate of extension, are equipped to draw stress-strain charts. These charts can frequently be used to give an indication of how the fabric damage occurred by comparing changes of fabric elongation and modulus. The charts also serve as permanent records of the testing data.

B. Tear Strength

The Elmendorf tear test (ASTM-D-1424) is also widely used for predicting end-use performance. The test is fast and easy to run. Sample preparation is easier and the results are more accurate if the samples can be die cut. The results can be sensitive to loss of softener in cleaning, especially if the fabric has a loose construction.

C. Burst Strength

Bursting strength is usually the only meaningful strength measurement that can be determined on knit fabrics. Mullen burst (ASTM-D-231-62) is the most common and is easier to run than the ball burst (ASTM-D-231-62) method. The final gauge reading on the Mullen test should always be corrected for the pressure needed to raise the rubber diaphragm. It is frequently helpful to use a monitor to check the accuracy or calibration of the equipment, especially if the data are to be compared with similar data from another laboratory. A "standard" fabric or aluminum foil can be used as the monitor.

The fabric strength that must be retained after multiple cleanings for the fabric to be acceptable is determined by end-use requirements. Many fiber producers, mills, and retail chain laboratories set their own specifications to ensure the quality of their products. In most cases, these specifications are backed up by extensive wear testing and can be relied on as practical guides to acceptable strength retention.

III. ABRASION

A. Direct Abrasion

The direct loss of fiber during the cleaning process, due to either flex or surface abrasion, is undesirable and consequently a subject of continuing interest to the cleaning researcher. The problems of direct abrasion during cleaning were magnified by the advent of resin-treated polyester/cotton blend (permanent press) garments. The accelerated abrasion of these garments is the direct result of the cross-linking and weakening of the cellulosic component [4].

This type of "wear" of fabrics can be simulated in the laboratory by repeated laundering and tumble drying, but, as with much testing, the interpretation of such a simple test is difficult because of the nonreproducibility of the results. In spite of the difficulties caused by lack of precision and accuracy in a repeated laundering test it is still the most commonly used technique for conducting accelerated wear trials on garments. This type of testing has been used with shirting fabrics to determine the effect of fabric construction and finish on the expected wear life of the garment. The results served as meaningful guidelines in development work. Such testing is apropos provided its shortcomings are understood. The AATCC research committee RA-29 on abrasion test methods made a thorough study of repeated laundering and tumble drying as an accelerated abrasion test method. Its findings [5] indicated that the method was reliable within a laboratory but could not be recommended as a standard AATCC test for use between laboratories. Some of the factors that caused variability were the age and surface condition of the laundry tub, the amount and type of wash load, the extraction efficiency, which can affect the drying time, the wash temperature, and the drying time and temperature. The variability of this type of testing was also reported by Markezich and Smith and the AATCC Gulf Coast Section [6, 7].

The RA-29 committee was unable to pin down the effects of all these variables and they did find considerable differences between laboratories even when holding most of these conditions constant. The committee also found that the makeup of the test swatches had a highly significant effect on the test results. The use of an interliner in the cuff or collar makeup accelerated the edge wear.

Handy et al. [8] reported that wear on dress shirts was largely due to laundering. The test method used was essentially the AATCC test method 124. A control item of known wear performance was always included and the garments were rated after every fifth laundering. The use of a control fabric of this type is very helpful in correlating a series of tests over a long period with a test method which is variable.

Another variable in abrasion testing is the technique used to measure the amount of abrasion that has occurred. When working with 100% undyed

4   3   2   1

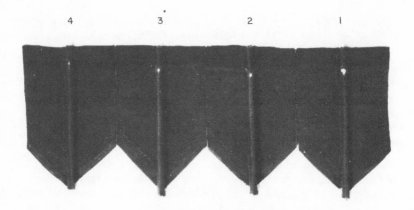

FIG. 1. Tentative Celanese durability standards.

cotton fabric the Goldthwait staining technique [9] can be used. Lint accumulation and weight loss are also useful techniques. Photographic standards
are probably the most common technique and are handier for relating laboratory testing to actual wear on garments. This technique requires that a
subjective rating is assigned by a technician comparing the test fabric with
photographs of similar fabric with various degrees of wear. The usual set
of standards will follow the AATCC rating principle of assigning a five (5)
rating for no wear and a one (1) rating for the most severe wear, with the
(2), (3), and (4) ratings the intermediate conditions. The Evaluation Laboratories of Celanese Fibers Marketing Company have developed such standards for hole formation during edge wear testing and for color change at a
crease during laundering of permanent press fabrics (see Figs. 1 and 2).

B. Abrasion Resistance

Most of the specialized test equipment designed to measure abrasion
resistance are intended to predict the performance of fabrics in wear. The
testing devices therefore attempt to simulate wear by rubbing or flexing
actions or combinations of both. Considering the variety of surfaces on
which fabrics can be rubbed and flexed, it is easy to understand the multiplicity of abrasion tests that have been developed. Correlation with wear
is even more difficult and most test methods have been developed and used
for specific purposes or end uses.

C. Appearance Change Due to Flat Abrasion: "Frosting"

"Frosting" is one of several abrasion problems peculiar to wash-and-
wear fabrics of resin-treated polyester/cellulosic blends. The more

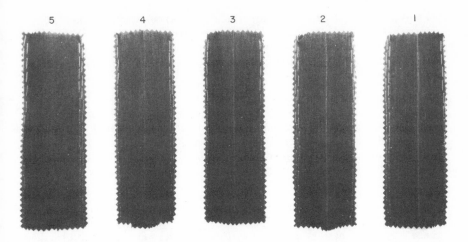

FIG. 2. Evaluation test standards for appearance change at the crease.

abrasion-resistant polyester outlasts the resin-treated cellulosic fiber, resulting in a significant change in the ratio of the two fibers during wear. If the two fibers are not dyed to good union shades, or if the dye penetration into the fabric is poor, then an objectional shade change occurs at points of surface abrasion on the garment. The term normally used to describe this problem is "frosting." The problem is so severe with permanent press garments that virtually no cross-dyed styling effects are available without resorting to complicated and expensive fiber blends. Two test methods were adopted by AATCC RA-29 committee on abrasion for measuring "frosting" (AATCC-119 and -120) and can be used to measure changes in resistance to "frosting" due to particular laundering and dry-cleaning procedures. Both tests are based on flat abrasion using the Stoll universal wear tester. The "O" emery method, developed at the Celanese Evaluation Laboratories will show up poor dye penetration as well as "frosting" problems due to cross-dyed shades. This method was introduced before permanent press fabrics became a major factor and was designed to predict approximately 50 wearings of casual slacks.

The screen wire method was developed specifically for permanent press fabrics [10] and is generally a milder test. The method will predict approximately 25 wearings of casual slacks and correlates well with wear on permanent-press-finished cross-dyed polyester/cellulosics. Problems arising from poor dye penetration are not picked up by this method.

A third frosting test method, the "280 A" emery, was developed and is in use at the Celanese Laboratories. The need for this third test arose when it was found that the "O" emery method did not correlate with wear when the polyester was dyed to a darker shade than the cellulosic. The "280 A" emery test is a combination of the "O" emery and the screen wire methods [11]. The "280 A" test uses the same fabric-mounting technique and the lighter load of the screen wire method but utilizes a coarser emery as an abradant.

The most widely accepted abrasion test for 100% cellulosics has been the Stoll flex test (ASTM-D-1175). This test is very useful if the blades in the flex tester are kept sharp and if the equipment is frequently standardized with a standard tape available from the instrument manufacturer. The method is practically useless on polyester blends because the abrading action prematurely wears the cellulose while the polyester is only slowly abraded.

Several types of abrasion tests are run to a fabric failure end point. These methods are usually used on very specific fabric types and end uses where a thorough history of fabric performance versus test results has been built up. Typical of these methods are the Stoll flex, Stoll flat, Tabor, and Wyzenbeek tests. None of these methods has a good overall correlation with wear in garments and they cannot be relied upon as good general indicators of garment wear resistance.

Edge abrasion testing is the favorite technique for predicting the wear that occurs at shirt collars or cuffs and trouser cuffs or pockets. The most widely accepted method is based on the Accelerotor (AATCC-93). The assessment of abrasion by this test is made by either weight loss or a visual judgment of the degree of wear along the folded edge. The reliability of the test is highly dependent on the speed control of the rotors and the condition of the abradant or the rotors. Markezich has reported on a set of photographic standards based on light transmittance for rating the degree of edge wear using this test method [12].

The Celanese Laboratories have based their edge wear testing on the Random Tumble Pilling tester using emery paper as an abradant with much the same principle as the Accelerotor but at a much slower, more controlled, speed. A modification of the Celanese test, called the folded edge test, closely duplicates the wear observed at trouser cuffs. A set of photographic standards for the folded edge test was developed by Celanese (see Fig. 1); these standards are very useful for assessing the wear observed during this type of testing as well as during actual garment wear. Investigators must be aware that the correlation with wear is not high in edge abrasion testing. Rough correlations have been established, but the techniques do not permit the determination of small differences between fabric abrasion resistances. Each of these tests has its place in predicting the losses of abrasion resistance due to laundering.

IV. FABRIC WRINKLING

The textile industry is steadily working toward the goal of removing the housewife's chore of ironing garments to achieve a smooth appearance. Crease-resistant finishes for cotton were a major step in that direction and the advent of "permanent" press was a logical extension which essentially achieved the goal provided garments were properly laundered and tumble dried. The term "properly laundered" is significant and has a major effect on laundered appearance.

The AATCC test method for durable press appearance (AATCC-124) after laundering is almost universally used in the United States. The details of the test method must be adhered to closely. In addition to controlling the obviously critical variables, such as wash temperature and time, and drying temperature and time, other variables are equally critical if not so obvious. Rinse temperatures, type and amount of load, speed of centrifuging, completeness of drying, dryer temperature variability, and speed of removal at the end of the drying cycle are all factors affecting laundered appearance. Nevertheless, this test can be controlled sufficiently within a given laboratory to guide the development of new fabrics and laundering products. Correlation between laboratories is difficult.

Fabrics can also wrinkle during wear in a more or less dry or semi-moist state. Frequently the ability of a fabric to resist dry wrinkling can be enhanced by a softening agent applied during fabric finishing or during home laundering. The removal of these softeners during laundering or the acid hydrolysis and subsequent breakdown of resin cross-linking in a cellulosic fiber can adversely affect the dry wrinkle performance of a garment. This property of fabrics is best measured by the Monsanto crease angle test (AATCC-66). This technique is reliable when comparing treatments on a specific type of fabric. Technician skill and training are, however, important to reproducibility. Recent reports [13] indicate that special fabric holders can improve the reproducibility of the Monsanto test. Unfortunately, this method cannot be relied on to predict wear performance of fabrics, and especially it cannot differentiate different blends and constructions.

A new dry wrinkle test method is being introduced by the AATCC test committee RA-6 based on the AKU apparatus (AATCC-128). This method is designed to give better correlation with wear. Other dry wrinkle tests are the CSI Wrinkleometer developed by Celanese and the FRL wrinkle tester developed by Fabric Research Laboratories. Both of these methods are designed to give better correlation with wear than the Monsanto test.

A. Laundry Shrinkage

While some might not consider shrinkage to be fabric damage, the loss of garment utility due to shrinkage qualifies shrinkage as damage within the term of reference for this chapter. The techniques and problems of testing shrinkage are similar to those involved in testing for change in laundered appearance. In fact, the same samples used for judging durable press in the AATCC method (AATCC-124) can be used for measuring shrinkage due to home laundering. The only additional precautions that should be taken are to use a stamping device that is preset for the base measurement (usually 10 in.) and to train the technicians on the importance of consistent and precise techniques.

In addition to home laundering, it may be desirable to determine shrinkage due to commercial laundering, and AATCC Test Method 96 is designed to do this. A washweel, centrifuge, and tumble dryer are necessary to carry out this particular test.

B.   Miscellaneous Effects

Frequently the detergent researcher is involved in determining the effect of his products on the more specialized properties of textile fabrics. The number and variety of special properties encountered are too varied for complete coverage in this work, but some properties of current importance are water repellency, flammability, and delamination of bonded fabrics.

Water repellency can be changed significantly by laundering techniques. The spray rating test (AATCC-22) is a fast, reliable test. The impact penetration test (AATCC-42) can be used where efficiency of rain protection is important, but this test is highly dependent on fabric construction. Frequently, it is necessary to iron the fabric after washing to restore the water-repellency properties of the finish, particularly if a fluorohydrocarbon type of finish is used, and this fact must not be overlooked during testing.

The effect of laundering on fabric flammability is important and will become increasingly so with the introduction of new government standards on flammability of apparel. The test methods used for apparel testing are the vertical and 45° angle methods (see AATCC-33 and -34). Flammability testing is currently undergoing such intensive investigation and redevelopment that it is difficult to predict which tests will be adopted. The government tests and standards, as issued, are a prerequisite in any studies of the effect of laundering on flammability.

Delamination is a continuing problem with bonded and foam-laminated fabrics. Delamination during laundering is usually less severe than delamination during dry cleaning. The standard laundering procedures for durable press testing should be adequate. Testing for delamination during dry cleaning is more difficult. Laboratories frequently test their samples in coin-operated dry-cleaning units, but this type of testing is unreliable since there is no control over the testing conditions. The installation of coin-operated type of dry-cleaning equipment or the Atlas Electric machine in the laboratory is more desirable and can give consistency of testing as well as convenience. AATCC test methods are available for dry-cleaning testing (e.g., AATCC-86). Unfortunately, it is difficult to run a sufficiently large sample vigorously enough to achieve reliable results.

As indicated at the beginning of this chapter, damage to the physical substrate is considered as practically any change that prohibits or significantly reduces the utilization of the product by the consumer. The testing of these changes is only straightforward where strength or shrinkage is involved. The testing of aesthetic properties, for example, color change or more particularly abrasion, is very complex, often subjective, and difficult to correlate with actual wear. However, specific tests can be used for predicting relative performance with reasonable accuracy. The researcher must be aware of the limitations of a test and draw only those conclusions which are valid.

The literature contains a number of excellent articles [14-19] of general interest on the subject of damage to textile substrates in domestic laundering.

REFERENCES

1. V. C. Ester, N. Hollen, and R. Edgar, Amer. Dyest. Rep., March 19, 1962, pp. 25-30.

2. M. A. Huisman and M. A. Morris, Tex. Res. J., No. 1, 30-32 (1972).

3. A. E. Johnson, Amer. Dyest. Rep., 55, No. 5, 163-166 (1966).

4. E. C. Peterson, Text. Chem. Color., 1, No. 24, 519 (1969).

5. Committee RA-29, Annual report, AATCC Technical Manual, Amer. Assoc. Text. Chem. Color., 45, 19 (1969).

6. AATCC - Gulf Coast Section, Amer. Dyest. Rep., 55, No. 25, 1056-1064 (1966).

7. A. R. Markezich and M. M. Smith, Text. Chem. Color., 3, No. 6, 140 (1971).

8. C. T. Handy, H. W. Arnold, D. C. Reitz, and P. R. Wilkinson, Amer. Dyest. Rep., 57, 529 (1968).

9. D. M. Cates, K. S. Campbell, and H. A. Rutherford, Text. Res. J., 22, No. 1D, 623-630 (1952).

10. N. B. Gobeil and P. L. D'Alessandro, Amer. Dyest. Rep., 54, No. 24, 992 (1965).

11. R. College, Can. Text. J., 85, No. 11, 61 (1968).

12. A. R. Markezich, Amer. Dyest. Rep., 55, No. 24, 992-994 (1966).

13. G. McLean, A. R. Markezich, and H. R. Copeland, Amer. Dyest.
     Rep., 57, No. 18, 650-653 (1968).

14. C. J. Pope and E. P. Parker, Text. Chem. Color., 1, No. 16, 345-
     353 (1969).

15. R. C. Davis, Text. Chem. Color., 1, No. 24, 524-527 (1969).

16. J. L. Bubl, Text. Res. J., 40, No. 7, 637-643 (1970).

17. M. A. Morris, Text. Res. J., 40, No. 7, 644-649 (1970).

18. E. J. Stavarakas, Amer. Dyest. Rep., 56, 708-710 (1967).

19. S. V. Vaeck, J. Soc. Dyers Colour., 82, 374-379 (1966).

Chapter 15

ANCILLARY TESTS

Paul Sosis[*]
Conoco Chemicals
Saddle Brook, New Jersey

I. INTRODUCTION

The complete evaluation of a surface-active agent, and particularly a detergent substance, must include tests that measure not only the primary effects such as soil removal, soil redeposition, rinsability, and the like, but also a large variety of other factors that will significantly affect the general performance and acceptability of the substance. Some of these

---

[*] Present address: Witco Chemical Corporation, Ultra Division, Paterson, New Jersey.

other parameters are microbiological activity, toxicity (acute and subacute), and environmental compatibility, including aquatic safety, phytotoxicity, teratological effects, foam characteristics, surface tension, interfacial tension, wetting, and fabric hand. This chapter deals with tests for measuring foam, surface tension, interfacial tension, wetting, and fabric hand.

All tests are imperfect and strive to achieve ultimate accuracy in their measurements. To this end, we are constantly developing "improved" procedures. But all tests are also compromises between maximum accuracy and the pragmatic requirements of the work. Hence, the choice of a test method is usually determined by considering the practical framework in which the scientific data will be applied. For example, one may sacrifice some accuracy to gain some time.

II. FOAM

While a variety of test methods have appeared, they do not necessarily help to clarify the very complex physiochemical system which is foam. In fact, Kitchener and Cooper [1] maintain that one cause of the current confused state "has been the multiplicity of isolated, ad hoc, experiments which have been carried out and the diversity of materials, often impure, which have been used."

Foams are colloidal systems in which a gas is dispersed in a liquid. They are agglomerations of gas bubbles separated by liquid films. They may be classified by their levels of stability. Foam bubbles and their agglomerations are never in a state of equilibrium and are usually undergoing a breakdown by liquid draindown or bursting of the foam films. At very best, we have a metastable system in some special cases.

We cannot go into the theory of foam formation and stability in this chapter. There are several excellent works on the physical chemistry of foam, emulsions, and colloids which are recommended for the more serious student of the subject [2-12]. This section reviews the most frequently used methods for measuring the lifetime or persistence of foams.

There is no one method or device which can provide a complete profile of foam behavior. The methods that have been employed to study and measure foam represent both practical and theoretical approaches. This development reflects the considerable academic interest which has been shown in the phenomenon, while the great importance of the many practical applications of foam demands relative empirical data.

Foam measurement methods have historically been divided into two classes, static and dynamic. Ross [13] states: "It is recognized that static and dynamic methods represent only an empirical distinction and that there exist more fundamental theoretical considerations upon which a final classification of methods must be based." However, the two terms are convenient to provide an approach to discussing foam measurement methods.

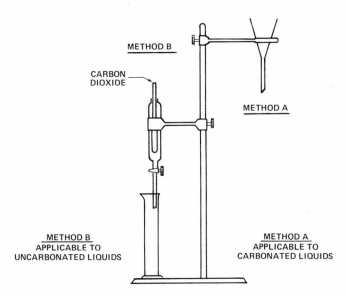

FIG. 1. Ross and Clark static foam apparatus. Method A applicable to carbonated liquids; method B uncarbonated liquids.

A. Static Methods

Static methods usually consist of forming a foam and observing the collapse through drainage as a function of time, commencing the measurement immediately after cessation of foam formation. Drainage is the main factor being measured in static methods and the methods are generally fairly reproducible. Foams themselves are more dependent on fundamental properties such as viscosity, density, surface tension, vapor pressure, cohesion, and charge. The foams may be generated in any of several ways. The simplest is the shake tube method. In this procedure, a volume of solution is shaken in a standard tube and the height and/or duration of the resulting foam is measured [14]. Preston and Richardson [15] measured the "foam number," a calculated value based on the volume of liquid not used in making the foam.

Figure 1 illustrates the Ross and Clark [16, 16A] method for carbonated (method A) and noncarbonated (method B) liquids. The Stiepel [17] foam meter (Fig. 2) is capable of greater accuracy. This foam meter can be used to measure not only the drainage but also the volume of foam produced.

Figure 3 illustrates a variation of a static method. The foam is produced by dropping test solutions into a porous plate connected to a vacuum filter. As the solution passes through the porous filter, it picks up air and bubbles. At some point, the liquid is permitted to drain from the foam by

FIG. 2.   Stiepel foam meter.

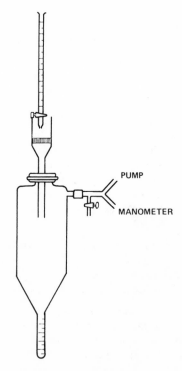

FIG. 3.   Static foam meter used by Abruzov and Grebenshchikov [18].

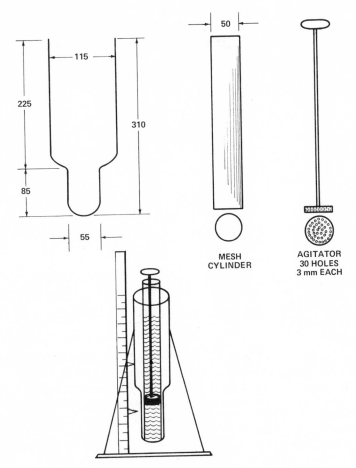

FIG. 4. Schlachter and Dierkes foam tester [19].

equalizing the pressure, and the foam stability is determined by the rate of liquid drainage. This method was developed by Abruzov and Grebenshchikov [18].

Schlachter and Dierkes [19] measured foam and drainage in the apparatus shown in Fig. 4. The foam is generated by beating air into the test solution with the illustrated beater.

Static foam tests may also be run by producing a foam with a high-speed blender or mixer in a closed container and observing the loss of bubbles or measuring the liquid drainage. One example of this procedure is the Star-mix method [20] which employs a mechanical mixer similar to a household blender and a graduated container to measure foam height and liquid volume.

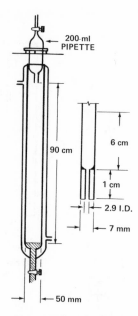

FIG. 5. Ross-Miles foam tester [21].

The procedure most often employed today to measure foaming power and foam stability is a static test developed by Ross and Miles [21] (Fig. 5.) It consists of a jacketed cylinder in which a portion of the test solution is placed. The foam is formed by directing a stream of a second portion of the test solution from a specified height through a standard orifice onto the first volume, thus creating a turbulence and foam. The method has proved so reproducible that the American Society for Testing Materials has adopted the procedure as official and designated it D1173-53.

B. Dynamic Methods

Dynamic test methods differ from static procedures in that measurements are taken during foam generation. Rate of foam formation or ultimate volume of foam formed during the test is the usual parameter measured. Dynamic tests suffer from a lack of proven mathematical formulas to describe these phenomena. The continuous growth and decay of the foam formation makes it more difficult to analyze these systems and correlations are substantially more difficult to describe.

Nevertheless, many workers in the field hold that dynamic foam testing is more meaningful than static procedures and have attempted to design test systems to yield reproducible data.

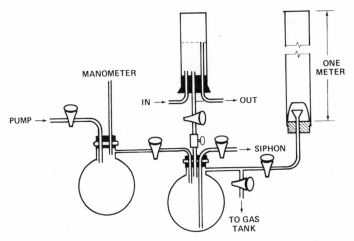

FIG. 6. Bikerman dynamic foam meter [25].

In dynamic tests, the foam is usually produced by passage of a gas through the liquid phase from a porous septum of some type. The capacity of a substance to foam and foam stability are separate phenomena and must be evaluated individually. There are several breakdown stresses during dynamic foam tests, such as (a) mechanical shock, (b) thermal shock, and (c) chemical change.

It is, of course, also impossible to prevent draining of the liquid from the foam and the consequent thinning and ultimate collapse of the liquid films; however, only the rate of collapse is actually measured in dynamic methods.

Ostwald, Siehr, and Mischke [22-24] from 1936 to 1940 developed a dynamic foam tester in which gas bubbles of a known size are passed into a liquid. For a constant gas flow, the initial rate of rise of the foam in the measuring cylinder is taken as a measure of the foaming capacity of the liquid. A strong similarity in the initial rate of rise for all substances tested suggested that the rate of air being passed into the liquid was the controlling factor and not the foaming power of the test substance. These methods are therefore considered inapplicable for strongly foaming solutions.

Bikerman [25] considered "establishing foaminess as a definite physical property of a liquid which must therefore be independent of the apparatus used and of the amount of material employed in measuring it." He designed a modification of the dynamic foam meter recommended by Foulk and Miller [26] and by Lederer [27]. Figure 6 illustrates his apparatus. Gas is forced at a measured rate through a porous membrane and through a layer of test solution. The foam builds up until a constant maximum volume is reached.

The unit recommended by Bikerman to designate foaminess is Σ. It is described as "the average lifetime of a bubble in the foam." $\Sigma = h/u$, where h equals the average maximum foam height and u equals the linear velocity of the gas in the foam. There are many limitations to this approach and the more detailed study by Bikerman [25] and the critique of the method by Sydney Ross [28] are recommended.

Pankhurst [29] adopted a modification of Foulk and Miller's [26] dynamic foam meter as seen in Fig. 7. He measured foaming power as a function of time for a moving foam front to reach a specified height (50 cm). The value θ_{50} is taken as an inverse measure of the foaming power of the liquid.

In 1942 Schutz [30] proposed a system to measure the time of foam collapse. The time F was measured at the time when half the foam surface was gone after carefully regulating foam generation. The apparatus is shown in Fig. 8.

C. Single-Bubble Methods

A single bubble lends itself more directly to theoretical mathematical treatment than does a bulk foam. This fact together with the relative ease of producing a single bubble floating on a liquid makes these techniques likely candidates for more prominent roles in studying the fundamentals of foam. Work by Hardy [31] and by Talmud and Suchowolskaja [32] using single-bubble methods has helped to gain information on the nature of interfaces.

D. Other Tests

Sinsheimer [33] modified two established procedures in order to provide better standardization. The sudsing test listed in Federal Specification P-S-536 was modified by using a mechanical shaker, an improved test cylinder, and recording the initial volume and a final volume of the foam for a period of 15 min following shaking. The dynamic foam-meter method of Hattiangdi [34] was modified by regulating the pressure of the gas used to produce the foam and calibrating the apparatus. He derived a factor for each bubble and used these factors for correlating data.

Sironval and Ramakers [35] showed some relationship between foam tests. They found that the method of Weeks [36] had the greatest precision and correlated well with the results of a consumer panel test for dishwashing.

Tschakert [37] surveyed the tests for foam evaluation and reported on a multiple-beating instrument designed by Sinner that was not mentioned elsewhere in the literature.

Goette [38] described the construction and mode of action of a fully automatic apparatus for measuring foam production. The device is based on mechanically operated reciprocating sieves.

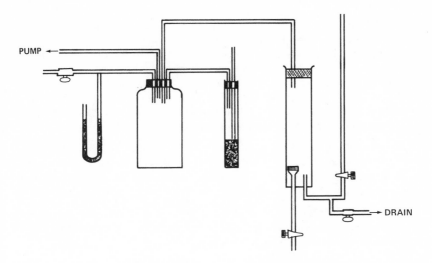

FIG. 7. Dynamic foam meter used by Pankhurst [29].

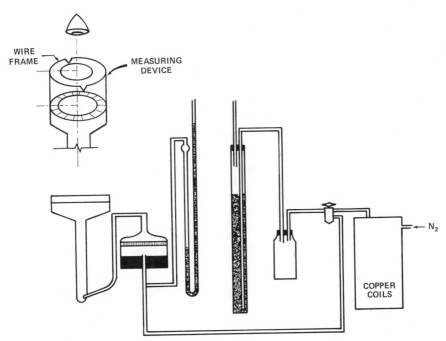

FIG. 8. Schutz apparatus to measure foam time and device used by Schutz [30] to observe when half-surface area is clear of foam.

Noll [39] studied the determination of foaming power of soaps and detergents. His apparatus consisted of a 250-ml graduated cylinder (about 30 cm tall, of which the upper one-sixth is ungraduated) provided with a removable cover through which passes a rod to the bottom of which is fixed a perforated plate (twelve 5-mm holes) with minimum clearance from the wall of the graduate. Place 50 ml of the solution to be tested in the graduate, put on the cover, read the level of the liquid, and raise and lower the perforated plate until the volume of foam remains constant. The increase in volume gives a measure of the foaming power.

Goette [40] studied foam with soaps and textile auxiliaries. Measurements were made with a jacketed, graduated glass cylinder. Air was introduced through fine openings in the bottom of the cylinder and a means for agitating the liquid was provided.

Peters [41] introduced the concept of minimum bubble size for comparing relative foaming power of materials. He utilized a simplified dynamic foam tester that generated foam by nitrogen bubbling.

Walling et al. [42] developed a unique dynamic foam meter. Nitrogen bubbling generates foam which is permitted to pass through a vertical tube and is thrown into an annular receiver by a rotating paddle. Drainage rate is determined by measuring the rate of transfer of solution through different vertical heights with the same nitrogen gas flow rate.

Burcik [43] studied the rate of surface-tension lowering and its role in foaming. Surface tension was measured as a function of time by the dynamic method of Addison for aquatic solutions of sodium laurate, and so on. The stability of foams was judged by measuring the average life of a single bubble and also the half-life of the foam. The solutions having high foam stability are those with low surface tension, high surface viscosity, and a moderate rate of surface tension lowering.

A special method of foam study was suggested by Chang et al. [44]. Bubble size and distribution were determined photomicrographically on frozen foams made from 1.5-6% solutions of heptadecylbenzimidazole, saponin, sodium dodecylsulfate, and so on. Sliding-vane and centrifugal pumps were used to generate foam.

Matalon [45-47] designed an apparatus to study formation and stability of foam laminas. The laminometer is well suited for studying foaming properties of aqueous detergent solutions. A rectangular platinum wire frame is pulled out of the surface of the solution to be tested. During this process, the variation of the force acting on the frame is recorded as a function of the height of the frame above the surface of the solution. Conditions resulting in foam formation of aqueous solutions are studied with the laminometer. This technique is useful in following the change in mechanical properties of a thin layer. Conditions for foam formation can be given more precisely.

Wilmsmann [48] described a foam generator that eliminates manual errors. The foam is developed by friction. A polyester brush rubs over a rotating sieve cylinder that is immersed in a surfactant solution. As a result of the horizontal frictional movement of the brush, the slowly increasing foam level is kept undisturbed, and the foam volume can be obtained as a function of time. The foam volume, the ability to hold water, and the fat-loading capacity can be determined at 20-90° with a reproducibility of $\pm$ 5%.

A number of potential foam tests have been suggested to measure foaming power of detergent systems. Hand dishwashing, washing machine tests (with and without soil), and titration of detergents with fats and oil have been in use in commercial laboratories for many years. These protocols are designed to evaluate the effectiveness of one or more surfactant components. Performance profiles are plotted by visual data observation, instrumental light beam devices, or photographically.

III. SURFACE AND INTERFACIAL TENSION

The measurement of surface tension or interfacial tension has been discussed in great detail by Adamson [49], Bikerman [50], Adam [51], Harkins and Chang [52], and others. It is a fundamental physical property of a substance and is independent of the method employed to determine its value.

The methods for determining surface tension fall into two general classes, static and dynamic. The static tests measure the tension of a surface that is in equilibrium with the interior. Dynamic methods measure the tension of a surface that is in the process of being expanded or contracted. In the case of pure liquids, there is usually no difference between static and dynamic methods. In the case of solutions, there may be large differences. In general, the concentration of solute differs at the surface or interface of a solution from the concentration in bulk. After formation of a fresh interface, a long period of time may be required to establish equilibrium with the solute concentration in bulk.

Static measurements depend largely on the principle of differential pressure across a curved interface caused by surface free energy. Capillary drop, bubble, and centrifugal methods are examples of methods of this type. Another and perhaps a more commercially important principle involves the slow extension of the surface or interface and the simultaneous measurement of the force necessary to create this extension.

Dynamic methods depend more on measuring the restoring forces of distorted flow patterns by observing the form of waves or oscillations in a rapidly moving fluid. This restoring force is due to the surface free energy.

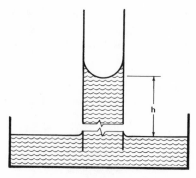

FIG. 9.   Capillary rise.

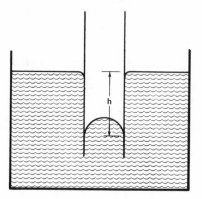

FIG. 10.   Capillary depression.

A.   Static Methods

1.   Capillary Rise

The classical method for determining surface tension is the capillary
rise procedure.   The height to which a liquid in a capillary will rise depends
on the radius of the tube, the contact angle between the tube wall, the air,
and the liquid, the surface tension of the liquid, and the density of the liquid.
A liquid that wets the walls of a capillary tube will rise in the capillary
(Fig. 9);   one that does not wet the walls will fall (Fig. 10).   The equation
$\gamma = (1/2)$ grhD, where g is the gravitation constant, h is the height of the
liquid rise in the capillary tube, r is the radius of the capillary tube, and
D is the density of the test liquid, provides an adequate treatment of this
phenomenon.   The expression includes a density factor D which has been
derived from the pressure differential.   The more common expression for
the capillary rise method is $\gamma = (1/2)$ grh ΔP.   This equation is applicable

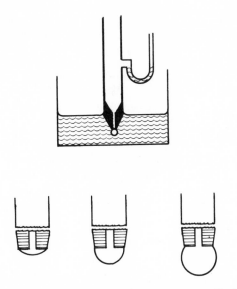

FIG. 11.   Maximum bubble pressure method.

if the liquid completely wets the walls of the capillary tube, giving a contact angle of zero.   If the liquid fails to wet the walls of the capillary, the contact angle is 180°.   The meniscus is convex, and h is the depth of the depression (Fig. 10).   If the contact angle θ is not 0 or 180°, then the expression is

$$\gamma \cos \theta = (1/2) \, grh \, \Delta P$$

The best discussions of the experimental aspects of the capillary rise method are given by Richards and Carver [53] and Harkins and Brown [54].

A number of variations in the capillary rise method have been developed. For ultimate accuracy, it is necessary to obtain capillaries with a uniform radius.   This can be avoided if the meniscus can always be brought to the same point.   This may be done by raising or lowering the outer liquid level until the meniscus stands at the reference point.   Urazovskii and Chetaev [55] provided an apparatus to do this.   Edwards [56] accomplished the same result by varying the pressure above the meniscus.   Jones and Ray [57] developed a very accurate apparatus that consisted of a U tube to measure differential capillary rise.

2.   Maximum Bubble Pressure Method

This procedure, as indicated in Fig. 11, is to blow bubbles of a gas (usually air) in the test liquid by means of a tube projected beneath the surface of a liquid.

As illustrated in the figure, a bubble is blown at the top of the tube. The sequence of shapes assumed by the bubble during its growth is such that its radius goes through a minimum when it is just hemispherical. At this point, the radius is equal to that of the tube and the pressure is at a maximum. Further growth causes a decrease of pressure so that air rushes in and bursts the bubble. The maximum pressure is $\Delta p = 2\gamma/r$, where r is the radius of the tube. It is evident that only a portion of the drop actually falls.

While some investigators [58, 59] have studied this method and calculations may be made to correct for this fact accurately, a set of empirically determined values by Harkins and Brown [60] is usually employed. Using the Harkins and Brown factor f, the correct expression for surface tension for this method is

$$\gamma = \frac{mg}{2\pi rf}$$

The instrument employed to produce standard drops for which the Harkins and Brown factors are accurate is called a stalogmonometer. These factors are included in the International Critical Tables.

Experimentally one measures the maximum gas pressure in the tube such that the bubbles are unable to grow and break away. Referring to Fig. 11, since the tube is some arbitrary distance t below the surface of the liquid, Δp max is equal to (P max - Pt) where P max is the measured maximum pressure and Pt is the pressure equal to the hydrostatic head t. If P max is expressed in terms of the corresponding height of a column of the liquid (ΔP max $= \Delta pgh$), then the relationship is identical to the capillary rise situation:

$$a^2 = \frac{2\gamma}{\Delta Pg} \qquad \text{or} \qquad \gamma = \frac{grhD}{2}$$

Experimental details and method variations and corrections are discussed by Snugden [61, 62]. Cuny and Wolf [63] discuss a variation using two tubes.

3. Drop Weight or Drop Volume Method

This accurate method is probably the most convenient laboratory procedure for measuring surface tension of a liquid-air or a liquid-liquid interface. The procedure is to form drops of the liquid at the end of a tube. Sufficient drops are collected so that the weight per drop may be accurately determined. The simplest expression relating to this procedure is Tate's law [64]:

$$W = 2\pi r\gamma$$

DIAGRAM OF A FALLING DROP

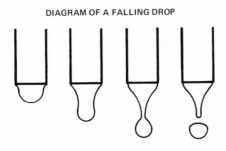

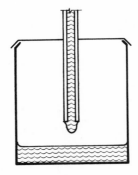

FIG. 12. Diagram of a falling drop; surface tension by the drop weight method.

In practice a weight W' is obtained. W' is smaller than ideal and may be as little as 60% of W. Figure 12 illustrates what actually happens.

4. Methods Based on the Shape of Static Drops or Bubbles

Small drops or bubbles will assume spherical shapes because surface forces depend on the area, which decreases as the square of the linear dimension, while distortions due to gravitational effects depend on the volume, which decreases as the cube of the linear dimension. When gravitational and surface forces are comparable, one can determine the surface tension from measurements of the shape of a drop or bubble.

The usual procedure is to employ photography to make certain measurements of carefully produced drops or bubbles. Figure 13 illustrates the shapes of sessile and hanging drops and bubbles.

These methods are particularly useful in studying the change of surface tension or aging.

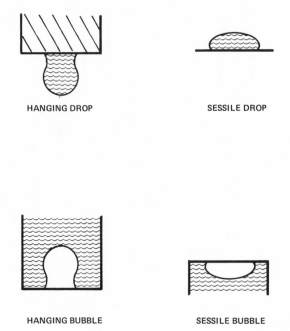

FIG. 13.   Shapes of sessile and hanging drops and bubbles.

5. Ring Method

The ring method is most widely used in commercial laboratories because it is capable of rapid, accurate, and easily reproducible data. The most favored apparatus is the du Nouy tensiometer. This instrument rapidly measures the interfacial tension between two liquids or the surface tension between a liquid and a vapor. The method consists of measuring the force required to pull a platinum ring of known diameter away from the surface of the liquid. Figure 14 is a diagram of the tensiometer.

The theory of the ring method is complex. In the diagram, R is the ring in elevation, L is the liquid being measured, and B is the balance to measure the force required to detach R from L. It is essential that the wire loop be completely wetted by the liquid. Elementary theory suggests that upon detachment of the wire loop, the total weight W tot = W ring + $4\pi r\gamma$, where R is the mean diameter of the ring (provided the ring is large in relation to the gauge of the wire).

This equation is in serious error, however, and Harkins and Jordan [65] worked out empirical correction factors for this procedure. An extension of the tables by Fox and Chrisman [66] is available for higher densities and lower surface tensions.

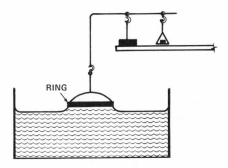

FIG. 14. Ring method of measuring surface tension.

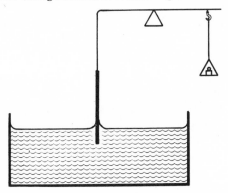

FIG. 15. Wilhelmy slide method [69].

The ring method demands a zero or near-zero contact angle, otherwise the results will be low. With surfactant solutions, adsorption on the ring changes its wetting characteristics. In such cases, a Teflon or polyethylene ring may be used [67].

This procedure was adopted by ASTM as standard and bears the designation D1331-56 (reapproved 1970) [68].

6. Wilhelmy Slide Method

This method is very simple to use, but has remained rather obscure. Wilhelmy [69] described it in 1863 and it entails none of the correctional factors required with the aforementioned methods. Figure 15 depicts the experimental arrangement for this procedure.

The ideal equation (assuming $0°$ contact angle) is

$$W \text{ tot} = W \text{ plate} + \gamma p$$

where p is the perimeter. This method may be used as a detachment method or the liquid level may be raised gradually until it just touches the hanging plate suspended from a balance arm. The increase in weight is then measured.

7. Other Methods

1. A procedure to estimate the surface tension of a liquid based on observing the spreading of immiscible liquids was described by Adam [70].

2. Brown [71] described the theory of a method to determine surface tension by observing the wavelength of a wave or ripple promulgated at a known frequency. The formula was suggested by Lord Kelvin:

$$\gamma = \frac{\lambda^3 D}{2\pi T^2} - \frac{g \lambda^2 D}{4\pi^2}$$

where λ is the wavelength, D is the density, and T is the period.

3. Ferguson [72] developed a method that employs very small quantities of liquid. If 1 mm^3 or less of a liquid is placed in a vertical capillary tube, its surface tension may be determined by applying pressure to the upper end of the tube and measuring the pressure necessary to force the liquid into such a position that the meniscus at the lower end of the tube is a plane.

4. Podlipny [73] described an apparatus to determine surface tension by measuring the height of the capillary column prepared by a new technique.

5. Schulze [74] studied the significance of surface tension measurements in view of characteristics of ore flotation agents, interaction of collectors and frothers, and the stability of froths and bubbles. He designed an apparatus based on the capillary rise method of Ferguson and Dawson in 1922.

6. Schwen [75] received a patent on a tensiometer using a U-tube manometer connected by a three-way stopcock to a capillary of radius r and to a source of pressure (tank of gas or a squeeze bulb). The capillary is immersed to a precise depth x in the experimental liquid. The manometer is first connected to the pressure source to build up a pressure. The stopcock is then turned to allow the pressure in the manometer to be released through the capillary into the liquid until bubbling ceases. The difference in liquid levels in the two sides of the U tube h is measured and the surface tension is calculated from

surface tension = (1/2)gr(Dh - dx)

where g is the gravitational acceleration, D is the density of the manometer fluid, and d is the density of the experimental liquid. For solutions of surfactants slow rotation to help bubble release gives better reproducibility.

7. A new method by Schwen [76] consists of measuring the static air pressure in a capillary tube, the open end of which is situated 10 mm below the surface of the liquid whose surface tension is desired. The pressure $p = 2\sigma/r$, where σ and r represent the surface tension and the radius of the capillary, respectively.

8. Cupples [77] described a method for evaluation of aqueous solutions of soaps and wetting agents by determination of their spreading coefficients with reference to a refined mineral oil. A du Nouy interfacial tensiometer is used for measuring the surface and interfacial tensions.

9. Guastalla et al. [78] developed a new tensiometer equipped with two blades which dip into the liquid and are connected with a suitable recording mechanism. This allows the simultaneous determination of surface tension and adhesion tension, and (indirectly) of contact angles, interfacial forces, and so on.

10. In 1964 Hilton et al. [79] described a tensiometer which automatically detaches a platinum stirrup from the liquid-air interface while continuously recording the force exerted by the liquid surface. Calibration of the instrument and use of a modified rectangular stirrup allow a direct reading of absolute surface tension eliminating the need for a ring correction.

11. Neumann and Tanner [80] have described an apparatus for static surface-tension determination of solutions. A Cahn Electrobalance RG is used to continuously record the change in weight of a solution on suspended steel plate.

12. Picon [81] developed a recording tensiometer. Surface tension is measured by a thin foil of material platinum operating at the level of the liquid and attached to one end of the beam of a torsion balance, sensible to 0.1 mg. The opposite end of the beam carries a pointer of platinum which closes a circuit through a drop of mercury causing a mechanism to move the rider. The rod for working the rider is attached to a stylus which records the displacement of the rider on a moving cylinder of paper.

13. Gaddum [82] measured surface tension in absolute units by measurement of the volume of drops by means of the micrometer syringe.

14. Peterson [83] described a film tensiometer for the continuous measurement of surface tension of liquids and solutions. Changes in surface tension, such as that caused by age, are measured by an apparatus in which a thin film of the test liquid moves downward between vertical rods, one of which is movable. Under the pull of the liquid film this rod moves against a suitable tension, and this movement is recorded by a differential transformer connected to an amplifier and a recorder.

15. A very unique and sensitive method for determining surface tension
was described by Shelduko and Velichkova [84]. A drop of paraffin containing magnetic iron filings is placed in the solution to be tested. The paraffin
is brought to the surface by motion through a magnetic field. Its velocity
is microscopically measured. This velocity is a measure of the surface
tension of the test material.

16. Vallee and Guillaumin [85] used a surface tension method to study
detergency. They reported that the stretchability of liquid molecules in a
special apparatus is an indication of their detergency. The method proposed
gives the surface tension, the effect of additives on detergency, and the
critical micelle concentration.

A new test by Spurny and Dobias [86] in 1968 was developed to measure
the liquid surface tension by the method of maximum bubble pressure. They
describe a modified instrument for the relative determination of liquid surface tension by the bubble-pressure method (Fig. 16). In this, pressure is
indicated by a column of water with which the bubble of gas is pressed into
the measuring liquid. The instrument must first be standardized by means
of a liquid of known surface tension, as well as with water, whose surface
tension can be obtained from tables.

B. Dynamic Methods

Dynamic methods are desirable for studying rapidly changing systems.
The calculations in dynamic methods are considerably more involved than
those for the static tests and the observations on moving fluids are also
more difficult. Fewer dynamic methods have been studied, although some
of the work dates back to Rayleigh in 1879.

A jet emerging from a noncircular orifice has a noncircular initial cross
section. Oscillations develop in the jet because the surface tension of the
liquid tends to correct the noncircular cross section; however, momentum
carries it past the desired circular cross section. The result is an oscil-
lation about the preferred circular cross section. The surface tension can
be calculated from the distance apart of the modes and swellings that appear
periodically. Rayleigh [87] originally laid down the theory for an ideal
case. The method has been discussed and corrected by Addison [88],
Hansen [89], and Netzel et al. [90].

A dynamic method based on the dependence of the shape of a falling
column of liquid on its surface tension was developed by Addison and
Elliott [91].

Netzel et al. [90] performed adsorption studies of surfactants at the
liquid-vapor interface. They developed an apparatus and a method for
rapidly determining the dynamic surface tension by a vibrating jet technique.
The former tedious method of photographing the wave was replaced by a

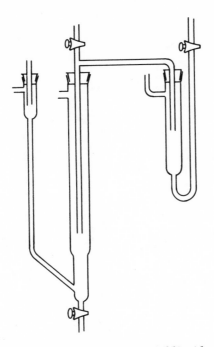

FIG. 16. Apparatus for the measurement of liquid surface tension by the modified bubble-pressure method.

traveling microscope which gathers reflected light from the nodes and anti-nodes of the standing wave and transfers the signals through a photomultiplier to a strip chart recorder

C. Surface Tension Values as Obtained by Different Methods [72]

The data given in Table 1 are provided as a reference to surface tension values for commonly studied interfaces.

IV.   WETTING

The wetting phenomenon is of considerable commercial interest. Practical operations in which wetting plays an important role are the removal of soil by washing, the dyeing of fabrics, mineral ore flotation, lubrication, corrosion inhibition, and printing. Even oil-well operators are concerned with the penetration of crude oil through various porosities of strata and wetting agents are used to facilitate secondary recovery from so-called dried-out wells.

TABLE 1

Surface Tension Values

Liquid	Temp. (^{o}C)	γ (dynes/cm)	Method
	Liquid-Vapor Interfaces		
Water	20	72.75	
		72.73	Capillary rise
		72.91	Maximum bubble pressure
		71.76	Drop weight
		71.89	Wilhelmy slide
		72.00	Pendant drop
Organic compounds			
Methylene iodide	20	67.00	Capillary rise
Dimethyl sulfoxide	20	43.54	Maximum bubble pressure
Propylene carbonate	20	41.1	
Ethylene bromide	20	38.75	
Dimethylaniline	20	36.56	Capillary rise
Nitromethane	20	32.66	Maximum bubble pressure
Benzene	20	28.88	
Toluene	20	28.43	Capillary rise
Chloroform	20	27.14	
Propionic acid	20	26.80	Drop weight
Carbon tetrachloride	20	26.77	
Butyl acetate	20	25.09	
Methanol	20	22.61	
Ethanol	20	22.27	
Octane	20	21.80	
Heptane	20	19.7	Pendant drop
Ether	20	17.01	
Perfluoromethyl cyclohexane	20	15.74	Maximum bubble pressure
Perfluoroheptane	20	10.98	Capillary rise
Low-boiling substances			
^{4}He	1°K	0.365	Capillary rise
H_2	20°K	2.01	
D_2	20°K	3.54	
N_2	75°K	9.41	Capillary rise
Ar	90°K	11.86	Capillary rise
O_2	77°K	15.7	
C_2H_6	180.6^{o}K	16.63	Capillary rise
Xe	163°K	18.6	Capillary rise
N_2O	182.5^{o}K	24.26	Capillary rise
Br_2	20	31.9	

TABLE 1 (continued)

Liquid	Temp. ($^\circ$C)	γ (dynes/cm)	Method
Metals			
Hg	20	476	Drop weight
	25	484.2	Sessile drop
	50	479.0	Sessile drop
	75	474.5	Sessile drop
	25	485.4	Sessile drop
	16.5	487.3	Sessile drop
Na	130	198	Drop volume
Ba	720	226	Drop volume
Sn	332	543.8	Maximum bubble pressure
Ag	1100	878.5	Maximum bubble pressure
Cu	mp	1300	Pendant drop
Ti	1680	1588	Pendant drop
Pt	mp	1800	Pendant drop
Fe	mp	1880	Pendant drop
Salts			
$BiCl_2$	271	66	Capillary pressure
$KClO_2$	368	81	Maximum bubble pressure
KNCS	175	101.5	Maximum bubble pressure
$NaNO_2$	308	116.6	Maximum bubble pressure
$K_2Cr_2O_7$	397	129	Maximum bubble pressure
$Ba(NO_3)_2$	595	134.8	Maximum bubble pressure

Liquid-Liquid Interfaces			
Liquid 1: water			
n-Butyl alcohol	20	1.8	
Ethyl acetate	20	6.8	
Heptanoic acid	20	7.0	
Benzaldehyde	20	15.5	
Nitrobenzene	20	25.2	
Benzene	20	35.0	
Carbon tetrachloride	20	45.0	
n-Heptane	20	50.2	
Liquid 1: mercury			
Water	20	415	Pendant drop
	25	416	Pendant drop
Ethanol	20	389	
n-Hexane	20	378	
n-Heptane	20	378	
Benzene	20	357	
Liquid 1: fluorocarbon polymer			
Benzene	25	7.8	
Water	25	57.0	

The basic mechanisms describing wetting are related to contact angles at the solid-liquid-air boundary. Direct correlations between wetting times and contact angles can be made. It is usually difficult to measure contact angles directly, hence some investigators have devised direct measurement methods. This is particularly important for fabrics and fibers.

It is often necessary or desirable to measure the wetting power of various surface-active agents, and here too direct measurement methods are desirable.

The two most widely used wetting tests for fabrics are the Draves [92, 93] skein test and the Seyferth-Morgan [94] canvas disc test. In the Draves test, a 5-g skein of gray cotton yarn is submerged in the test solution and the time recorded for the air in the yarn to be replaced by penetration of the solution. The end point is observed as that moment when the skein sinks. Figure 17 illustrates the test apparatus setup. This test has been accepted as the official method of the American Association of Textile Chemists and Colorists [95] and as the standard method of the American Society for Testing Materials (D2281-68).

In the canvas disc test, the disc is held under the surface of the test solution and the liquid penetrates the fabric until it sinks of its own weight. Figure 18 shows this setup.

In the Draves skein test and the canvas disc test, the end point is taken as the moment of sinking. At this point the yarn is not completely wet. It represents that point where the buoyancy decrease due to air displacement and the specific gravity of the skein or disc, air, and attached weights (Draves) exceeds unity. Considerable interest in complete wetting and penetration is generated at textile processing plants, where finishing chemicals and dyes are required to be thoroughly distributed in the yarn or fabric.

The relationship between Draves wetting time, surface tension, and contact angle was studied by Fischer and Gans [96]. Figure 19 shows this correlation.

A test was designed by Powney [97] which measured penetration electrically. He measured conductance across a fabric swatch subjected to a wetting agent solution. This procedure could offer data relating to wetness in ranges inaccessible to sinking tests. Trommer [98] used an electric circuit to signify the end point of penetration through a standard fabric bundle. This method attempted to study the difference between surface wetting and penetration of textiles.

The phenomenon of complete wetting and the relative difference from the Draves test was studied by Gruntfest et al. [99] using a unique hydrometer (Fig. 20). This technique allows one to determine the escape of air contained in the fibers in relation to time. This method provides the ability to conduct fundamental studies of the action of surface-active agents on

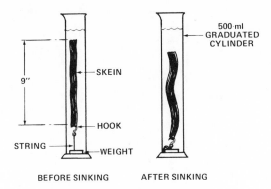

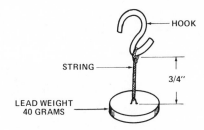

FIG. 17. Draves wetting test apparatus.

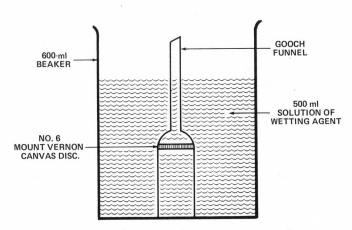

FIG. 18. Canvas disc wetting test apparatus.

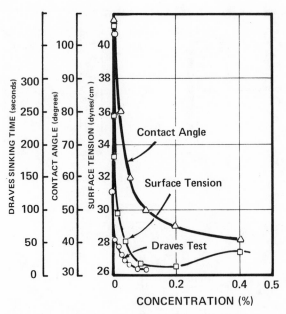

FIG. 19. Curves showing Draves test sinking times, surface tension values, and contact angle measurements in relation to concentration of reagent (sodium salt of octyl ester of sulfosuccinic acid).

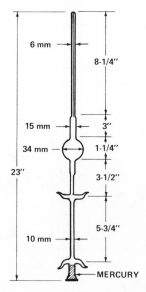

FIG. 20. Gruntfest et al. [99] hydrometer.

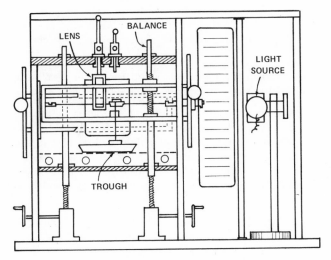

FIG. 21.   Guastalla torsion surface tensiometer.

textiles.   Anomalies between methods were discussed by Reutenauer et al. [100].

A unique method designed to measure wetting and penetration utilizing a centrifuge to remove nonabsorbed liquid was described by Herbig [101]. Forster and Venkataraman [102] used a similar centrifugal method to measure wetting power of surface-active agents, and Lenker and Smith [103] devised an improved centrifugal method for the evaluation of textile penetration assistants.

Physical chemists have continued efforts to design and calibrate methods and equipment to study the fundamental relationship associated with the wetting phenomenon.   Guastalla and Guastalla [104] suggested an apparatus to measure contact angle.   It employs a torsion balance and is similar to a Wilhelmy plate surface tensiometer.   Figure 21 is a diagram of this wetting tensiometer.

Sinking test modifications have been numerous.   A very early test designed to measure immersion time of a fabric placed on the surface of a liquid was developed by Erban [105].   Ristenpart [106] offered a modification of the Erban test.   The Draves skein test and the canvas disc method are very widely used even today.   Shapiro [107] recommended a modification of the Draves test.   He used a woven tape in place of skeins.   Shapiro reported that textile mill operators preferred woven fabrics to directly interpret the test data better.   Edelstein and Draves [108] reviewed the most popular wetting tests in studying chemical properties and wetting.   They concluded that more reliable data are attainable by use of the canvas square test.

This test is very similar to the original Erban method of measuring the time of immersion of a square of canvas dropped on the surface of the test solution.

Bernett and Zisman [109] generated wetting curves by plotting the cosine of the contact angle versus the surface tension of the test solution.

Desalme [110] developed an improvement of the rondelle method which is based on penetration of test solutions through a felt disc. A small metallic tube placed on a support, the bottom of which is closed by an exchangeable disc of felt 43 mm in diameter and 7 mm thick, is filled up to a fixed mark with the test solution. With the aid of a mirror, the lower face of the disc is observed and the time required by the liquid to penetrate the felt is recorded.

Durham and Camp [111] designed an apparatus that accurately measures the rate of wetting of cotton by detergent solutions. Three electrodes, one of which is positioned in the center of a circular piece of cotton, bear against the cotton surface; as the wetting solution proceeds from the central electrode to a nearby electrode it provides a conducting path and the resulting current actuates a relay which switches on an electronic times. As the wetting solution advances to the third electrode, a second relay is actuated to stop the timer.

Getmanskii et al. [112] suggested a method for determining the cloth-wetting capacity of solutions of surfactants based on the measurement of the rate of penetration of the liquid or solution into the cloth. The wetting rate is characterized by the time necessary to impregnate a cloth with a constant amount of the test liquid. The time is measured with a photoelectric device.

Getmanskii et al. [113] obtained a patent on a device to measure wetting capacity by fluorescence of the wetting solution washing a fabric which had first been contaminated with a compound containing a luminophor to the fluorescence of a solution of a standard substance, for example, sodium lauryl sulfate, expressed in percent, or from the difference in fluorescence of the fabric being tested or of the solution before and after laundering.

Goette [114] developed an improved method for the determination of wettability of surface-active agents. Using DIN 53901 as a basis, a standard method is being developed for this measurement. Wetting agents are to be rated according to the minimum concentration in grams per liter required to penetrate a small circle of cotton gauze after 100 sec of immersion. Laboratories in eight countries have already collaborated on this procedure. Ultimate internationalization of this method is being delayed by the present inability to furnish large quantities of cotton patches of the desired degree of reproducibility. In the meantime satisfactory standardization may be achieved against sodium dodecyl sulfate.

Kretzschmar and Fruhner [115] received a patent on a device that measured temperature changes accompanying the wetting of textiles in the presence of various concentrations of the surfactants. The changes are measured with a resistance thermometer. The apparatus and all materials are enclosed in a thermostat.

Melikhov and Tutunov [116] studied wetting agents in the textile industry. Wetting power was determined by (a) measuring the height of rise in a cotton fabric of a colored aquatic solution to which was added 0.5, 1.0, and 2.0 g/liter of wetting agent; (b) the time in minutes it took a cotton fabric 3 x 3 cm to submerge in 1-, 5-, and 10-g/liter solutions of the wetting agent at 20 and 50°C; (c) the gain in weight of a 100-mm strip of raw cotton fabric submerged for 1 min in an aquatic 0.5-. 1.0-, and 2-g/liter solution of the wetting agent at 20 and 50° and allowed to drain for 3 min.

Neudert [117] developed a spreading test for characterizing wetting. Wettability can be characterized by the constants A, B, C in the equation $R = Av^B - Cv$, where R is the measured radius of drops of known volume, v, on a solid surface. These values are rapidly determined by dropping liquid or solution from a buret onto a level plate and measuring R conveniently by a scale of concentric circles.

Shmeleva [118] developed a unique test for wetting properties using two immiscible liquids. The method consists in shaking the material to be tested, for example, chopped rabbit hair, in a cylinder, with two immiscible liquids, one polar and one nonpolar, for example, an aquatic solution of Igepon and dichloroethane, and after allowing the cylinder to stand for some time, determine distribution of the hair between the two layers.

V. FABRIC HAND

"Hand" or "handle" is a term used primarily in the textile trade. It refers to a subjective evaluation of a fabric and is in fact a composite value. Hand is composed of many variables and is often described by one or more of the following textile terms:

Softness	Coarseness
Smoothness	Thickness
Firmness	Heaviness

Since laundry detergents are designed to remove soil from a fabric, it is expected that the use of a particular detergent system could and probably does affect the hand of the textile substrate.

Hand is essentially a subjective preference factor, hence it is difficult to design test methods to measure this parameter objectively. It is, however, a factor of considerable commercial interest, particularly for detergent products utilizing precipitating hardness builders such as carbonate and silicate.

The primary application of hand measurements has been to evaluate the net effect of finishing agents on textiles during processing in the mills. Household fabric softener treatments have also become widespread, and producers of these chemicals are vitally concerned with measuring the efficacy of their research developments. These tests almost always demand comparison with standards. While panel testing is reasonably accurate, it entails working with large numbers of people resulting in relatively expensive operations for data accumulation, control, and statistical treatment. The data also are not available immediately, which represents a significant hardship to planning research programs.

The most common methods used to measure hand are based on observation of people's reaction to samples of fabric previously subjected to a particular treatment. Paired comparisons [119] of large numbers of panelists are required to obtain statistically significant results. A treatment may consist of a laundering cycle or the specific application of a substance designed to affect the hand of the fabric, such as fabric softeners [119-121].

Of the factors influencing hand, smoothness and stiffness are of primary importance. No entirely satisfactory objective test to measure smoothness has been developed so far; however, Huffington [122] pointed out that a technique was developed [123, 124] for measuring smoothness which operates in a similar way to the sense of touch. It is postulated that roughness as a sensation is due to small indentations in the skin. These indentations are in contact with pressure-sensitive nerve endings and the degree of roughness is detected as an average across the entire surface.

Huffington [122] suggests preparing a model of the test surface by using a silicone rubber disc that is placed in contact with the sample to produce a replica of the substrate. The indentations are then examined and comparisons made.

A hand-measuring device was designed by Okamura [125]. His apparatus (Fig. 22) measures the thickness and pressure of fabric on the test head. By assigning numerical values to the comparative materials, the "feeling" can be scored and compared.

Correlating hand with a physical property seemed to suggest a means of deriving an objective relationship for hand evaluation. The coefficient of friction would appear to be related to this phenomenon, and hence several workers [126-129] have attempted to derive such a relationship.

Röder [126] reported the use of an inclined plane to measure coefficient of friction of fabric after treatment with various substances. His method is based on the formula $Ms/Mo = e^{\mu\alpha}$ where Mo and Ms are, respectively,

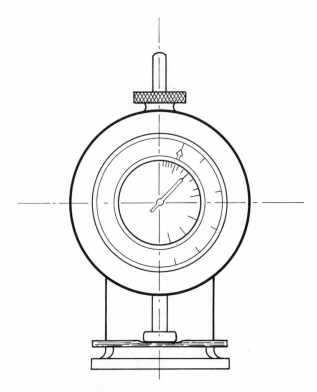

FIG. 22. Okamura device for measuring hand [125].

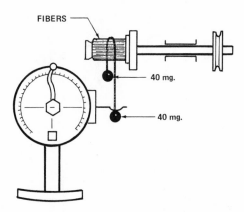

FIG. 23. Röder apparatus for measuring interfiber friction [126].

TABLE 2

List of Terms Relating to the Hand of Fabrics

Physical property	Explanatory phrase	Terms to be used in describing range of corresponding component of hand
Flexibility	Ease of bending	Pliable (high) to stiff (low)
Compressibility	Ease of squeezing	Soft (high) to hard (low)
Extensibility	East of stretching	Stretchy (high) to nonstretchy (low)
Resilience	Ability to recover from deformation	Springy (high) to limp (low). Resilience may be flexural, compressional, extensional, or torsional
Density	Weight per unit volume (based on measurement of thickness and fabric weight)	
Surface contour	Divergence of the surface from planeness	Rough (high) to smooth (low)
Surface friction	Resistance to slipping offered by the surface	Harsh (high) to slippery (low)
Thermal character	Apparent difference in temperature of the fabric and the skin of the observer touching it	Cool (high) to warm (low)

the tensions before and after the rubbing surface has been passed, μ is the coefficient of friction, and α is the angle of contact between fiber and the rubbing surface. While this method is useful, he required and designed an apparatus (Fig. 23) for measuring coefficients of friction. The tensions are measured in a single fiber which slides on a layer of similar fibers arranged on a metal spool. The coefficient of friction is calculated from the formula mentioned above.

Two fairly common machines in general use for measuring hand are the Twing-Albert Handle-O-Meter and the Friction Meter. The Handle-O-Meter is an instrument that measures the combined effects of flexibility and surface friction of a fabric and expresses these effects as an integrated numerical value of hand. The instrument measures the force required for an arm to push the center portion of an 8 in. x 8 in. piece of fabric a certain depth into a slot. The results claim to be dependent on both the stiffness of the fabric and the surface characteristics of the fabric which produce friction above the edges of the slots. The higher the value, the stiffer is the fabric.

The Friction Meter is an instrument that measures the friction of a fabric against a fabric as a function of the force required to steadily pull the top fabric over the bottom fabric under a standardized loading of 1 lb on a 7 x 9 cm area, and at a specified speed. The higher the tension reading, the greater is the friction between fabric surfaces.

The American Association for Testing Materials has listed terms relating to hand fabrics in ASTM D123-689 Appendix III, 1968 Book of Standards. These are given in Table 2.

BIBLIOGRAPHY: STANDARD TEST METHODS

American Association of Textile Chemists and Colorists:
AATCC 17-1952, Evaluation of Wetting Agents
AATCC 27-1952T, Evaluation of Rewetting Agents
AATCC 39-1952, Evaluation of Wettability

American Society for Testing Materials:
ASTM D-1173-53, Foaming Properties of Surface Active Agents
ASTM D-1331-56, Surface and Interfacial Tension of Solutions of Surface Active Agents
ASTM D-2281-68, Evaluation of Wettability

USA Standards Institute:
USAS No. L 14. 11-1956 (AATCC 17-1952)
USAS No. L 14. 75-1956 (AATCC 39-1952)
USAS No. L 14. 106-1961 (AATCC 27-1952T)

Belgian Committee for Detergency:
CBD 67-1, Foaming Power (Ross-Miles Method)

Deutsche Industrie Norm (Germany):
DIN 53901, Determination of the Immersion-Wettability of Wetting
Agents
DIN 53902, Testing of Surface Active Agents; Foam Power and Foam
Stability Guidelines
DIN 53902 Sheet 1, Foaming Power (Beating Method)
DIN 53902 Sheet 2, Foaming Power (Ross-Miles Method)

International Organization for Standardization:
ISO-R304-1963, Surface Active Agents, Determination of Surface and
Facial Tension
Proposal ISO/TC 91, Foaming Power (Modification of Ross-Miles Foam
Test)

REFERENCES

1. J. A. Kitchener, and C. F. Cooper, Chem. Soc. Quart. Rev. (London),
   13, 71-97 (1959).

2. J. L. Moilliet, B. Collie and W. Black, Surface Activity, 2nd ed.,
   Van Nostrand -Reinhold, Princeton, N.J., 1961.

3. J. J. Bikerman, Foams: Theory and Industrial Applications, Van
   Nostrand-Reinhold, Princeton, N. J., 1953.

4. E. Manegold, Schaum, Strassenbau, Chemie und Technik, Heidelberg,
   1953.

5. A. J. deVries, Foam Stability, Mededel Rubber-Stichting, Delft, No. 326
   (1957).

6. K. Mysels, K. Shinoda, and S. Frankel, Soap Films, Pergamon Press,
   1959.

7. S. Berkman and G. Egloff, Chem. Rev., 15, 377 (1938).

8. W. M. Sawyer and F. M. Fowkes, J. Phys. Chem., 62, 159 (1958).

9. A. M. Schwartz and J. W. Perry, Surface-Active Agents, Wiley-
   Interscience, New York, 1949.

10. A. M. Schwartz, J. W. Perry, and J. Berch, Surface Active Agents
    and Detergents, Vol. II, Wiley-Interscience, New York, 1958.

11. L. I. Osipow, Surface Chemistry, ACS Monograph 153, Van-Nostrand-
    Reinhold, Princeton, N. J., 1962.

12. A. W. Adamson, Physical Chemistry of Surfaces, 2nd ed., Wiley-
    Interscience, New York, 1967.

13. S. Ross, Ind. Eng. Chem., Anal. Ed., 15, 329 (1943).

14. S. R. Trotman and J. E. Hackford, J.S.C.I., 25, 104 (1906).

15. W. C. Preston and A. S. Richardson, J. Phys. Chem., 33, 1142 (1929)

16. S. Ross and G. L. Clark, Wallerstein Labs., Commun. Sci. Practice Brewing, 46, No. 6 (1939).

16A. S. Ross and G. L. Clark, Ind. Eng. Chem., 32, 1594 (1940).

17. C. Stiepel, Seifensieder Ztg., 41, 347 (1914).

18. K. N. Abruzov and B. N. Grebenshchikov, J. Phys. Chem. (USSR), 10, 32 (1937).

19. A. Schlachter and H. Dierkes, Fette und Seifen, 53, 207-209 (1951).

20. A. Schlachter and H. Dierkes, Fette und Seifen, 54, No. 12, 772 (1952).

21. J. Ross and G. D. Miles, Oil and Soap, 18, 99 (1941).

22. W. Mischke, Kolloid-Z., 90, 77 (1949).

23. W. O. Ostwald and W. Mischke, Kolloid-Z., 90, 17, 205 (1949).

24. W. O. Ostwald and A. Siehr, Kolloid-Z., 76, 33 (1936).

25. J. J. Bikerman, Trans. Faraday Soc., 34, 634 (1938).

26. C. W. Foulk and J. N. Miller, Ind. Eng. Chem., 23, 1283 (1931).

27. E. L. Lederer, Seifensieder Ztg., 63, 331 (1936).

28. S. Ross, Ind. Eng. Chem., Anal. Ed., 15, No. 5, 330 (1943).

29. K. G. A. Pankhurst, Trans. Faraday Soc., 37, 496 (1941).

30. F. Schutz, Trans. Faraday Soc., 38, 85 (1942).

31. W. Hardy, J. Chem. Soc., 127, 1207 (1925).

32. D. Talmud and S. Z. Suchowolskaja, Phys. Chem. A, 154, 277 (1931).

33. J. G. Sinsheimer, Soap Sanit. Chem., 26 (8), 38-41, 157 (1950).

34. G. S. Hattiangdi, W. W. Walton, and J. I. Hoffman, J. Res. Natl. Bur. Standards, 42, 361 (1949).

35. L. Sironval and H. Ramakers, Compt. Rend. Congr. Int. Chim. Ind., 31^e Liege, 1958.

36. L. E. Weeks, J. C. Harris, and E. L. Brown, J. Am. Oil Chemists Soc., 31, 254 (1954).

37. H. E. Tschakert, Tenside, 3, 317-322, 359-365, 388-394 (1966).

38. E. Goette, Melliand Textilber., 32, 210-212 (1951).

39. A. Noll, Seifensieder Ztg., 73, 41-42 (1947).

40. E. Goette, Melliand Textilber, 29, 65-68, 105-108 (1948).

41. D. Peters, Angew. Chem., 64, 586-590 (1952).

42. C. Walling, E. E. Ruff, and J. L. Thornton, Jr., J. Phys. Chem., 56, 989-993 (1952).

43. E. J. Burcik, J. Colloid Sci., 5, 421-436 (1950).

44. R. C. Chang, H. M. Schoen, and C. S. Grove, Ind. Eng. Chem., 48, 2035-2039 (1956).

45. R. Matalon, J. Soc. Cosmet. Chem., 3, 216 (1952).

46. R. Matalon, Surface Chem., 1949, 195-201; Mem. Services Chim. Etat (Paris), 34, 345-352 (1948).

47. R. Matalon, Mem. Services Chim. Etat (Paris), 34, 345 (1948).

48. H. Wilmsmann, Fette, Seifen, Anstrichm., 66 (11), 955-961 (1964).

49. A. W. Adamson, Physical Chemistry of Surfaces, Wiley-Interscience, 1960.

50. J. J. Bikerman, Surface Chemistry, Academic Press, New York, 1958.

51. N. K. Adam, The Physics and Chemistry of Surfaces, Oxford Univ. Press, London and New York, 1941.

52. W. D. Harkins and R. C. Chang, J. Amer. Chem. Soc., 43, 36 (1921).

53. T. W. Richards and E. K. Carver, J. Amer. Chem. Soc., 43, 827 (1921).

54. W. D. Harkins and F. E. Brown, J. Amer. Chem. Soc., 41, 499 (1919).

55. S. S. Urazovskii and P. M. Chetaev, Kolloid-Z., 11, 359 (1949).

56. P. R. Edwards, J. Chem. Soc., 744 (1925).

57. G. Jones and W. A. Ray, J. Amer. Chem. Soc., 59, 187 (1937).

58. T. Lohnstein, Ann. Phys., 22, 767 (1957); Z. Phys. Chem., 84, 410 (1913).

59. H. Dunken, Ann. Phys., 41, 567 (1942).

60. W. D. Harkins and F. E. Brown, J. Amer. Chem. Soc., 41, 499 (1919).

61. S. Snugden, J. Chem. Soc., 858 (1922).

62. S. Snugden, J. Chem. Soc., 27 (1924).

63. K. H. Cuny and K. L. Wolf, Ann. Phys., 17, 57 (1956).

64. T. Tate, Phil. Mag., 27, 176 (1864).

65. W. D. Harkins and H. F. Jordan, J. Amer. Chem. Soc., 52, 1751 (1930).

66. H. W. Fox and C. H. Chrisman, J. Phys. Chem. Soc., 56, 284 (1952).

67. J. A. Krynitsky and W. D. Garrett, J. Colloid Sci., 18, 893 (1963).

68. Annual Standards ASTM, Part 22, 206 (1972).

69. L. Wilhelmy, Ann. Physk., 119, 177 (1963).

70. N. K. Adam, Proc. Roy. Soc. (London) B, 122, 134 (1937).

71. R. C. Brown, Proc. Roy. Soc. (London), 48, 312 (1936).

72. A. Ferguson, Proc. Phys. Soc. (London), 36, 37-44 (1923).

73. V. Podlipny, Chem. Listy, 59 (10), 1223-1228 (1965).

74. H. K. Schulze, Freiberg. Forschungsh, A408, 37 (1967).

75. G. Schwen, German Pat. 1,167,066 (4/2/64).

76. G. Schwen, Melliand Textilber., 42, 457 (1961).

77. H. L. Cupples, Ind. Eng. Chem., 27, 1219 (1935).

78. J. Guastalla, L. P. Guastalla, and H. L. Rosano, Bull. Mens. ITERG
(Inst. Corps Gras), 6, 60, 111 (1952).

79. T. B. Hilton, M. E. Tuvell, and E. A. Casey, Soap Chem., 40, 48
(1964).

80. A. W. Neumann and W. Tanner, Tenside, 4, 220 (1967).

81. M. Picon, Compt. Rend., 219, 22-24 (1944).

82. J. H. Gaddum, Proc. Roy. Soc. (London) B, 109, 114 (1931).

83. E. C. Peterson, Kolloid-Z., 183, 141 (1962).

84. A. Sheludko and V. Velichkova, Godishnik Sofiiskiya Univ., Fiz-Mat.
Fak. Khim., 50, Pt. 1-2, 135 (1955/56).

85. J. Vallee and R. Guillaumin, Vortraege Originalfassung Int. Kongr.
Grenzflaechenaktive Stoffe, 3, Cologne, Ger., 3, 151 (1960).

86. J. Spurny and G. Dobias, Tenside, 5, 77-79 (1968).

87. L. Rayleigh, Proc. Roy. Soc. (London), 29, 71 (1879).

88. C. C. Addison, Phil. Mag., 36, 73 (1945).

89. R. S. Hansen, J. Phys. Chem., 68, 2012 (1964).

90. D. A. Netzel, G. Hock, and T. I. Marx, J. Colloid Sci., 19, 774
(1964).

91. C. C. Addison and T. A. Elliott, J. Chem. Soc., 2789 (1949).

92. C. Z. Draves and R. G. Clarkson, Amer. Dyest. Rep., 20, 201 (1931).

93. C. Z. Draves, Amer. Dyest. Rep., 28, 421 (1939).

94. H. Seyferth and O. M. Morgan, Amer. Dyest. Rep., 27, 525 (1938).

95. Standard Test Method 17-43, AATCC Year Book, 1949, p. 143.

96. E. K. Fischer and D. M. Gans, Ann. N. Y. Acad. Sci., 46, 389 (1946).

97. J. Powney, Wetting and Detergency, A. Harvey, London, 1937.

98. C. R. Trommer, Amer. Dyest. Rep., 39, 811 (1956).

99. I. J. Gruntfest, O. B. Hager, and H. B. Walker, Amer. Dyest. Rep., 36, 225 (1947).

100. G. Reutenauer, J. P. Sisley, and S. Dupin, Proc. AATCC, 25 (1952).

101. W. Herbig, Melliand Textilber., 1, 9 (1927).

102. R. B. Forster, I. S. Uppal, and K. Venkataraman, J. Soc. Dyers Color., 54, 465 (1938).

103. S. Lenker and J. E. Smith, Ind. Eng. Chem., Anal. Ed., 5, 376 (1933).

104. J. Guastalla and L. Guastalla, Compt. Rend., 226, 2054 (1948); Bull. Mens. ITERG, 6, 60 (1952); Mem. Services Chem. Etat (Paris), 34, 373 (1948).

105. F. Erban, Die Anvendung der Fettstaffe und dorous hergestellen produkte, 160 (1911).

106. E. Ristenpart, Z. Gr. Textil., 13, 173 (1926).

107. L. Shapiro, Amer. Dyest. Rep., 39, 38 (1950).

108. S. M. Edelstein and C. Z. Draves, Amer. Dyest. Rep., 38, 343 (1949).

109. M. K. Bernett and W. A. Zisman, J. Phys. Chem., 63, 1241 (1959).

110. R. Desalme, Rev. Fr. Corps Gras, 4, 545 (1957).

111. K. Duerham and M. Camp, Proc. Int. Congr. Surface Activity, 2nd, London, IV, 3-11 (1957).

112. I. K. Getmanskii, L. I. Bavika, and A. P. Kolugin, Vses. Soveshch. po Sintetich. Zhirozamenitelyam, Poverkhnostnoaktivn. Veshchestvam i Moyushchim Sredstvam, 3rd Sb. Shebekino, 1965, 373.

113. I. K. Getmanskii, L. I. Bavika, A. G. Pisareva, and A. M. Prokopenko USSR Patent 189,113 (1966).

114. E. Goette, Chem. Weekbl., 58, 201 (1962).

115. G. Kretzchmar and H. Fruhner, German (East) Patent 42,484 (1965).

116. S. A. Melikhov and M. A. Tutunov, Legkaya Prom., 4, 23 (1944).

117. W. Neudert, Kolloid-Z., 118, 113 (1950).

118. T. A. Shmeleva, Colloid J. (USSR), 3, 265 (1937).

119. E. Larrat and G. L. Templeton, Amer. Dyest. Rep., 15 (1966).

120. M. E. Ginn, F. A. Shenoch, and E. Jungermann, J. Amer. Oil Chem. Soc., 42, 1084 (1965).

121. W. M. Linfield, J. C. Sherrill, G. A. Davis, and R. M. Raschke, J. Amer. Oil Chem. Soc., 35, 590 (1958).

122. J. D. Huffington, University of London, Ph.D. Thesis, 1965.

123. J. D. Huffington, Nature, 198, 948 (1963).

124. J. D. Huffington, Proc. Roy. Soc. (London), 279, 161 (1964).

125. I. Okamura, Teijin Times, 19, 39 (1949).

126. H. L. Röder, J. Text. Inst., 44, T247 (1953).

127. M. Lipson and P. Howard, J. Soc. Dyers Color., 62, 29 (1946).

128. A. R. Martin and R. Mittlemann, J. Text. Inst., 38, T269 (1947).

129. G. King, J. Text. Inst., 41, T135 (1950).

Chapter 16

ENZYMES

Theodore Cayle[*]
Wallerstein Company
Division of Travenol Laboratories, Inc.
Morton Grove, Illinois

I.   INTRODUCTION

Among the terms that have become household words during the past de-
cade are weightlessness, transplant, moonwalk, and enzyme. In each case
the expression was well known to a relatively limited group of specialists
prior to its becoming a generally discussed and accepted part of virtually
every language on earth.

In 1971 it was estimated that approximately three-fourths of all laundry
products contain enzymes, and the importance of this group of additives to
both the housewife and the detergent industry was common knowledge. In
the last few years enzyme use has declined markedly; Chapter 17 explains
the reason for this decline.

———————
[*]Present address: CCF Consulting Corporation, Highland Park,
Illinois.

Enzymes have been used for over 30 years by dry cleaners to remove stains from fabrics. Why did it take the laundry product developers so long to recognize the potential of enzymes as detergent additives? The answer is twofold. On the one hand, product development usually follows established practices, and in the United States the propensity for automating household chores seemed to preclude the use of additives requiring what was believed to be specialized handling. On the other hand, the enzymes suitable for use by the dry cleaner did not have characteristics that made them compatible with the laundry products.

Both of these drawbacks were overcome, each in its own way. Instead of the developments taking place in the United States, thereby bucking established trends, they took place in Europe, where laundry practices were more compatible with enzyme behavior. And, of course, new enzyme systems were developed which, for the first time, had characteristics that made them more suitable for use as detergent additives.

What are enzymes, and why are they so effective in the laundry room?

II. ENZYME CHARACTERISTICS

If one regards a living organism as a mixture of reacting chemicals, it soon becomes apparent that during the evolution of biological systems a mechanism had to arise by which these reactions could take place at temperatures and within time periods favorable to the maintenance of life as we know it on earth.

As evolution proceeded there arose a class of compounds that were capable of accomplishing distinct chemical reactions within the living cell under the mildest of conditions. The general term applied to a reagent that aids in a chemical reaction without itself being changed is catalyst, and biological catalysts are called enzymes.

Microbial enzymes have been produced on an industrial scale since before the turn of the century. Methods include the growing of the microorganism in either deep tanks or on semisolid mash, separating the cells from the enzyme secreted into the growth medium, and chemically isolating the enzymes by a series of fractionation procedures designed to separate unwanted metabolic by-products from the desirable enzymes of commerce. Beckhorn et al. [1] have disclosed typical procedures used by enzyme manufacturers today and have described the lengths to which the producers go to maintain the quality of the final product.

All enzymes isolated to date have proved to be protein in nature, though some combine with nonprotein components while functioning as catalytic agents. Each enzyme operates optimally at a particular pH and temperature, and on a particular substrate. Obviously, the pH and temperature requirements of many enzymes are similar, but most enzymes attack only one specific type of linkage, as found in one particular type of compound.

Hydrolytic enzymes are usually described in accordance with the class of substrates they degrade. Thus, the proteases attack proteins, amylases starch, and lipases fats.

Discussion in this chapter is limited to the enzyme currently enjoying most favor as a laundry additive, alkaline protease, derived from varieties of Bacillus subtilis and its close relatives.

III. PROTEASES

The term protease is applied to that group of enzymes capable of hydrolyzing peptide bonds:

$$\underset{NH_2CHCO}{\overset{R}{|}} \underset{NHCHCOOH}{\overset{R'}{|}} + H_2O \rightarrow \underset{NH_2CHCOOH}{\overset{R}{|}} + \underset{NH_2CHCOOH}{\overset{R'}{|}}$$

While all proteins contain such linkages and thus serve as potential substrates for the proteolytic enzymes, a requirement on the part of the catalyst for specific amino acid residues on either or both sides of the peptide bond serves to confer a degree of specificity to each of the many proteases found in nature.

The conditions under which an enzyme would be expected to function as a laundry additive are quite removed from those under which it would normally operate in a living cell. For example, the laundry product typically acts at a pH between 9.5 and 10, at a temperature between 40 and 50°C, and in the presence of high concentrations of polyphosphates, surfactants, metasilicates, and other components normally found in detergent formulations.

The proteolytic enzymes derived from varieties of Bacillus subtilis that function in the high pH range are generally termed subtilisins and have been classified as the Carlsberg, Novo, or BPN[1] type. Olaitan et al. [2] have shown that subtilisin Novo and BPN[1] are one and the same, whereas the Carlsberg type is distinctive. Since it is the latter subtilisin that appears to be most commonly employed as a detergent additive, comment is limited to it.

In a series of excellent publications, Smith et al. have reported on the characteristics of subtilisin Carlsberg [3-10]. This enzyme has a molecular weight of 27,600, contains 274 amino acid residues, and exists as a single peptide chain. It is characterized as a "serine protease," and appears to utilize one or more histidine residues as part of its reaction mechanism. The enzyme exhibits peptidase and esterase activities as well as the ability to catalyze transesterification reactions.

The protease enzymes of commerce, sold under a variety of brand names such as Alkaline Protease 201 or 301 by Wallerstein Company,

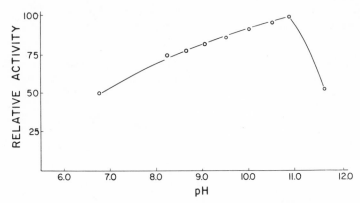

FIG. 1.   Activity as a function of pH, Alkaline Protease 201.

Division of Travenol Laboratories, Alcalase by Novo Industries, and Maxa-
tase by Charles Pfizer and Company, have similar characteristics.   The
following has been established for Alkaline Protease 201 [11]:

1.   An extremely high pH optimum which is in excess of 10 on a casein
     substrate at 37°C (Fig. 1).
2.   A suitably high temperature optimum.   Figure 2 shows this to occur
     at approximately 60°C for the enzyme concentrate at pH 8.5.   How-
     ever, it has been found that the pH-activity curve is altered if it is
     run at the temperature optimum.   For example, Fig. 3 shows the
     shift toward the acid side when the curve is repeated at 61°C, re-
     sulting in a new optimum at pH 9.6.   This characteristic is well
     known to enzyme chemists and is the result of a competition between
     activity and destruction of the enzyme at the higher temperature and
     pH.   As the temperature and pH are raised, a point is reached where
     the destructive influence of both of these on the enzyme protein is
     manifested by the shift of the optimum away from the harsher envi-
     ronmental conditions.
3.   Superior pH-stability characteristics, as can be seen from the broad
     plateau shown in Fig. 4.   These data were obtained by incubating
     the enzyme in solution at the indicated pH, for 19 hr at 35°C, after
     which the standard assay was performed to determine residual
     activity.
4.   Compatibility with sodium tripolyphosphate.   Many related proteases
     are inhibited by this ubiquitous detergent ingredient.   In fact, U.S.
     Patent 3,037,870 [12] discloses the use of sodium tripolyphosphate
     to control the activity of a neutral bacterial protease used to tender-
     ize hams.   The presence of the phosphate prevents the overtender-
     ization of the meat by destroying the activity of the enzyme within a
     relatively short period of time.

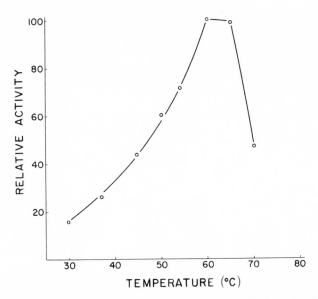

FIG. 2. Activity as a function of temperature, Alkaline Protease 201.

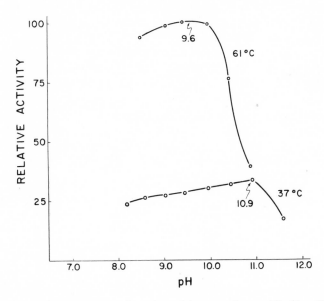

FIG. 3. pH-Activity as a function of temperature, Alkaline Protease 201.

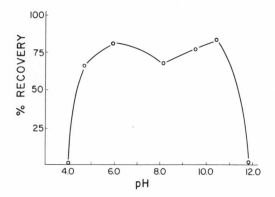

FIG. 4. Stability as a function of pH, Alkaline Protease 201.

As will be seen in the following section, it is recommended that sodium tripolyphosphate be incorporated in the assay of alkaline protease to make certain that the activity being measured is exclusive of any neutral protease that may be present as a contaminant.

In addition to compatibility with higher phosphates, a successful laundry additive must also be stable in the presence of the other components normally found in laundry products. This has been established by Cayle [11] with enzyme assays and by Langguth and Mecey [13] and Stensby et al. [14] with laundry tests. Ingredients or adjuvants so tested include sodium perborate, sodium hypochlorite, sodium metasilicate, carboxymethylcellulose, nitrilotriacetic acid, linear alcohol ethoxylate, sodium lauryl sulfate, alkyldimethylethyl- and ethylbenzyl ammonium chloride, fluorescent whiteners, and bacteriostats.

It was found that chlorinated oxidizing agents are the most harmful to these enzymes. In addition, concentrations of sodium perborate in excess of approximately 10% also shorten their life expectancy, as do cationic surfactants. The other components mentioned appear to be suitably compatible, if the pH of the final formulation is not allowed to exceed approximately 10.5.

IV.   ASSAY METHODS

Several assay procedures are currently in use in a number of laboratories. Most of these depend on the hydrolysis of casein or hemoglobin, with either the increase of end product or the decrease of substrate used as the criterion of activity. Either method is acceptable as long as certain restrictions are observed:

1. Substrate must be present in excess during the period that hydrolysis is being measured.
2. The rate of the reaction must be linear during the period that hydrolysis is being measured. To assure this, modification of substrate generally is not allowed to proceed to an extent greater than 20%.
3. The conditions of pH and temperature should be selected so that very slight changes (due to day-to-day and lab-to-lab variation) do not cause inordinately large changes in reaction rate.

Typical of the assays that have been recommended to the detergent industry are those described by Cayle [11] and Green [15]. The former is based on the hydrolysis of casein at a pH of 8.5 and a temperature of 37°C. The hydrolysis products in a trichloroacetic acid extract are measured in a suitable spectrophotometer as tyrosine equivalents absorbing at 277 nm. The latter assay is a modified Anson method based on the hydrolysis of hemoglobin at a pH of 7.5 and a temperature of 25°C. The hydrolysis products are measured in a manner similar to that described above.

Several automated procedures have also been published, an example of which is that of Paixao et al. [16]. A Technicon AutoAnalyzer is employed, with a casein substrate, a pH of 9.4, and a temperature of 50°C. Liberated amino groups are determined colorimetrically with trinitrobenzenesulfonic acid.

The American Society for Testing and Materials (ASTM) established a task group to study the available assay methods and derive a single procedure incorporating the suggestions and experiences of the detergent industry. The resulting method is to be evaluated by the participating laboratories and, upon ultimate adoption by ASTM, would assume a quasi-official status. The following is the procedure currently being evaluated by ASTM:

1. Principle

The test is based on the hydrolysis of casein which is followed by the determination of tyrosine equivalents in a TCA extract measuring absorption at 275 nm in a spectrophotometer.

2. Main Conditions

Temperature, 50°C; duration of hydrolysis, 15 min; pH 9.0; borate buffer.

Ratio of ingredients to enzyme: STPP 100:1; LAS 20:1; nonionic 20:1 (LAS is Witco Sulframin 1345; nonionic is Witco Alfol 1618-65).

3. Solutions

a. Borate, 0.2 M. Dissolve 12.4 g H_3BO_3 in 100 ml 1 N NaOH and dilute to 1 liter with water; pH 9.3.

b. **Buffer to dissolve enzyme.** Dissolve 12.0 g NaCl in about 500 ml water and add 237 ml 0.2 M borate solution. Adjust to pH 9.0 with 0.1 N NaOH. Approximately 18 ml will be needed. Make to 1.0 liter with water.

c. **STPP-Alfol-Sulframin solution.** Dissolve 0.3 g Alfol in 350 ml water; this requires stirring for 10 min at 37°C. Add 0.36 g Sulframin, 82.6% active (i.e., 0.3 g 100% active Sulframin) and 1.5 g STPP (Fisher Catalog No. S-645). Stir to dissolve and adjust to pH 9.0 with about 6 ml 0.1 N HCl. Make with water to a volume of 500 ml. Five milliliters of this solution contains 3.0 mg Alfol, 3.0 mg pure Sulframin, and 15 mg STPP.

d. **TCA reagent.** (1) Prepare a stock solution of 6.67 M acetic acid by dissolving 400 g glacial acetic acid (CP) to 1000 ml with water. (2) Dissolve 18.0 g trichloroacetic acid (reagent grade) and 19.0 g sodium acetate (crystalline 3 H_2O) in about 300 ml water, add 50.0 ml 6.67 M acetic acid solution, and transfer to a 1-liter volumetric flask. Make to volume with water. The solution should have pH 3.5 ± 0.1. The TCA solution decomposes with time and should be discarded after one week.

e. **Substrate solution.** Slurry 6.0 g casein (Hammersten, Nutritional Biochemicals Corporation) in 200 ml water, add 120 ml 0.2 M borate (a) and heat 20 min in a boiling water bath. Cool to room temperature and adjust to pH 9.0 with 0.1 N NaOH. About 30 ml will be needed. Make to 500 ml with water, pH 9.0. The solution may be used for one week but should be stored under refrigeration.

f. **Enzyme solutions.** Prepare all solutions and serial dilutions with borate buffer (solution b). Stock solutions should be stirred for 30 min before serial dilutions are made.

Final enzyme solutions should contain between 20 and 60 units/ml. This will impart between 40 and 120 units to an assay mixture which will then give absorbancy readings in the preferred range of 0.200-0.600. For unit definition see below.

4. Assay Procedure

Mix 5.0 ml substrate solution and 5.0 ml STPP solution in a 25 x 150 mm tube and place for 10 min in a bath at 50°C. Add 2.0 ml enzyme solution and place for exactly 15 min in a bath at 50°C. Add 10.0 ml TCA reagent, shake vigorously, and keep 30 min with intermittent shaking at 37°C. Filter the precipitated mixture after thorough shaking through an 11-cm Whatman No. 42 paper. To obtain perfectly clear filtrates refilter the first portion of the filtrates through the same filter. Read the absorbance of the filtrate in a 10-mm cell at 275 nm against the substrate blank.

To prepare the substrate blank mix 5.0 ml substrate solution and 5.0 ml STPP solution (c), incubate 10 min at 50°C, add 2.0 ml borate buffer (b), mix well, and keep 15 min at 50°C. Add 10.0 ml TCA reagent, shake vigorously, and keep 30 min at 37°C with intermittent shaking. Filter as directed above.

5. Enzyme Blank

The readings of the enzyme tests are corrected by subtracting the value of the enzyme blank. To prepare an enzyme blank incubate about 5 ml enzyme solution in a separate tube for 15 min at 50°C. Pipet 5.0 ml substrate solution and 5.0 ml STPP solution (c) into another tube. Incubate 15 min at 50°C, add 10.0 ml TCA reagent, shake well, and hold 1 min. Add 2.0 ml of the separately incubated enzyme solution and mix well. Place the tube in a 37°C bath for 30 min with intermittent shaking and filter as described before. Read the absorbancy of the filtrate against the substrate blank.

6. Definition of Units

One unit of activity is that amount of enzyme which releases in 1 min under the conditions of the test a hydrolyzate that contains the equivalent of 1 μg of tyrosine per milliliter in the final reaction volume.

To find the value for the tyrosine solution proceed as follows: Dissolve 100 mg L-tyrosine (Mann Research Laboratories Catalog No. 1654, dried in a vacuum desiccator with H_2SO_4 before use) in 60 ml 0.1 N HCl. Be certain that the tyrosine is completely dissolved and dilute to 1 liter with water. This stock solution contains 100 μg tyrosine/ml. Prepare three subsequent dilutions containing 25, 40, and 75 μg tyrosine ml and determine the absorbancy of each for a path of 100 mm at 275 nm. Plot the results. A straight line passing through the origin must be obtained. Take the value for 60 μg/ml from the graph and divide by 60 to obtain the absorbancy for 1.0 μg/ml. A figure close to 0.0072 will result.

7. Calculation of Units

The number of units in the digestion mixture is

$$\frac{A_{275} \text{ of hydrolyzate}}{A_{275} \text{ of } 1.0 \ \mu g \ ty/ml} \times \frac{vol \ (ml)}{time \ (min)}$$

$$= \frac{A_{275} \text{ of hydrolyzate}}{0.0072} \times \frac{22}{15}$$

$$= A_{275} \text{ of hydrolyzate} \times 204$$

The units obtained with this method are designated APB units. The number of APB units per gram of a preparation is called the APB of the preparation.

Thus,

$$APB = \frac{A_{275} \text{ of hydrolyzate x 204}}{\text{grams of enzyme prep. in test}}$$

A comparison of the approximate results obtained with a sample of Alkaline Protease 201 when assayed by several methods currently in use is as follows:

APB	760,000
PCA	195,000
Anson	1.5
Loehlein-Volhard	125,000
Delft	300,000
PV	114,000

V.   EVALUATION METHODS

In order to evaluate the effectiveness of the enzymes as laundry additives under practical conditions, but at the same time with some degree of standardization and reproducibility, standard test fabrics are employed and a soaking or full-cycle operation is approximated in the laboratory.   There are several pieces of equipment suitable for such studies, including the Terg-O-Tometer and Launder-Ometer.

The test fabrics virtually universally used to establish efficacy of the proteolytic enzymes is EMPA 116, uniformly soiled with blood, milk, and Japanese ink, and available through Test Fabrics Inc., New York.

A procedure we have successfully employed is discussed below [11].

A.   Method

Cloth swatches cut to 2 in. x 4 in. are used. The wash liquor containing 0.5% of the detergent mixture is preheated to 50°C by adding 200-ml portions to each 1-pint Launder-Ometer jar and allowing it to equilibrate for 2 min in the constant-temperature bath.   The test cloth and 10 steel balls are then added, and washing is allowed to proceed for 15 min.   Each swatch is rinsed twice for 1 min with 100-ml portions of water at 50°C. Neutralization is provided by adding 100 ml of water containing one drop of 28% acetic acid.   This is held for 1 min at 27°C, after which the cloth is rinsed for 1 min in 100 ml of fresh water at 27°C, squeezed between towels, and ironed.

Reflectance measurements are made with a Gardner Automatic Reflectometer, Gardner Laboratory, Inc., Bethesda, Maryland, using the blue filter. Readings are taken on both sides of the fabric and the values are averaged.

B. Results

Figure 5 shows the results of an experiment to determine the optimum level of Alkaline Protease 201 required with an anionic detergent formulation. Maximum reflectance is exhibited with an enzyme level of 1.5%, though though there is only a 10% difference in reflectance obtained between 0.5 and 1.5% enzyme. It is possible, however, to distinguish visually between EMPA 116 laundered with 0.5 and 1.5% enzyme.

Figure 6 shows a temperature-activity curve obtained using this laundry test with the test fabric, the anionic base, and 0.8% Alkaline Protease 201. It can be seen that the detergent plus enzyme has a temperature optimum between 40 and 50°C, rather than above 60°C previously described for the enzyme alone.

VI. QUICK IN-PLANT TEST

The final method to be discussed is one described by Cayle et al. [17] for establishing the presence of enzyme in a product on the production line. This procedure utilizes processed 8mm black-and-white movie film as the test reagent. A piece of the film is immersed in a solution of the enzyme-containing detergent and the resulting hydrolysis of the protein emulsion is a measure of protease activity.

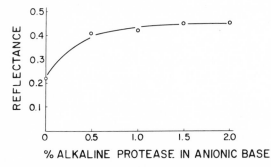

FIG. 5. Effect of enzyme level on laundering of EMPA 116.

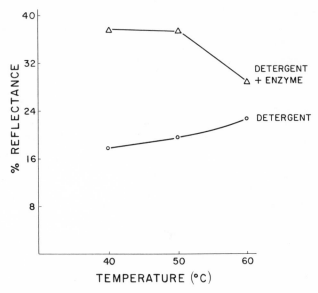

FIG. 6. Activity as a function of temperature, EMPA 116, Alkaline
Protease 201.

A. Method

1. Add 100 ml of water at 50°C to a beaker.

2. Add 100 ml of the detergent-enzyme mixture. Mix thoroughly.

3. Suspend a 2-in. strip of developed 8mm movie film from a hinged
paper clip and immerse the lower half in solution 2.

4. After 10 min, remove the strip and wipe on both sides with a facial
tissue by pulling the strip between the fingers starting from the top down.
The extent of emulsion loss is dependent on enzyme concentration and the
time of incubation.

B. Results

Figure 7 shows the results of a 10-min incubation with several different
anionic bases alone and in the presence of Alkaline Protease 201-HA at a
level of 0.5%. Figure 8 shows film strips incubated for 10 min in detergent solutions containing 0, 0.1, 0.25, 0.5, 0.75, and 1.0% enzyme, indica-
ting the semiquantitative nature of this procedure.

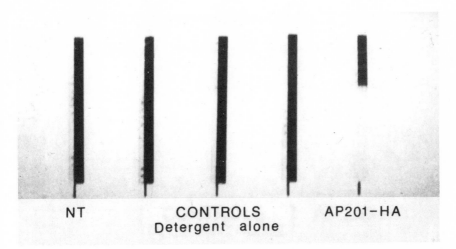

NT   CONTROLS   AP201-HA
            Detergent alone

FIG. 7. Eight-millimeter film strips incubated for 10 min in several anionic bases alone and in a base plus Alkaline Protease 201-HA. NT stands for no treatment.

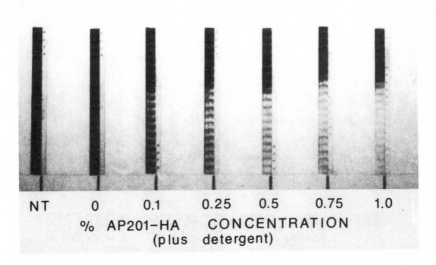

NT   0   0.1   0.25   0.5   0.75   1.0

% AP201-HA   CONCENTRATION
        (plus detergent)

FIG. 8. Eight-millimeter film strips incubated for 10 min in detergent solutions containing 0, 0.1, 0.25, 0.5, 0.75, and 1.0% Alkaline Protease 201-HA. NT stands for no treatment.

REFERENCES

1. E. J. Beckhorn, M. D. Labbee, and L. A. Underkofler, J. Agr. Food Chem., 13, 30 (1965).

2. S. A. Olaitan, R. J. DeLange, and E. L. Smith, J. Biol. Chem., 243, 6296 (1968).

3. R. J. DeLange and E. L. Smith, J. Biol. Chem., 243, 2134 (1968).

4. R. J. DeLange and E. L. Smith, J. Biol. Chem., 243, 2143 (1968).

5. M. Landon, W. H. Evans, and E. L. Smith, J. Biol. Chem., 243, 2165 (1968).

6. W. H. Evans, M. Landon, and E. L. Smith, J. Biol. Chem., 243, 2172 (1968).

7. E. L. Smith, R. J. DeLange, W. H. Evans, M. Landon, and F. S. Markland, J. Biol. Chem., 243, 2184 (1968).

8. A. N. Glazer, J. Biol. Chem., 242, 433 (1967).

9. E. L. Smith, F. S. Markland, C. B. Kasper, R. J. DeLange, M. Landon, and W. H. Evans, J. Biol. Chem., 241, 5974 (1966).

10. A. O. Barel and A. N. Glazer, J. Biol. Chem., 243, 1344 (1968).

11. T. Cayle, J. Amer. Oil Chem. Soc., 46, 515 (1969).

12. H. Schleich and R. S. Arnold, U.S. Pat. 3,037,870 (1962).

13. R. P. Langguth and L. W. Mecey, Soap Chem. Spec., 45, 60 (1969).

14. P. S. Stensby, W. R. Findley, and C. W. Liebert, Deterg. Spec., 6, 29 (1969).

15. S. R. Green, Soap Chem. Spec., 44, 86 (1968).

16. L. M. Paixao, S. W. Babulak, S. M. Barkin, D. K. Shumway, and S. D. Friedman, J. Amer. Oil Chem. Soc., 46, 511 (1969).

17. T. Cayle, R. Hoerle, and R. Brier, Soap Chem. Spec., 45, 37 (1969).

Chapter 17

TEST METHODS IN TOXICOLOGY

Leonard J. Vinson
Lever Brothers Company
Research and Development Division
Edgewater, New Jersey

I. INTRODUCTION

There are many published reports citing the low toxicity of surfactants
that go into the formulation of a wide variety of household detergents

available to the consumer [1-8]. Records kept by the detergent industry and statistics made available by Poison Control Centers point to a remarkably low incidence of systemic toxicity linked to the regular home use of such products, and, more significantly, even from misuse as in accidental ingestion or inadvertent contact with the eye.

II. GOVERNMENT REGULATIONS OF HAZARDOUS HOUSEHOLD SUBSTANCES

In assessing the safety of household detergents, government regulations and definitions of hazardous household substances provide important guidelines. The need for regulating household products to better ensure consumer safety was recognized many years ago with the passing of the Caustic Poisons Act of 1927 requiring precautionary labeling for 12 listed hazardous substances. As the number and complexity of household products increased, further safeguards became readily apparent. The Federal Hazardous Substances Labeling Act, enacted in 1961, was prompted by the need to combat a rising incidence of poisonings and other accidental injuries, especially to children, caused by common household substances.

The law defines a hazardous material as a substance or mixture of substances that may cause substantial personal injury or illness as a proximate result of any customary or reasonably foreseeable handling or use, including reasonably foreseeable ingestion by children. Hazardous materials are broken down into six classes: (a) a toxic substance, (b) a corrosive substance, (c) an irritant, (d) a strong sensitizer, (e) a flammable substance, or (f) a pressure-generating substance. A toxic substance is one that has the capacity to produce personal injury or illness to man through ingestion, inhalation, or absorption through any body surface. A corrosive substance is one that, in contact with living tissue, will cause irreversible destruction of tissue.

Hopper [9] noted that a product may fall within one or more of the categories defining hazard and still not necessarily be a hazardous substance under the law. "To be a hazardous substance, it must come within the so-called 'if' clause which reads as follows: If such a substance or mixture of substances may cause substantial personal injury or substantial illness as a result of any customary or reasonably foreseeable handling or use, including reasonably foreseeable ingestion by children." Therefore, an appraisal of a household product, whether it is hazardous as defined by the act, calls for the exercise of sound judgment and involves the consideration of such matters as methods of sales distribution, size and form of container, the physical form (liquid, solid, or paste), the type of closure, color, odor, and taste, its emetic properties, as well as any available data on human experience.

The Federal Hazardous Substances Labeling Act requires labeling that provides information about hazardous household products, defines their potential hazard, and cites precautions to minimize the danger of exposure. Also, those products deemed hazardous by toxicological tests require labeling information relative to emergency treatment for accidental eye contact, inhalation, or ingestion of the product. A statement common to all precautionary labels is "Keep Out of Reach of Children."

Prior to 1972, the Bureau of Product Safety of the Food and Drug Administration regulated hazardous household substances. With the passing of the Consumer Product Safety Act, October 1972, regulatory responsibilities were transferred to a new independent regulatory agency headed by the Consumer Product Safety Commission.

Cleaning products claiming sanitizing or disinfecting actions do not come under the jurisdiction of the CPSA, which regulates the FHSLA; they are regulated by the Environmental Protection Agency under the Federal Insecticide, Fungicide and Rodenticide Act. The regulations under this act require caution statements on the labels of such products.

III. ACCIDENTAL INGESTIONS OF HOUSEHOLD DETERGENTS

Since accidental ingestion of household products, principally by young children, is a major factor in defining hazard, particular attention should be given to accidental poisonings and the involvement of household detergents. Soaps and household detergents account for 4-5% of all substances that are accidentally ingested by children under five years of age, as documented by the Poison Control Centers.

Poison Control Centers, first organized in Chicago in 1953, serve as central information agencies where data on toxicity of products and treatment are readily available. There exist today more than 500 local Poison Control Centers in the United States providing instant information on a wide variety of poisonous and potentially poisonous substances that are likely to find their way into the American home. Most of these centers are associated with hospitals or medical schools and usually provide treatment facilities. The National Clearinghouse for Poison Control Centers in Washington, D.C., a unit of the FDA's Bureau of Product Safety, distributes information to the centers and analyzes toxicological reports such as cases of accidental ingestion. Poison Control centers have received the cooperation of manufacturers of household soaps and detergents who have provided the centers with data on the biological and chemical properties of products, such as alkalinity, irritancy, corrosiveness, and toxicity. Locations of Poison Control Centers can be obtained from the Directory of Poison Control Centers which is available from the Superintendent of Documents [10].

There are a number of factors influencing the nature and extent of the hazard involved in accidental ingestions. The physical, chemical, and biological considerations of cleaning products involved in accidental ingestion incidents are discussed by Calandra and Fancher [11].

About two-thirds of all accidental ingestions of detergents occur as a result of drinking liquids from bottles. Powders are less likely to be consumed in toxic quantities because of their bulky nature. Also, in such instances, emesis usually occurs which serves to limit sharply the quantity retained. Jones and Work [12] reported that the average volume of three to four normal swallows corresponds to an average intake of material of about 1 ml/kg for men, women, and children. This observation, coupled with the relatively low acute oral toxicity of soaps and detergents and the difficulty of retaining even one swallow without emesis occurring, points up the unlikelihood of ingesting such products in hazardous amounts.

The acute oral toxicity (LD_{50}) is a convenient parameter for making a comparison of toxicity of materials and assessing the potential hazard which may result from accidental ingestion by human beings. Hayes [13] calculated probable lethal oral doses for a human adult based on rat LD_{50} values. His data are shown in Table 1. Swisher [14], in a comprehensive review of the safety of surfactants, presented acute LD_{50} values of various types of surfactants used in detergents. Some of these values are given in Table 2, from which it can be observed that the anionic and nonionic surfactants, for the most part, have the same acute oral toxicity ranges. The hazard of oral ingestion can be considered low for either type of material. Most cationic surfactants are more toxic by the oral route than are the other classes of surfactants.

A more meaningful picture of detergent acute oral toxicity is provided in Table 3, as given by Calandra and Fancher [11], where a variety of finished household products are listed. For a better understanding of the significance of the LD_{50} values, data on common solvents and well-known household substances such as NaCl and $NaHCO_3$ are also included in Table 3. Griffith and co-workers [15, 16] observed that the emetic effects of household detergents were similar to that of syrup of ipecac. Thus, it is unlikely that potentially toxic amounts of such household producus could be ingested without induction of vomiting.

Calandra and Fancher [11] related that in 1970, 83,313 accidental ingestion cases among all age groups were processed by the Poison Control Centers as reported to the National Clearinghouse. Under the category of soaps, detergents and specialty cleaners, 3446 cases of children under five years of age were recorded. Those children that required treatment exhibited symptoms confined primarily to minor gastrointestinal or pharyngeal mucous membrane irritation. No fatalities were reported.

TABLE 1

Rat LD_{50} versus Probable Lethal Oral Dose for a Human Adult

Animal acute LD_{50} (mg/kg)	Quantity
Less than 5	A few drops
5-50	A pinch to one teaspoonful
50-500	One teaspoonful to two tablespoonfuls
500-5000	One ounce to one pint (1 lb)
5000-15,000	One pint to one quart (2 lb)

TABLE 2

Some Acute Oral LD_{50} Values for Surfactants

Surfactant	Rat LD_{50} (g/kg)
Anionics	
Linear alkylbenzenesulfonate (C_{12}-C_{14})	1.3-2.5
Lauryl sulfate	1.3
Lauryl alcohol ethylene oxide (3)[a] sulfate	1.8
Octylphenol ethylene oxide sulfate	3.7-5.4
Alkane sulfonate	3.0
Oleoyl methyl tauride	4.0
Dioctyl succinate	1.9
Nonionics	
Stearoyl EO (8)[a]	53.0
Lauryl alcohol EO (4)	8.6
Lauryl alcohol EO (7)	4.1
Lauryl alcohol EO (23)	8.6
Stearyl alcohol EO (2)	25.0
Stearyl alcohol EO (10)	2.9
Stearyl alcohol EO (20)	1.9
Fatty acyl sorbitan EO (20)	20.0
Nonylphenol EO (9-10)	1.6
Lauric diethanolamide	2.7
Cationics	
Cetyltrimethylammonium bromide	0.4
Cetylpyridinium chloride	0.2
Lauryl imidazoline	3.2

[a]Numbers in parentheses signify number of ethylene oxide (EO) units.

TABLE 3

Acute Oral LD_{50} Values for Detergents and
Other Household Products[a]

Product type	Rat LD_{50} (g/kg)
Toilet bar soap	7–20
General-purpose granular detergent	3–7
General-purpose liquid detergent	4–9
Scouring cleanser	10+
Enzyme laundry presoak product	3–7
Dishwashing liquid detergent	4–12
Automatic dishwasher detergent with or without bleach	3–5
Bubble bath	7.6
Bleach, liquid	10+
Fabric softener	5.6–12
Fabric whitener	5+
Shampoo	5–10
Shampoo (antidandruff)	3–4
NaCl (table salt)	3.1–4.2
Sodium bicarbonate (baking soda)	4.3
Ethyl alcohol	13.7
Gasoline	0.5–5
Ethylene glycol (antifreeze fluid)	5.5

[a]Reprinted from Calandra and Fancher [11, pp. 7 and 8] by courtesy of the Soap and Detergent Association.

IV. GUIDELINES FOR ASSESSING TOXICITY OF HOUSEHOLD DETERGENTS

Regulations issued August 12, 1961, pursuant to the Federal Hazardous Labeling Act, require that the toxicity of chemicals contained in household substances be determined by the manufacturer. The regulations deal with maximal toxic doses for certain experimental animals, when administered by inhalation, oral ingestion, or percutaneous absorption, as well as corrosive, irritant, and sensitizing actions.

Excellent guidelines have been prepared for assessing the toxicity of household substances by the Committee on Toxicology of the Division of Chemistry and Chemical Technology, National Academy of Sciences, National Research Council [17]. Another publication of particular value in helping to plan toxicological programs for household products is Appraisal of the Safety of Chemicals in Foods, Drugs, and Cosmetics, edited by the Editorial Committee of the Association of the Food and Drug Officials of the United States [18].

In assessing the safety of household detergents, toxicological methods are used that are oriented toward the kind of possible exposures these products may have during use or foreseeable misuse by the consumer. These exposures are (a) accidental ingestion; (b) skin contact leading to percutaneous absorption, (c) eye contact, and (d) skin contact; primary irritation and sensitization. Toxicological procedures for assessing the likelihood of household detergents to cause injury by the first three routes mentioned above are discussed herein. Primary irritation and sensitization aspects of household detergents are described in the next chapter.

The tests commonly employed in assessing the safety of household detergents are those recommended in the regulations under the Federal Hazardous Substances Labeling Act (Part 191, Chapter 1, Title 21, Code of the Federal Regulations) [19].

V. FHSLA REGULATIONS RELATING TO HOUSEHOLD DETERGENTS

A. Toxic Substances

Toxic substances is any substance falling within any of the following categories:

1. Any substance that produces death within 14 days in one-half of a group of white rats each weighing between 200 and 300 g, at a single dose of more than 50 mg/kg but not more than 5 g/kg of body weight, when orally administered. Substances falling in the toxicity range between 500 mg and 5 g/kg of body weight will be considered for exemption from some or all of the labeling requirements of the act under 191.62, upon a showing that, because of the physical form of the substances (solid, a thick plastic,

emulsion, etc.), the size or closure of the container, human experience
with the article, or any other relevant factors, such labeling is not needed.

  2. Any substance that produces death within 14 days in one-half of a
group of white rats each weighing between 200 and 300 g when inhaled continuously for a period of 1 hr or less at an atmospheric concentration of more
than 200 ppm but not more than 20,000 ppm by volume of gas or vapor or
more than 2 mg but not more than 200 mg/liter by volume of mist or dust,
provided such concentration is likely to be encountered by man when the substance is used in any reasonably foreseeable manner.

  3. Any substance that produces death with 14 days in one-half of a
group of rabbits weighing between 2.3 and 3.0 kg each, tested at a dosage
of more than 200 mg/kg of body weight but not more than 2 g/kg of body
weight, when administered by continuous contact with the bare skin for 24 hr
by the method described in the Federal Register [19] under Section 191.10.

  4. Any substance that is "toxic" (but not "highly toxic") on the basis of
human experience.

B. Irritants

  1. The term irritant includes "primary irritant to the skin" as well as
substances irritant to the eye or to mucous membranes.

  2. The term primary irritant means a substance that is not corrosive
and that the available data of human experience indicate it as a primary
irritant; or which results in an empirical score of 5 or more when tested
by the method described in the Code of Federal Regulations under Section
191.11 [19].

  3. A substance is an irritant to the eye mucosa if the available data on
human experience indicate that it is an irritant for the eye mucosa, or,
when tested by the method described in Section 191.12 of 21 CFR, there is
at any of the readings made at 24, 48, and 72 hr discernible opacity or ul-
ceration of the corneum or inflammation of the iris, or such substance produces in the conjunctivae (excluding the cornea and iris) a diffuse deep-
crimson red with individual vessels not easily discernible, or an obvious
swelling with partial eversion of the lids.

C. Corrosives

  A "corrosive substance" is one that causes visible destruction or irreversible alterations in the tissue at the site of contact. A test for a corrosive substance is whether, by human experience, such tissue destruction
occurs at the site of application. A substance would be considered corrosive
to the skin if, when tested on the intact skin of the albino rabbit by the technique described in 21 CFR, Section 191.11 [19], the structure of the tissue

at the site of contact is destroyed or changed irreversibly in 24 hr or less. Other appropriate tests should be applied when contact of the substance with other than skin tissues is being considered.

VI. RABBIT-EYE TEST

A substance is an irritant to the eye if the available data on human experience indicate that it is an irritant to the eye, or if a positive test result is obtained when the substance is tested by the rabbit-eye method described in the 21 CFR under Section 191.12. The procedure used is as follows [20]:

1. Six albino test rabbits are used for each substance tested. The cages housing the animals are so designed as to exclude sawdust, wood chips, and other extraneous materials that might enter the eye. The eyes of the animals in the test group are examined before testing, and only those animals without observable eye defects are used. One tenth of a milliliter of the test substance, or in the case of solids or semisolids, 100 mg of the test substance, is allowed to fall on the everted lower lid of one eye of each rabbit; the upper and lower lids are then gently held together for 1 sec before releasing, to prevent loss of material. The other eye, remaining untreated, serves as a control. The eyes are not washed following instillation. The eyes are examined at 24, 48, and 72 hr after instillation of the test material. An animal is considered as giving a positive reaction if there is, at any of the readings, discernible opacity of the cornea, or inflammation of the iris [other than a slight deepening of the folds (rugae) or a slight circumcorneal injection], or if such substance produces in the conjunctivae (excluding the cornea and iris) an obvious swelling with partial eversion of the lids, or a diffuse deep-crimson red with individual vessels not easily discernible.

2. The test is considered positive if four or more of the animals in the test group exhibit a positive reaction. If one animal exhibits a positive reaction, the test is regarded as negative. If two or three animals exhibit a positive reaction, the test is rerun, using a different group of six animals. The second test is considered positive if three or more of the animals exhibit a positive reaction. If only one or two animals in the second test exhibit a positive reaction, the test is repeated with a different group of six animals. Should a third test be needed, the substance is regarded as an irritant if two or more animals exhibit a positive response. Ocular reactions may be read with the unaided eye or aided by the use of a binocular loupe, the hand slit lamp, or any other expert means available. The diagnosis of corneal damage may be confirmed by instilling one drop of 2% fluorescein sodium ophthalmic solution into the treated eyes of two additional test rabbits. (The original group of six animals is not treated with fluorescein solution.) After flushing the excess fluorescein solution, the injured area of the cornea appears yellow, in contrast to the surrounding clear

cornea. Fluorescein staining may be better visualized in a dark room under ultraviolet illumination.

The Draize rabbit-eye test is widely used as a predictive test for determining the possible injury to the human eye on accidental contact with household products. Some questions have been raised concerning its value as a reliable predictive test because of the anatomical differences between the rabbit's eye and the human eye which may account for the rabbit's greater sensitivity to eye irritants [21-24]. The two major differences between the rabbit eye and the human eye are (a) the presence of the nicitating membrane or third eyelid of the rabbit which serves presumably as a protective device for the eye, and (b) the absence of an effective tearing mechanism as found in the primate. In a comprehensive report on a comparison of eye irritation in monkeys and rabbits, Buehler and Newmann [24] described results which indicate that the rhesus monkey is a more reliable subject for predicting human ocular responses to detergent preparations than the rabbit. The investigators state that "using the rabbit as a test animal, one could conclude that the anionic formulation, for instance, is a severe eye irritant when any of the grading systems are used; whereas, data obtained by monkey eye and extensive human experience after accidental factory exposures to similar formulations have shown such materials to be completely non-hazardous."

In defense of the Draize rabbit-eye test, it should be mentioned that it has proved valuable as a relatively simple means for obtaining preliminary information on the potential of a substance to cause eye damage. Negative results in the rabbit-eye test provide good assurance that a problem would not occur to the human eye on accidental exposure. On the other hand, if ocular damage does develop in the rabbit-eye test, the test product does not have to be rejected. Comparisons in this test can be made with a similar product with proven safety under use conditions that would serve as a useful reference standard. Also, one can resort to the rhesus monkey as a test subject to further assess product safety.

Toxicologists are not in complete agreement on the predictive value of the rabbit-eye test for assessing the degree of hazard of household detergents to the human eye. Scientists at the Consumer Product Safety Agency are in the process of modifying the rabbit-eye procedure to increase its predictive reliability. Toward this end, use will be made of comparative data obtained in a collaborative study* on eye responses of rabbits and monkeys to common household preparations, covering a spectrum of mild to irritating eye effects.

---

*Soap and Detergent Association, Government Cooperative Study supervised by Dr. Richard Green, Professor of Opthalmic Pathology of Johns Hopkins University.

VII. DERMAL TOXICITY TESTS

In addition to the selected toxicity tests in the regulations describing acute oral toxicity, skin and eye irritancy, and corrosiveness, it may be desirable to run subacute dermal toxicity tests, particularly on detergent formulations containing new surfactant or builder ingredients. Draize [25] has described 20- and 90-day subacute toxicity tests employing rabbits, which can be valuable in predicting the safety and the nature of the effect of the product on repeated application to skin.

A. Twenty-Day Subacute Dermal Toxicity Test

In this test, relatively large doses of the test substances are applied daily to intact and abraded skin sites. The adult albino rabbit is the animal of choice because of the large surface available for treatment.

Three dosage levels are chosen, one usually being a realistic concentration, and the other two, exaggerated levels. A minimum of four male and four female rabbits is included in each group. Rabbits are immobilized in stocks and applications are made by inunction to an uncovered area of intact and abraded skin. The area inuncted is approximately 10% of the total body surface and is covered with a rubber dam to prevent evaporation. Each animal is patched six days a week for three weeks (18 applications). All animals are observed for a two-week period following the final exposure.

During the course of the test, animals are observed grossly for any abnormalities in general appearance or behavior. Any irritancy at the site of application is graded and recorded. Body weight data are obtained prior to the first treatment, after the second and third weeks, and just prior to sacrifice. Hematology studies are conducted initially, after the last treatment, and finally just prior to sacrifice. This includes hemoglobin level, total and differential white blood cell counts, and packed cell volume determined by microhematocrit method as percent hematocrit. Urine is collected before the first treatment and just prior to sacrifice, and examined for pH, protein, glucose, ketones, and occult blood.

On autopsy, organs are weighed, examined for visible lesions, and portions fixed in buffered formalin for histopathologic examination. Typical organs examined are liver, heart, lung, kidneys, adrenals, and spleen.

B. Ninety-Day Subacute Dermal Toxicity Test

In this longer term study, an attempt is made to determine the effects of the test materials on intact skin at different exaggerated levels of the product. Dosage levels may be chosen at either 1, 3, and 10 times, or 1, 2, 4, and 8 times the baseline dose. It may be desirable in some instances to vary only the concentration of a particular ingredient rather than the whole product. In any event, the test solution is applied by gentle inunction to an area of closely clipped skin which comprises approximately 10% of the body surface. The animal is then returned to its cage. Doses are applied six days a week for 15 weeks (90 applications). Each test group usually consists of four male and four female adult albino rabbits.

Evaluation procedures are similar to those used in the 20-day study. These include gross observations, evaluation of local effects, body weight data, hematology (initially, after four and eight weeks, and terminally), urinalyses (initially, after six weeks, and terminally), gross pathology at autopsy, and histopathologic evaluation of all vital organs.

VIII.   RECENT DEVELOPMENTS IN DETERGENT FORMULATIONS

In recent years, household detergent formulations containing microbial enzymes (alkaline protease) became almost an overnight success because of enhanced stain removal properties. Extensive toxicological studies on animals and humans indicated that enzyme detergent products exhibited essentially the same safety as nonenzyme detergent products [26, 27]. However, serious reservations were voiced by allergists about the potential of the microbial enzymes to induce respiratory allergy and skin rashes in the consumer. Such adverse publicity has prompted the withdrawal of these enzymes from most of the household detergents despite the fact that government regulations do not bar their use.

Another important development is the growing use of nonphosphate builders in household detergents because of the concern of environmentalists over the eutrophication potential of phosphates. The use of carbonates is gaining favor as a replacement of phosphate in detergent formulations. Such formulations may satisfy the environmentalists but, in some cases, there is reason for concern as to safety if accidentally ingested. To better define this type of toxic effect, the Consumer Product Safety Agency has publicized and actively employed a provisional test for screening potentially corrosive products, called the esophageal corrosivity test.

The procedure used is as follows: Four rabbits (New Zealand, albino), either sex (weight range 2-3 kg), are used for the test. The animals are fasted for 48 hr prior to testing (water ad libitum). Each animal is anesthetized (sodium pentobarbital) and the oral cavity is examined with the aid of a binocular loop (magnification 2-3 X) and examining lamp. After recovery from anesthesia, the animal is placed in a plastic restrainer of one's own design. The animal's mouth is forced open with a plastic bit with a 1/2- to 3/4-in. hole in the center. The tongue is drawn forward through the hole with a pair of long forceps. A curved spatula containing a weighted sample (300-500 mg) of powder is placed on the posterior aspect of the tongue. For liquid products or semisolids, use 1 ml volume dispensed from a syringe. The tongue is released immediately, allowing the animal to complete swallowing reflex. The animal is returned to its cage with access to water, but no solid food. Treated animals are observed after administration of the product but no physical examination is attempted. At 24 hr, two of the test group are sacrificed by overdose of anesthetic (pentobarbital intravenously, marginal ear vein). The tongue, adjacent pharyngeal structure, and esophagus down to the cardiaca incisura are removed. The stomach is also examined. After gross macroscopic examination (pictures included) the specimen is fixed in formalin for histological examination. The remaining test animals are allowed solid food and water after 24 hr and are sacrificed at 96 hr. The tissues are removed, examined, and fixed as described above.

Evaluation of oral cavity, pharyngeal, and esophageal structures is as follows:

1. Negative: No visible irritation or injury when examined at 24 and 96 hr. Histopathology may not be necessary as determined by gross examination.
2. Irritant: Patchy areas of beefy redness with or without edema present at 24 hr but not at 96 hr. Histologic examination of tissue from the animals sacrificed at 96 hr should be normal in appearance.
3. Corrosive: Necrotic lesions (i.e. esophageal perforation, stricture, etc.) apparent at 24 or 96 hr are confirmed by microscopic examination.

Since the test is primarily concerned with corrosive action, it is considered positive if any of the test animals at 24 or 96 hr shows signs of necrotic lesions in the mouth, pharynx, larynx, or esophagus. The extent of injury is confirmed by histologic examination.

In summary, test methods for assessing the toxicology of household cleansing products have been described. For the most part, standard toxicological tests for evaluating topical, eye, and systemic effects in animals have sufficed to establish the low order of toxicity of this class of commonly used products. This conclusion is supported by the very low incidence of irritation complaints associated with the use and possible misuse of soaps and detergents. Recently, questions have been raised whether the toxicity tests employed can adequately predict potential use hazards of detergent formulations in view of expanding changes being made in their makeup, for example, phosphates being replaced by carbonates, silicates, and other builders.

The Consumer Product Safety Agency is currently proposing new and modified testing procedures for assessing the irritation effects of household products on skin, eye, and mucous membrane.

REFERENCES

1. O. G. Fitzhugh and A. A. Nelson, J. Amer. Pharm. Ass., Sci. Ed., 37, 29-32 (1948).

2. G. Woodward and H. O. Calvery, Proc. Sci. Sec. Toilet Goods Ass., No. 3, 11-14 (1945).

3. H. C. Hodge and W. L. Dowas, Toxicol. Appl. Pharmacol., 3, 689-695 (1961).

4. H. F. Smyth, Jr., in the Public Health Significance of Synthetic Detergents, University of Durham, King's Coll., Dept. Civil Eng. Bull. 2, 1955, pp. 41-43.

5. H. M. Cann and H. L. Verhulst, Amer. J. Dis. Child., 100, 287-290 (1960).

6. M. N. Gleason, R. E. Gosselin, and H. C. Hodge, Clinical Toxicology of Commercial Products, 2nd ed., Williams & Wilkins, Baltimore, 1963.

7. F. H. Snyder, D. L. Opdyke, J. F. Griffith, H. K. Rubenkoenig, T. W. Tusing, and O. E. Paynter, Toxicol. Appl. Pharmacol., 6, 689-695 (1961).

8. D. L. Opdyke, F. H. Snyder, and H. L. Rubenkoenig, Toxicol. Appl. Pharmacol., 6, 141-146 (1964).

9. G. Hopper, Proceedings of the 49th Chemical Specialties Manufacturers Association, Inc., New York, 1962, pp. 75-77.

10. Directory of Poison Control Centers, Public Service Publication No. 1278, Superintendent of Documents, U.S. Government Printing Office, Washington, D. C., 1967 (price, $0.20).

11. J. C. Calandra and O. E. Fancher, Cleaning Products and Their Accidental Ingestion, The Soap Detergent Association, New York, Scientific and Technical Report No. 5R, 1972.

12. D. V. Jones and C. E. Work, Amer. J. Dis. Child., 102, 427 (1961).

13. W. J. Hayes, Jr., Clinical Handbook on Economic Poisons, U.S. Dept. of HEW, Public Health Service Publication No. 476, 1963.

14. R. D. Swisher, Arch. Environ. Health, 17, 232-246 (1968). Also available Surfactant Effects on Humans and Other Animals, The Soap and Detergent Association, New York, Scientific and Technical Report No. 4, 1966.

15. J. F. Griffith and R. O. Carter, Arch. Environ. Health, 11, 678-685 (1965).

16. J. E. Weaver and J. F. Griffith, Toxicol. Appl. Pharmacol., 14, 214 (1969).

17. Principles and Procedures for Evaluating the Toxicity of Household Substances, Publication 1138, National Academy of Sciences, National Research Council, Washington, D.C., 1964.

18. Appraisal of the Safety of Chemicals in Foods, Drugs, and Cosmetics, second printing (1965), published 1959 by the Association of Food and Drug Officials of the United States, Business Office, P. O. Box 1494, Topeka, Kansas.

19. Part 192, Chapter 1, Title 21, Code of the Federal Regulations, reprinted from Federal Register of August 12, 1961.

20. Federal Register, Vol. 28, No. 110, June 6, 1963, p. 5582.

21. J. Mann and B. D. Pullinger, Proc. Reg. Soc. Med., 35, 229-244 (1942).

22. J. H. Beckley, Amer. Perfum. Cosmet., 80, 51-54 (1965).

23. J. H. Beckley, T. J. Russell, and L. F. Rubin, Toxicol. Appl. Pharmacol., 15, 1-9 (1969).

24. E. V. Buehler and E. A. Newmann, Toxicol. Appl. Pharmacol., 6, 701-710 (1964).

25. J. H. Draize, "Dermal Toxicity," in Appraisal of the Safety of Chemicals in Foods, Drugs and Cosmetics, Association of Food and Drug Officials of the United States (see Ref. 18).

26. J. F. Griffith, J. E. Weaver, and H. S. Whitehouse, Fed. Cosmet. Toxicol., 7, 581-593 (1970).

27. M. H. Hendricks and R. O. Carter, Deterg. Spec., 7, 25-27, 55, 62 (1970).

Chapter 18

TEST METHODS IN DERMATOLOGY

Christian Gloxhuber
Toxicological Laboratories
Henkel & Cie. GmbH
Düsseldorf, West Germany

K. H. Schulz
Dermatology Clinic
University of Hamburg
Hamburg, West Germany

I. INTRODUCTION

By far the greatest use of synthetic surface-active agents is in the production of washing, cleansing, and rinsing agents. Not even the ever widely spreading use of washing machines can prevent the human skin from getting into contact with surface-active agents. Testing how these surface-active agents are tolerated by the skin is therefore of great practical interest, since irritating products must be excluded.

Beside testing how the skin tolerates these agents, it is of great impor- tance, primarily in the case of products intended for use in shampoos, to establish that they are tolerated by the mucous membrane, especially of the eye. The testing should comprise both finished products and any in- gredient of a new type. For this purpose an adequate test can be selected from the tests described in the following. This selection should always be adapted to the respective product and its intended usage, and should be left to the criterion of the tester and manufacturer. This is especially the case when new finished products differ only in insignificant formula changes from well-established products which are being used without difficulty. The testing of novel ingredients will have to be done more extensively than that of finished products. Although surface-active agents and detergents are widely used today, their testing for compatibility is basically wholly empirical. Very little is yet known about how surface-active agents, and other components of detergents, react with the proteins and other substances of the skin, and what effects these provoke which eventually may damage the skin surface or its inner layers. Only recently were there attempts [1-5] which can be referred to for the explanation and understanding of these processes. It is assumed that a great deal of knowledge will still be acquired from this field of work.

The number of skin sensitivity reactions, which can be definitely traced back to detergents, is small percentagewise. The experimental prediction that a product will probably be tolerated is very difficult. A series of points of reference, however, can be gathered from animal experiments and dermatological studies. It is of special importance to use in the investigations comparative commercial products whose harmlessness under conditions of usage is known. Data on expected incidence of skin sensitivity reactions cannot be found in experiments with animals and dermatological studies but there is a trend that shows whether a new product can be expected to behave better, identically, or worse than the material selected for comparison. Such investigations are all experimental models. The more convincing the result, the greater is the number of such experimental models that can be used. If, for example, in all models, it was the new product that was tolerated less than the known preparation, one could conclude that the incidence of skin sensitivity reactions will increase. Primarily, dermatological studies and not animal studies alone warrant conclusions of this type.

II. TEST METHODS

Different in vitro methods, experimental animal, and dermatological test models adequate for such type of investigations are described in the following.

A. In Vitro Methods

For obtaining information on skin sensitivity under certain conditions, the zein test, as described by Götte [6], is useful. Although it is not in all cases possible to obtain conclusive results with this test, it does show a new and interesting direction. It is based, in principle, on bringing together zein (a protein obtained from corn, belonging to the prolamins) with a solution of the surface-active agent to be examined. The experimental mixture is shaken slightly at constant temperature for an hour and after filtering, the quantity of dissolved zein is determined in an aliquot part of the filtrate. The more irritating a substance is to the skin, the more zein will be taken over by it into the solution.

For the sake of completeness, the saccharase test described by Wilmsmann and Marks [7] is also mentioned. In our opinion, however, in this test the correlation between the test result and the tolerance is restricted to an even greater degree than in the zein test described by Götte.

B. Test Methods with Experimental Animals

Experimental animal tests to find out whether substances are locally tolerated are run mostly subsequent to or concurrent with tests for systemic toxic effects. In doing this, it is practical to study first the new chemical alone and subsequently in the formulation of its usage. In such investigations it is desirable, if at all possible, to include for the sake of comparison a similar known substance or a commercial product.

1. Regarding the action on connective tissues of the corium (true skin) intracutane tests are informative. To the casual observer such experiments might seem unnecessary; in fact, the behavior of the skin at these sites is not indifferent, since substances in usage very often can penetrate through skin fissures into the corium and thus cause inflammatory reactions.

These experiments can be run according to the procedure described by Barail [8]. In the Toxicological Laboratories of Henkel and Cie. GmbH, Düsseldorf, this test is carried out on mice. The mice are injected in the depilated skin of their abdomen with solutions of the material to be tested in increasing concentrations (0.05 ml per application; five animals for each concentration; two comparative blisters, test preparation and control preparation, for each animal). This test has the advantage that after only 24 hr a reading is possible. For this purpose the animals are killed, their skins are peeled off, and the skins' inner sides are examined. Light damages are characterized by a brownish discoloration, and severe damages by necrosis of the skin. Since the products to be compared are applied to the same animal and in identical concentrations it is easy to establish which of the two products caused the slighter reaction. Figure 1 shows the results of such experiments carried out with a homologous series of alkyl sulfates.

2. Further tests with experimental animals deal with the action of externally applied raw materials and formulated products on the intact skin. The test by Draize [9] uses the back of rabbits, and is especially favored because it is frequently accepted as a semiofficial test procedure. When applied, however, some points must be observed. Results are very often discrepant. For this reason, results of one laboratory can be compared with those of another only with reservations. This actually refers also to

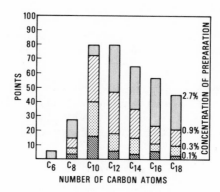

FIG. 1. Results of tissue compatibility testing of alkyl sulfates of different chain lengths (C_6-C_{18}) by intracutaneous injection. Judgment: Bleeding 0-8 points; skin defect 0-8 points. The represented result per preparation and concentration is calculated from the sum of single-point evaluations of the animal groups.

other tests using experimental animals (see Griffith [10]). In evaluating results one can follow the rating scale, as suggested by Draize. However, it is more appropriate to evaluate a new product by comparing it with a known one on the market. For all practical purposes a rating of better, equal, or worse is sufficient. We have to restrain ourselves from a more detailed description of the method here. Nevertheless, one thing must be pointed out. In this test it is necessary that the concentration of the control product and the time period of its action be increased until a slight reaction is observed. Only then can the study of the experimental sample, under identical conditions, be started and evaluated in comparison with the control product.

Since the skin of rabbits, or of other experimental animals, reacts differently from the human skin, it is advisable to run analogous experiments with different animals species, for example, guinea pigs, rats, mice. The resulting trend can be used as a prediction for humans.

In cases where comparative products are not available the testing with humans will have to follow the animal experiments. However, a security factor must be included as far as concentration and time period of action are concerned. The conditions will have to be gradually tightened until results demonstrate that the material or product is sufficiently well tolerated by the skin.

3. A test method for skin sensitivity, which closely approximates real usage, was described by Opdyke and Burnett [11]. In this test guinea pigs are bathed in solutions of the experimental products for a certain period of time and subsequently examined for changes of their skin. Gloxhuber

FIG. 2. Testing of skin compatibility on hairless mice in the bath test.

further developed this test using hairless mice, which are especially suited for such experimentations. In a bath of a constant temperature of +37.0°C, the animals are bathed daily for 1 hr for a period of five days (bath test). The concentration of washing agents is mostly 2.5%. After the last bath the animals are examined for alterations of the skin and the results are registered. In cases when earlier skin reactions had already appeared and therefore the continuation of the experiments with the animals was not advisable, the experiments would be stopped and this period of action would be considered in the evaluation. Five animals are always needed for this test. It is an appropriate one for testing different products side by side. A test unit is shown in Fig. 2.

4. In experimental testing, whether detergents or their ingredients are tolerated, a repeated application of the product is often required. This is closer to the real usage than the single application. In certain cases the reaction of the skin is also different when applications are repeated than when there is only a single one. These tests are carried out in a way analogous to the single-application test.

5. A further test model is one in which rabbits are used, and effect on the mucous membrane of the eye is examined. This test, which can also be carried out according to the description of Draize [9], predicts the expected reactions in case of accidents in which a concentrated product gets into the eye. Here again comparison with a product of the market is of great importance. During the study of different products one finds time and again

that the results of the tests for mucous membrane sensitivity are parallel with those obtained in other tests. Here again we waive a more detailed description. For evaluation of experimental results the aforementioned is also applicable.

6. Another method of importance is used for testing the sensitizing properties of detergents on guinea pigs. Substances with sensitizing properties are not adequate ingredients of household detergents. The examination should be extended to both finished products and new types of raw materials, both of which should be appliable to the skin in the form of a solution or a paste. After a period of sensitization of three to four weeks, during which the experimental substances are applied repeatedly (three to four times weekly) to the same area, an interval of 10-14 days should follow. After this a skin reaction can perhaps be induced by a single application of the substance, in different concentrations, to another site, preferably to a contralateral skin region. If within 24-48 hr in the region of the application skin rash and swelling appear, the substance possesses sensitizing properties. The sensibility of this method can be increased by using the adjuvant of Freund (see Maguire and Chase [12]).

7. In a series of cases, substances provoke allergic reactions only when the skin is simultaneously exposed to sunlight. This is called photoallergy [13, 14]. In testing for photoallergic properties one proceeds in a way as described before in the case of substances that had to be tested for sensitizing properties. In the present case it is necessary that after each application of material the skin also be irradiated with a sufficient dose of ultraviolet light to cause erythema. In inducing reaction one proceeds as explained before but the dose of the simultaneously applied irradiation will have to be so small that by itself it would not cause any reaction. If inflammatory reactions, like reddening or swelling, appear, one can conclude that the substance or the product has photosensitizing properties. (With simultaneously observed control groups, which were only irradiated or to which only the substance was applied to the skin, one can demonstrate that only the two factors, materials and light together, bring about the hypersensibility reaction.)

8. A certain group of materials is able to increase the photosensibility of the skin to such a degree that a minimal quantity of ultraviolet light, which could be tolerated by the untreated skin without difficulty, would be sufficient to develop inflammatory reactions. Such substances are called phototoxic. The test using experimental animals can be carried out in a way that a certain area of the skin is retreated with the experimental material, for example, in the case of rabbits the area would be compared with one area of ultraviolet light below the threshold of causing erythema. If we are dealing with a phototoxic product, subsequent to the first application of the product and to the irradiation, inflammatory reaction will be seen in the area of application and irradiation; while areas of the skin which are only treated with the substance remain free of reaction.

The described experimental animal tests offer a selection of test models adequate for testing local tolerance. In certain cases such investigations will have to be complemented by other tests.

C. Investigations on the Human Skin

The results obtained with experimental animals represent the basis for further experiments now to be carried out on the human skin [15-18]. In doing this it should always be borne in mind that results obtained with animal experiments cannot directly apply to humans, since the structure and biology of the human skin differ essentially from those of the skins of all experimental animals utilized (thickness, quality of the horny layer, number and size of the hair follicles).

While the objective of investigations with experimental animals is only to prepare a product for the testing on humans, it is the task of dermatological experimentation to establish, as far as possible, the health risks connected with the introduction of a new product. Just as the step from animal experiment to testing with humans is full of uncertainty factors, the applicable dermatological test methods will also not offer absolutely certain predictions about the expected damages in the usage, unless an extensive comprehensible, true usage test is applied in the procedures. In most cases of dermatological investigations model tests are used which when compared to real practice can only be applied to a small number of persons. Model experiments can only furnish approximate results. It is therefore expedient, as in the case of animal experiments, to compare the new product to a known and established preparation.

Detergents exert different action on the skin. They can extract important components from the horny layer, such as fat, water-soluble substances, and with them water, which in turn might result in roughness of the skin surface. They can react with the scleroproteins of the horny layer and by this liberate sulfhydryl groups. Further, one can assume that in high concentrations they enhance the penetration of other substances through the barrier of the horny layer. And finally, they can induce, through their action on living components of the epidermis and cutis, inflammation of the skin.

Correspondingly to these effects different test methods were developed which comprise one or more functions.

1. Changes of the skin surface in the form of roughness and brittleness are complaints that are brought up by users after the intensive action of aggressive products. The experimental observation of such changes is therefore of great practical interest. Götte and Kling [19] by applying the observations of Jäger and Jäger [20] reported a method which makes it possible to observe the gradual changes of skin roughness. For this purpose

the surface of the skin is stained with Primuline O and observed under a fluorescence microscope. Roughness of the surface can be very well observed with this method, and corresponding to a rating scale developed by Götte and Kling [19] it can be classified into different grades. The area best suited for this testing method is the back of the hand. Comparison of different preparations is definitely possible.

Also Tronnier and Bussius [21] and Sommer [22] studied the problem of the determination of skin roughness. According to their method the skin is stained with a colorant. The quantity of the fixed colorant is in relationship with the roughness of the skin surface. By the help of reflection measurements the grade of roughness can be determined.

2. Methods suitable for studying the phenomena of swelling and dryness caused by the action of some, primarily alkaline, detergents were suggested by Tronnier and Wagener [23]. In these the resonance frequency is measured By means of a transmitter rod, impulses are sent to the skin, and a neighboring receiving rod receives these impulses more or less strongly, depending on the distance between the uppermost epidermis layers.

3. As Blank [1], Jacobi [5], and Spier and Pascher [2] have demonstrated, the roughness of the skin surface caused by detergents is explained by their extraction of essential components like water-soluble substances and fat. The elution of amino acids and proteins can be determined by putting gloves, into which certain quantities of the test solution are filled, on one hand of persons used in the experiment. After a period of action of 30 min or more, the solutions in the gloves are examined for their content of amino acids and proteins.

The method described by Vermeer and deJong [24, 25] is based on this same principle. However, they developed an instrument by which a defined area of the skin can be washed under standardized conditions (temperature, time, and intensity of washing). The washing solution can be subsequently analyzed for its content of proteins and amino acids. Smeenk and Polano [26] improved this method by changes in the equipment.

4. The reaction of certain surface-active agents with the keratin of the horny layer results in the liberation of sulfhydryl (SH) groups. A method for the determination of the SH groups was published by Van Scott and Lyon [27].

5. The degreasing effect of detergents is connected with the fat-emulsifying property of surface-active agents. By determination of the fat content of the skin after extraction with organic solvents, for example, petroleum ether, the degreasing effect can be tested [28].

6. One of the functions of the horny layer of the epidermis is that of alkali neutralization. This function is basically connected with water-soluble components. The testing for alkali-neutralizing ability of the skin

before and after the action of surface-active agents thus permits direct information regarding impaired functioning of the horny layer. The method for the determination of alkali neutralization is that of Burckhardt [29]. This test method was later somewhat modified by Tronnier and Bussius [30], Werdelmann [31], and others, and applied to the examination of detergents and cleansing agents. The method is principally based on applying a certain amount of alkali and a pH indicator (phenolphthalein) to a defined area of the skin and measuring the time elapsed until the turning point of the indicator, that is, the time needed for the applied quantity of alkali to be neutralized.

7. In order to determine the effect of surface-active agents on the penetration of other substances through the barrier of the horny layer, the method published by Bettley [32] can be used, by which the penetration of potassium ions through the total epidermis is measured under the influence of soaps and detergents.

8. A relatively rudimentary method for the determination of direct irritating effect, is the so-called patch test, whereby a small piece of cotton or linen 1-2 cm^2 in area is soaked with the test solution and applied under a plaster for about 22-24 hr, to the healthy skin of volunteers. Positive reaction appears in the form of inflammation limited to the area to which the product was applied (erythema, infiltration, blister). The number of volunteers should be as great as possible and be at least 100. Since the interpretation of experimental results is sometimes difficult, it has proved to be expedient to test new products by comparing them to well-known ones.

9. In order to examine the tolerance of the skin in conditions which are closer to practice, Burckhardt et al. [33] recently published a method called the "epicutane test by repeated moistening." The test is carried out by applying the test solution with a cotton swab to a marked area of the skin every 30 sec for a period of 30 min. The concentration can be between 1 and 10%. Positive reaction is characterized by a more or less distinct reddening. When comparing two substances distinguishable irritating effects can easily be verified.

The procedure described above can be combined with the test of Burckhardt [29] for alkali resistance. This test gives information about the defense and protective function of the horny layer and is carried out in a way that one drop of N/2 sodium hydroxide solution is applied to an area of the skin and then is covered with a glass block of definite size. The area is dabbed at intervals of 10 min and the treatment is repeated up to three times in the same way. Positive reaction is marked by spotty reddening and possibly by formation of blisters.

10. Another method by which the substances are repeatedly applied to a defined area of the skin is that of Shelanski and Shelanski [34] and is used for testing cumulative effects. In this the experimental substances are applied with the patch test methods repeatedly until an inflammatory reaction

appears. Blohm [35] examines the tolerance to detergents in a similar way; however, he uses a glass bell into which the test solution is filled and is brought in contact with a certain area of the skin for 2 hr daily. The method published by Blohm has the advantage over the patch test that greater volumes are applied. With this it is ensured that the experimental area is uniformly moistened, which is not always the case in the patch test. According to our own experience the method of Blohm proved to be very appropriate for comparative testing of several solutions (see Schulz and Rose [36].

11. A reliable method for testing the tolerance of surface-active agents and detergents is the so-called immersion test [26, 37]. In this test, the hands and the lower arms up to the elbow are immersed in the solutions to be tested once or twice a day for 20 min. The optimal concentration is about 0.1-0.2% and the temperature at the beginning of the experiment is +40°C. In evaluating results one has to consider that the changes that occur can be of different kinds. In certain persons distinct reddenings will appear or also several diffuse ones, while others will only have scalings or roughness of the surface of their skin. The intensity of scaling and reddening can be classified into several grades.

12. Although surface-active agents or detergents only rarely cause allergic sensitization, it may sometimes become necessary to test the sensitizing effect of certain raw materials or detergents. In humans this can be done with the epicutane patch test by which the substances to be tested are applied repeatedly (three times a week for three weeks) to an area of the skin. After an interval of 8-14 days inducement of a reaction will be tried in another area preferably contralaterally situated.

In the German Federal Republic there are some considerations, from legal and dermatological standpoints, against tests on humans to establish sensitizing effects, especially because once acquired, an allergy will evidently last for a long time, and the possibility of the sensitized person later coming into contact with the sensibilizer, or with closely related substances, cannot be excluded.

13. There is no doubt that the usage test, in which the method is extensively adapted to the foreseen application of the product, is the closest to real practice and is the most practical. The test can be carried out according to different conditions, while dermatological examinations will be necessary before and after the test period. Even this test procedure shows difficulties regarding its evaluation since there are several unforeseen possibilities of variations in product application. That is why the test must be carried out with a relatively great number of persons.

III. CONCLUSION

In conclusion, one can state that there is a series of methods for experimentation both with animals and humans which can supply information on how detergents will be tolerated by the skin. Since different methods are based on different mechanisms it is expedient to use several methods in testing a product. As emphasized before, comparative tests are especially important.

REFERENCES

1. I. H. Blank, J. Invest. Dermatol., 18, 433-440 (1952).

2. H. W. Spier and G. Pascher, Aktuelle Probleme der Dermatologie, Vol. 1, Karger, Basel, 1959.

3. M. K. Polano, J. Soc. Cosmet. Chem., 19, 3 (1968).

4. A. Szakall, Arch. Klin. Exp. Dermatol., 206, 374 (1957).

5. O. Jacobi, Berufsdermatosen, 6, 35 (1958).

6. E. Götte, CID/Chemistry, Physics and Application of Surface-Active Substances, Proceedings of the IVth Int. Congr. Surface-Active Substances, Brussels, 7, (Sept. 1964), Vol. III (Section C of the Congress).

7. H. Wilmsmann and A. Marks, Fette, Seifen, Anstrichm., 61, 965 (1959).

8. L. C. Barail, J. Soc. Cosmet. Chem., 11, 241 (1960).

9. J. H. Draize, Appraisal of the Safety of Chemicals in Foods, Drugs and Cosmetics, Bulletin, Association of Food and Drug Officials of the United States, 1959.

10. J. F. Griffith, Toxicol. Appl. Pharmacol., 6, 726 (1964).

11. D. L. Opdyke and C. M. Burnett, Proc. Sci. Sec. Toilet Goods Ass., 3, No. 44 (1965).

12. H. C. Maguire and M. W. Chase, J. Invest. Dermatol., 49, 460 (1967).

13. R. L. Baer, Der Hautarzt, 19, 82 (1968).

14. I. Willis and A. M. Kligman, J. Invest. Dermatol., 51, 378 (1968).

15. W. Schneider, H. Tronnier, and H. Wagner, in Dermatologie und Venerologie (H. A. Gottron and W. Schönfeld, eds.), Band 1 (2. Teil), 1043, G. Thieme Verlag, Stuttgart, 1962.

16. H. Tronnier, Fette, Seifen, Anstrichm. 67, 930 (1965).

17. E. Götte and J. J. Herzberg, Fette, Seifen, Ansstrichm., 59, 747 (1957).

18. W. Burckhardt, Dermatologica, 129, 37 (1964).

19. E. Götte and W. Kling, Fette, Seifen, Anstrichm., 59, 820 (1957).

20. R. Jäger and F. Jäger, Z. Wiss. Mikroskop. Tech., 56, 273 (1939).

21. H. Tronnier and H. Bussius, Berufsdermatosen, 7, 274 (1959).

22. K. Sommer, "Uber den Effekt unterschiedlicher Konzentrationen und Einwirkzeiten von Waschmittellösungen an der menschlichen Haut," Inaugural Dissertation, Tubingen, 1966.

23. H. Tronnier and H. H. Wagener, Dermatologica, 104, 135 (1952).

24. D. J. H. Vermeer and J. C. deJong, Dermatologica, 132, 305 (1966).

25. D. J. H. Vermeer and J. C. deJong, Dermatologica, 135, 131 (1967).

26. G. Smeenk and M. K. Polano, Trans. St. John's Hosp. Dermatol. Soc., 51, 90 (1965).

27. E. J. Van Scott and J. B. Lyon, J. Invest. Dermatol., 21, 199 (1953).

28. C. Carrie and H. Neuhaus, Arch. Dermatol. Syphilis, 192, 261 (1951).

29. W. Burckhardt, in Dermatologie und Venerologie, (H. A. Gottron and W. Schönfeld eds.), Band 1 (1. Teil), S. 196 G. Thieme Verlag, Stuttgart, 1961.

30. H. Tronnier, H. Bussius, and I. Vollbrecht, Parfüm. Kosmet., 42, 13 (1961).

31. B. Werdelmann, Berufsdermatosen, 6, 250 (1958).

32. F. R. Bettley, Brit. Med. J., 1675 (1960).

33. W. Burckhardt, R. Schmid, and P. Schmid, XIII Congr. Int. Dermatol., Band I, Springer-Verlag, Berlin and New York, 1968.

34. H. A. Shelanski and M. V. Shelanski, Proc. Sci. Sec. Toilet Goods Assoc., No. 19, 46 (1953).

35. S. -G. Blohm, Acta Dermato-venereol., 37, 269 (1957).

36. K. H. Schulz and G. Rose, Arch. Klin, Exp. Dermatol., 205, 254 (1957).

37. R. P. Suskind, M. M. Meister, S. R. Scheen, and D. J. A. Rebello, Arch. Dermatol., 88, 117 (1963).

Chapter 19

CLEANING OF METALS

E. B. Saubestre[†]
Enthone, Inc.
New Haven, Connecticut

[†]Deceased.

I. INTRODUCTION

What is a clean surface? It is one on which undesirable films have been replaced by acceptable films during the cleaning process. What is an acceptable film? One that is compatible with the end use of metal cleaning, be it electrodeposition, painting, lacquering, enameling, or other related processes. Sometimes cleaning is an end use in itself. A classic example is the anodizing of aluminum. Why must a film remain? Because, with few exceptions (certain noble metals), a truly "metallic" surface cannot be seen except in a vacuum.

What are the undesirable films that must be removed? They may be conveniently divided three ways: (a) those due to the metallurgy of the basis metal, (b) organic soils, and (c) inorganic films. Their removal is considered in turn.

II. METALLURGY OF THE BASIS METAL

There are remarkably few data available on the role of basis metal metallurgy on cleaning. Yet, crystalline anisotropy (continuation of the basis metal crystal structure into subsequent metallic deposits) must be of great importance in metal cleaning, unless only etching (mechanical keying) is to be relied on as the principal mechanism involved in metal cleaning. Yet (to cite a typical example) when zinc is plated on steel, adhesion on a properly cleaned surface is equal to the tensile strength of zinc, although such crystalline growth is not possible in this system.

Plating conditions that favor reproduction of basis metal crystal structure are those which, through use of proper organic addition agents, favor deposition of a refined grain structure. This assumes little or no mechanical working of the basis metal during the cleaning process, an example of the relation between the cleaning process and the end use thereof. Mechanical working of the surface may set up internal stresses in the basis metal which may be reflected in subsequent finishing operations. Nonmetallic inclusions may be present on basis metal substrates. These invariably complicate the cleaning process. In particular, being relatively nonconductive, they cause pits in electrodeposits, should this be the final finishing treatment. Such inclusions may arise from slag entrapped in metal during pouring of ingots and "tramp metal" picked up from refractory furnaces. Generally speaking, mechanical finishing will help, but not totally relieve this problem. Nonmetallic impurities seriously affect use of such techniques as electropolishing.

III. MECHANICAL FINISHING

The basic purpose of mechanical finishing is to rectify problems involved with substrate metallurgy. This technique, primarily for economic reasons, is not especially useful for removal of either organic or inorganic soils. While many metallurgical shortcomings are overcome by these processes, mechanical finishing can, in itself, give rise to new problems. For example, mechanical finishing can result in raising metal slivers which severely interfere with any subsequent operations. Such treatments frequently give rise to a metallurgically disturbed surface layer called the Beilby layer. The presence of such a disturbed surface layer may give rise to inadequately prepared subsequent coatings or finishes.

A. Polishing

This is basically a mechanical abrading operation. Its fundamental purpose is to ameliorate metallurgical problems involving the basis metal. Considerable metal may be removed in this step. Polishing is generally achieved on wheels made of woven cotton, felt, leather, or canvas. Design of the wheel is often conditioned by the exact shape of the part being cleaned. So-called hard wheels are usually made of separately cemented discs of woven cotton or muslin sewed together. Sewed sections, bound together by adhesives, are commonly used.

On irregularly shaped articles, pressed felt wheels are normally used, with relatively fine abrasive grit size. By contrast, solid leather wheels are used when finishing large, flat surfaces. The most accurate polishing is done on compress wheels. These are wheels composed of small pieces of leather or other fabric placed endwise as segments to a mandrel, with the edge at 90° to the wheel. Generally speaking, more rigid wheels are used for coarser, more rapid metal removal, while softer, more flexible wheels are used for more careful polishing where required. When adhesives are used to attach abrasive grains to polishing wheels, they are usually high-grade glue or silicate-based types. The former are better known, but the latter have the advantage of room-temperature application. Hence, such wheels are more convenient to set up.

Polishing wheels commonly contain an abrasive head. The most commonly used abrasives are aluminum oxide, silicon carbide, emery, and corundum. For polishing relatively tough metals, aluminum oxide is preferred. Speeds of polishing wheels are generally 6000 to 10,000 surface ft/min, the higher speeds requiring silicated adhesives.

B. Buffing

Buffing is used to provide lustrous, satin, or brushed finishes on metals. Buffing wheels are usually made of muslin, and, as a class, are considerably more flexible than polishing wheels. Buffing wheels are generally sewn, with full-disc muslin sections sewn spirally, concentrically, or radially. Spiral sewing is the most common.

Satin finishing is performed by applying to the buffing wheel greaseless compounds containing aluminum oxide or silicon carbide abrasives in an adhesive binder (usually glue). Wheel speed is about 5000 surface ft/min. Cut-down buffing, used to achieve a preliminary luster on the metal surface, generally involves use of grease-base compounds on the wheel. Commonly used are stearic acid, hydrogenated fatty acids, and tallow. These binders, in turn, are blended with buffing powders such as tripoli and aluminum oxide. Color buffing is used to provide maximum luster to a metal surface by mechanical finishing. Such buffing compounds contain relatively fine abrasive compounds, since significant metal removal is not desired in such operations. Also, burrs, scratches, and other metallographic imperfections must not be observable after color buffing. Silicon oxide (fine powder), unfused aluminum oxide, lime (fine powder), rouge (a form of fine iron oxide powder), and chromium oxide are used as the required abrasive. Binders are generally grease based (see above). Wheel speeds are 6000-8000 surface ft/min.

Liquid spray buffing compounds have become increasingly popular in recent years. Generally speaking, they have been replacing bar-type grease-based buffing compounds. The abrasives used are similar to those used in buffing bars. However, the binder is quite different. The greases used are in the form of oil and/or water emulsions, permitting application of the compound by spray gun. This permits automation and reduces labor costs involved in applying bar-type compounds. It also permits tight control over the quantity of compound present on the buff, eliminating presence of unusable nubbins, and reduces wear on the buffing wheel due to application of the compound.

C. Barrel Finishing

This technique is used primarily for the bulk finishing of small parts. Three variations upon the basic technique may be described. Barrel rolling imparts friction upon metallic surfaces by regular moving of small parts under circumstances which markedly reduce mechanical impact. Abrasive barrel finishing adds certain abrasive media to the system just mentioned, such as use of aluminium oxide. Burnishing is used to describe a system of barrel finishing which produces results on metallic surfaces similar to those obtained on larger parts by color buffing techniques. Basically, barrel finishing of small parts offers the advantages of low labor cost factors and generally slightly lower reject factors.

Barrel finishing of small parts is most useful for removing burrs and other metallurgical defects from castings. Removal of heat scale from forgings is another example of the value of barrel finishing of small parts. Media containing some abrasive action, noted above under polishing and buffing, are desirable in removing burrs, flash, etc., from mechanically finished metals. Otherwise, they are not used in fine finish barrel finishing operations. Where abrasive media are not desired, steel balls, plastic pyramids, and related materials are used. Frequently, barrel finishing is used as the last step, after other mechanical finishing operations.

Details of barrel design and usage are beyond the scope of this chapter. Such details may be found in Electroplating Engineering Handbook (Van Nostrand-Reinhold, Princeton, N.J., 1962).

IV. REMOVAL OF ORGANIC SOILS

Organic soils may be divided into three categories: mineral oils, animal (vegetable) oils, and cleaning and descaling residues.

A. Mineral Oils

In general, these oils are insoluble in water, acid, and alkaline solutions. They are unsaponifiable. Water emulsions are not stable. Such oils are soluble in chlorinated hydrocarbons, although this in turn presents serious waste-disposal problems.

B. Animal (Vegetable) Oils

Unlike the previously discussed materials, these are saponifiable; however, the reaction may often be incomplete. They are insoluble in water and (generally) ammoniacal cleaners. They are generally soluble in chlorinated hydrocarbons. These organic soils arise mostly from use of buffing compounds, machining and lubricating oils, and the like. Thermal decomposition of coolant oils presents an especially difficult situation. Such compounds are typified by paraffin-based mineral oils, sulfurized mineral oils, fatty oils, and sulfurized fatty oils.

C. Cleaning and Descaling Residues

Metals may pick up organic residues as a result of other preparations. For example, metal soaps form in situ when certain alkaline soak cleaners are used. Also, acid pickling inhibitors can adsorb to metallic surfaces. Such residues must be removed prior to final finishing operations, such as plating, painting, lacquering, or enameling.

D. Solvent Cleaning

Historically, solvent cleaners have been used "at the head of the line" for removal of the bulk of organic soil. Common industry belief has been that 90% of oil and grease should be removed by a solvent degreaser, 10% by subsequent alkaline cleaning (q. v.). Ideally, solvent cleaners should meet the following industrial requirements: (a) degrease at room temperature, hot, or in the vapor state; (b) stable, nontoxic, not inflammable; and (c) chemically inert to the substrate.

Chlorinated hydrocarbons come closest to meeting the requirements just given. However, for reasons of toxicity and cost, they fail to meet marketing needs fully. Hence, their use is declining. The most commonly used compounds in this area are tri- and perchloroethylene, trichlorotrifluoroethane (Freon), and 1,1,1-trichloroethane. The work to be cleaned may be dipped in the hot liquid solvent. On removal, any adhering liquid vaporizes, leaving the work hot and dry, except for the presence of a thin oil-containing film that must be removed in subsequent alkaline cleaning. Another method is to place the unheated work to be cleaned in a vapor chamber. The vapor condenses on striking the cold work, thus forming a liquid film which dissolves organic soil. This solvent-oil film drains off the work about as fast as it forms. The oil, because of its high boiling point, is not largely revaporized from the heated sump below so that the vapor condensing on the work being cleaned remains nearly pure solvent. As the work becomes heated in the vapor chamber, condensation gradually ceases, and the process comes to an end. Thus, a heavy object can be almost completely cleaned of even heavy oil films, whereas a thin sheet will not be cleaned of even light films.

A variant on solvent cleaners is the use of solvent-emulsion cleaners. Because of generally lower toxicity than the solvent cleaners, they have become quite popular industrially. However, they may be flammable, and also present waste-disposal problems in rinse tanks. Such solvent-emulsion cleaners are used in either of two ways:

1. The work to be cleaned is dipped into a solution of a petroleum-based hydrocarbon solvent, such as naphtha, which contains emulsifying agents such as rosin or oleate soaps, or any of a large number of anionic surfactants that are high in emulsifying characteristics. The hydrocarbon solvent dilutes the oil on the work and spreads the emulsifying agent over the soil particles. The work is then rinsed with a water spray to remove most of the contaminants by immediate emulsification action.

2. The work to be cleaned is either immersed in, or sprayed with, a stable oil-in-water emulsion, such as a mixture of kerosene or similar hydrocarbon fraction dispersed in water, stabilized by soaps, anionic surfactants, amines, and (for steel cleaning) alkalis. This is followed by a standard water rinse. Very rarely, invert emulsions are used (water-

in-oil emulsions). However, high drag-out losses mitigate against widespread use of such cleaners, despite their considerable effectiveness (since
oil is the continuous phase).

Some years ago, diphase cleaners were introduced to the market. These
were a special form of solvent-emulsion cleaning, in which the bath consisted of a layer of nearly emulsified solvent on top of an aqueous emulsified
layer. While seeming to show promise when introduced, diphase cleaners
never became established in the market, due in part to control and waste-
disposal problems.

E. Alkaline Cleaning

This is the oldest and most widely used method of removing organic soil.
While it is more expensive to remove heavy soils in alkaline cleaners than
in solvent cleaners, alkaline cleaners are capable of removing every last
trace of organic soil prior to subsequent processing of metal surfaces.
This cannot be done in either solvent or solvent-emulsion cleaners. Alkaline
cleaners are commonly used as either immersion, spray, or electrolytic
cleaners. The number of cleaner formulas in the literature is legion, and
it is not possible to detail them all or discuss their relative merits. Table
1 gives a few representative formulas for immersion alkaline cleaners.
These formulas may also be used for spray cleaners, provided that specially designed low-foaming surfactants are used. Table 2 gives a few representative formulas for electrolytic alkaline cleaners. In soak cleaning, the
metal to be cleaned is simply immersed in the cleaner for as long a period
of time as is found to be required. Temperatures used are quite elevated,
often not far from the boiling point, except in the case of spray wash cleaners, which operate at about 140-160°F and more rarely, at even lower
temperatures. Agitation of immersion cleaners is occasionally, but not
often, practiced. Cleaner concentration is generally 6-16 oz/gal. Since
oil and other organic matter may well float on top of the immersion cleaner
tank, unless strongly emulsifying and dispersing surfactants are used, steps
may have to be taken to avoid recontamination of the work on removal from
the cleaning tank. These include periodic skimming of the top of the tank,
use of an overflow dam, and so forth. In spray cleaning, the spray heads
must be so designed as to provide for direct impingement of the sprayed
cleaner over the entire surface of the work being cleaned. Cleaner concentrations are generally 1/4 to 1 1/2 oz/gal.

While immersion cleaning will often suffice to prepare metal surfaces
for final finishing, electrocleaning is frequently used next. Reduced to
fundamentals, electrocleaning is alkaline cleaning as described above, with
the aid of electric current, either anodic or cathodic. Anodic current is
most commonly used for cleaning ferrous surfaces in general, and for magnesium. Nonferrous surfaces, such as copper, brass, and zinc die casting

TABLE 1
Immersion Cleaners

Compound	Weight % used in cleaning						
	Steel		Copper and brass			Aluminum	
$Na_3PO_4 \cdot 12H_2O$	32	35	50	—	35	30	50
$Na_4P_2O_7$	—	5	—	—	—	—	—
$Na_6P_4O_{13}$	—	—	—	—	15	—	—
Na_4SiO_4	85	—	—	—	—	—	—
$Na_2SiO_3 \cdot 5H_2O$	—	50	30	52	30	65	30
$NaOH$	16	8	—	—	—	—	—
Na_2CO_3	46	—	13	46	13	—	13
Anionic surfactant	4	2	5	2	5	5	5
Nonionic surfactant	2	—	2	—	2	—	2
Concentration (oz/gal)	6-18	4-10	4-12	4-12	4-12	6-8	4-6
Temperature (°F)	190-200	190-200	180-190	180-190	180-190	180-190	180-190

TABLE 2

Electrocleaners

Compound	Weight % used in cleaning					
	Steel: anodic	Steel: anodic	Copper and brass: anodic	Copper and brass: anodic	Copper and brass: cathodic	Copper and brass: cathodic
$Na_3PO_4 \cdot 12H_2O$	35	—	25	25	47	—
$Na_4P_2O_7$	5	7	—	—	—	10
$Na_2SiO_3 \cdot 5H_2O$	50	35	—	20	20	60
NaOH	8	55	20	—	10	—
Na_2CO_3	—	—	53	51	20	25
Anionic surfactant	—	—	—	1	1	1
Nonionic surfactant	2	3	2	3	2	4
Concentration (oz/gal)	6–18	6–18	4–8	4–8	4–8	4–8
Temperature (°F)	190–200	190–200	180–190	180–190	180–190	180–190
Current density (A/ft^2)	50–100	60–120	25–40	25–40	20–30	20–30

alloys, may be cleaned either anodically or cathodically. Some years ago, only the latter was used, but the former has gained in relative popularity in more recent years. Sensitive metals, such as aluminum and its alloys, are rarely electrocleaned. When electrocleaning is used to depassivate metals prior to subsequent finishing operations, it is always cathodic. Such cathodic cleaning is common in depassivating stainless steel, nickel, and high-nickel and nickel-chromium alloys prior to further finishing operations. Time of electrocleaning is generally shorter than that of immersion cleaning, only rarely exceeding 2-3 min. While elevated temperatures are common-place, they are often a little lower than those in immersion cleaning. Agitation is provided solely by the gases evolved at the electrodes. Since the evolution of gas at the electrodes can cause excessive foaming of the surfactants present, leading to occasional hydrogen implosions, it has been historically common to use considerably lower foaming surfactants in electrocleaners than in immersion cleaners. This, however, necessitated very thorough rinsing between the immersion cleaner and the electrocleaner to avoid drag-in of high foaming surfactants. In recent years, to avoid such costly rinsing procedures, the trend has been markedly toward the use of surfactants compatible in both cleaners. This has been made possible by the development of improved nonionic surfactants which permit good cleaning action with only moderate foam development, and by the use of defoaming agents in electrocleaners. When cathodic cleaning is employed, care must be taken to minimize presence of metallic impurities in the cleaner, or else loose metallic smuts will form on the work, interfering with subsequent finishing operations. Cathodic cleaning may also cause hydrogen embrittlement of the work being cleaned, especially in the case of high-alloy, high-strength aerospace ferrous materials. Anodic cleaning may cause some staining or tarnishing of the work, due to superficial oxidation, but this is easily removed by subsequent acid dipping. Anodic cleaning at high current densities ($80-100$ A/ft^2) is also useful in removal of hard-water films on the work which may form in the course of immersion cleaning.

Other specialized forms of alkaline cleaning include ultrasonic cleaning (using $18-1000$ kHz energy), used especially for the precision cleaning of small parts, as in the electronics industry. Solution formulas are similar to those in Table 1, except that care must be taken not to use inorganic builders or organic surfactants which present colloidal micelles in the solution which lead to considerable power attenuation.

F. Formulation of Alkaline Cleaners

Because the formulation of alkaline cleaners is so complex, it is helpful to review briefly the role of some of the individual constituents that go into alkaline cleaners.

Caustic soda is a very common ingredient in such cleaners. There are three fundamental reasons for this: (a) it provides a high degree of

TABLE 3

Relative Alkalinity of Various Chemicals Used in
Alkaline Cleaning

Compound	pH (1% solution)	Total Na_2O (%)[a]	Active Na_2O (%)[b]	Equivalent cleaner[c]
NaOH	13.4	77.5	75.5	1.0
Na_4SiO_4	13.3	67.5	65.8	1.1
Na_2CO_3	11.4	58.0	29.0	2.6
$Na_2SiO_3 \cdot 5H_2O$	12.5	29.2	28.0	2.7
$Na_6Si_{10}O_{23}$	10.2	23.8	21.3	3.5
$Na_3PO_4 \cdot 10H_2O$	12.0	18.0[d]	10.0	7.6
$Na_2B_4O_7 \cdot 10H_2O$	9.2	16.3	8.4	9.0
$Na_4P_2O_7$	10.1	23.3[e]	8.1	9.3

[a]Based on the methyl orange end point (pH 4.5-5.0).

[b]Based on the phenolphthalein end point (pH 8.2-8.4).

[c]This column gives the number of grams of alkaline compound required to give the same amount of active Na_2O as a gram of NaOH.

[d]Taken to NaH_2PO_4 at this end point.

[e]Taken to $Na_2H_2P_2O_7$ at this end point.

alkalinity (Table 3) which generally assists the cleaning action; (b) it is fairly inexpensive; (c) in electrocleaners, it provides for maximum conductivity. As noted in Table 3, virtually the total alkalinity present is active (i.e., available at a pH above 8, below which alkaline cleaners have no real effectiveness). Caustic soda alone, however, will not suffice in an alkaline cleaner. It is a very poor surfactant and emulsifying agent. Because of its high percentage of active alkalinity, little buffering is provided. Too high a caustic content may even break down the effectiveness of emulsifying agents, many of which reach a peak of performance at a pH of 11.5-12.0. Caustic soda is also hard to rinse from amphoteric metals such as aluminium, zinc, tin, lead, and so on.

Soda ash is quite commonly found in alkaline cleaners, both of the immersion and electrocleaner types (see Tables 1 and 2). There can be only one major justification for such widespread industrial usage. The extremely low cost of soda ash means that more total inorganic builder action is designed into an alkaline cleaner containing soda ash per dollar cost of designing the cleaner than by use of other, considerably more effective, builders. While soda ash can be used as an alkaline buffer, about 50% of this buffering action occurs at a pH too low to be of practical use in alkaline cleaners for metals (Table 3). Soda ash, like caustic soda, is a very poor surfactant and emulsifying agent. In electrocleaners, it contributes only modestly to conductivity. Rinsability from amphoteric metals (see caustic soda, above) is poor to moderate. Traditionally, soda ash has also been used to moderate caking of caustic soda in preblended alkaline cleaners. In recent times, however, this usage has been largely replaced by use of organic anticaking agents.

The use of phosphates in alkaline cleaners may be divided into two basically differing groups. The orthophosphates are widely used (Tables 1 and 2) because they are fairly effective buffers and wetting agents, and also possess a degree of emulsifying action. Rinsability, even on amphoteric metals, is excellent. They are excellent inorganic builders when used in conjunction with both anionic and nonionic surfactants. Complex phosphates, such as $Na_4P_2O_7$ and $Na_6P_4O_{13}$, are used as excellent, inexpensive chelating agents for hard water and metallic impurities in cleaners (especially valuable in cathodic alkaline cleaners). In their own right, complex phosphates have moderately good detergent action. Unfortunately, both orthophosphates and complex phosphates tend (by fertilizing algae growth) to accelerate the eutrophication of small lakes and other relatively stagnant bodies of water. For this reason, nonphosphate cleaners must be used in ever-increasing areas of the country. These developments are so recent, that at the time of this writing, formulas for nonphosphate cleaners are not yet widely published. However, it has already been noted publicly that the following materials are being used to replace phosphates in metal cleaners: silicates, higher soda ash content in many nonphosphate metal cleaners; for complexing or chelating action, the following are used: alkylamines, alkanolamines, EDTA and its derivatives, NTA and related equivalents, and so on. It should be noted, however, that chelating agents such as NTA may tie up toxic metals and prevent their removal in ordinary waste-disposal operations. Thus, the "cure may be worse than the illness."

Silicates are a mainstay of many alkaline cleaners. As can be seen in Table 3, they may be good buffers. More importantly, of all inorganic builders, the silicates as a class are the best buffering agents, and the best wetting, emulsifying, and deflocculating agents. Because of potentially high active alkalinity, the silicates do not have good rinsability characteristics with amphoteric metals. Also, due to chemisorption phenomena, silicates present serious problems when used in cleaning highly reactive metals such as aluminium and its alloys, aluminium casting materials, and zinc die casting alloys. In all cases, a subsequent treatment in a fluoride-ion-containing material is mandatory prior to final finishing. In terms of detergent action, the optimum silicate is Na_4SiO_4. However, as illustrated in Table 2, this compound is virtually synonymous with NaOH. Hence it is used primarily for cleaning ferrous surfaces and magnesium. For other metals, $Na_2SiO_3 \cdot 5H_2O$, while less effective as a total cleaning agent, is safer and is far more widely used. In the case of cleaning aluminum, not only is a mild silicate commonly used, but often even a very mild silicate resembling water glass may be used. The higher the ratio of SiO_2 to Na_2O, the better is the degree of inhibition. Therefore, the ratio selected for aluminum cleaning should clearly reflect the end use of cleaning desired for the given finishing operation. A high SiO_2/Na_2O ratio compound, such as $Na_6Si_{10}O_{23}$, may be used. As seen in Table 3, it has a relatively efficient "equivalent cleaner" rating, yet has a relatively low pH. On the other hand, such silicates are the hardest to remove in rinsing, and invariably require subsequent use of fluoride-containing acid dips.

Borax and other borates are widely used in laundry cleaning and other soft surface cleaning. However, because of relatively low pH, and limited detergent qualities, they have not found widespread use in metal cleaning compositions. They have found a niche of sorts in such applications as aluminum cleaning and some spray wash compounds. However, with the growing emphasis on phosphate-free cleaners, borax is being more extensively employed in metal cleaners. As shown in Table 3, however, considerably more borax must be used in replacing phosphates, in order to obtain an "equivalent cleaner" rating, which is most important in metal cleaning.

Soaps and synthetic detergents are added to most alkaline cleaners to decrease surface and interfacial tension at the metal-cleaner interface, thereby enhancing the effect of the inorganic compounds in the cleaner. In addition, they are used to emulsify oil and deflocculate suspended matter. Soaps, such as coconut fatty acid types, are used in soak cleaners, but quite rarely in spray or electrolytic cleaners because of their tendency to stabilize foam. Nonionic surfactants are often used in soak cleaners and spray cleaners without any other synthetic surfactant. They are used in conjunction with anionic surfactants in electrocleaners. Anionic surfactants are occasionally used in soak cleaners, in which case they are of the high-foaming type. Cationic surfactants are hardly ever used in metal cleaning, except for specialized applications (often involving inhibition). Virtually all surfactants used currently in metal cleaning compositions are biodegradable.

Finally, a specialized yet important class of alkaline cleaner compositions should be mentioned. These are compositions that are designed not only to remove organic soils but to simultaneously deposit a film on the metal surface which is desirable for subsequent metal-finishing operations. A few examples follow, although there are many others. Prior to painting and other organic finishing operations, such as porcelainizing or enameling, it is generally desirable to have a phosphate coating on the metal surface.

Thus cleaners used prior to such finishing operations not only meet previously discussed criteria but contain a sufficiently large amount of phosphate compounds (ordinary orthophosphates are usually used) so as to leave behind a significant phosphate coating on the surface after cleaning. Some metals are relatively difficult to electroplate because of hydrogen overvoltage problems in the electroplating tank. Examples are cast and malleable irons and carbonitrided steels. Again, in these cases, it is often desirable to use a cleaner which leaves behind at least a very thin phosphate film. In some cases, no finishing operations are contemplated, but it is desirable to remove all chemical residues from the metal surface to prevent subsequent staining or other discoloration. In such cases, the cleaner must possess a degree of water-displacing power. This is achieved by using synthetic surfactants that adsorb very strongly to the metal surface. Both cationic and anionic surfactants may be used for this purpose. Nonionics are never used.

V.   REMOVAL OF INORGANIC FILMS

Inorganic films may be divided into four categories: scale and smut; rust and tarnish;   cleaning residues;   and dirt.

A.   Scale and Smut

Prior heat treatment of the metal may result in formation of scale on the surface. Pickling of high-carbon steels may result in the formation of bloom, or smut, composed largely of carbon and phosphides and/or oxides thrown out on the surface during pickling. Parts subjected to heat during normal usage may build up residues derived from the materials to which they are exposed. For example, engine parts are generally coated with carbon residues. Generally speaking, these materials are usually very troublesome to remove.

B.   Rust and Tarnish

This includes oxides, sulfides, and other inorganic films that form on metal surfaces because of corrosive atmospheres. Ferrous surfaces generally suffer from oxide corrosion;   cuprous surfaces may suffer from oxide, carbon dioxide, and sulfide corrosion;   silver surfaces suffer from sulfide corrosion;   aluminum, zinc, and magnesium surfaces generally suffer from oxide corrosion, but since the film formed is thin and self-healing, it can be removed in the alkaline cleaning operation and requires no pickling treatment.

These films, generally speaking, are not readily soluble in water or alkaline cleaners (except as noted above), but react readily with acid and cyanide (or other strongly complexing or chelating solutions) to form water-soluble compounds.

C. Cleaning Residues

Alkaline cleaning operations may leave behind films of oxides, phosphates, silicates, passive layers, adsorbed surfactants, hard-water fatty soap films, and adsorbed hydrogen (in the case of cathodic cleaning). Cathodic cleaning may also result in deposition of loosely adherent metallic smuts. Mechanical finishing operations may leave behind such residues as polishing and buffing compound residues, fine abrasive particles, burrs, torn metallic slivers, and the like. The worst such example is the smut left behind after vapor degreasing of buffed parts. These smuts are extremely difficult to remove. In general, such cleaner residues must be removed in the pickling or acid dipping operation (except for some specific cases noted above).

D. "Dirt"

This is a sort of miscellaneous title for all other inorganic residues which must generally be removed. It is characterized by being water insoluble, often admixed with oil originally present on the surface prior to alkaline cleaning. Perhaps the best way to define dirt is to call it any residue present on the metal surface which does not intrinsically result from prior metal-treating and cleaning operations.

E. Acid Pickling Baths and Acid Dips

The most common chemicals used for this purpose are sulfuric acid (least expensive) and hydrochloric acid (more effective for activation purposes prior to plating). Such baths are normally used by immersion, although electrolytic pickling is not uncommon. Anodic pickling is not especially effective because passive oxide layers are often produced. Cathodic pickling is more effective, but if metallic salts are present in the pickling bath, smuts will deposit on the work. When the primary purpose of this step is activation of the metal surface prior to electroplating, the preferred acid is hydrochloric acid, and the preferred usage is cathodic; sometimes, nickel chloride is added to the cathodic acid dip to deposit nickel simultaneously (Wood's nickel strike). Details of this procedure are beyond the scope of this chapter, but may be found in any general text on electroplating. In the case of chromium plating, it is common to pickle the surface anodically in a solution resembling a chromium plating solution and then immediately plate cathodically. Again, details may be found in general texts on electroplating. Since most acid treatments may attack the basis metal, it is common to employ inhibitors in such baths to minimize such attack. Among inhibitors commonly used are organic thiocompounds (for ferrous and cuprous subtrates), nitro compounds (for cuprous substrates), and strongly adsorbing cationic surfactant compounds (for all substrates). Use of phosphoric acid is a special case considered in the next section. When cleaner residues must be removed, especially silicate films, hydrofluoric acid is used, generally in combination with other mineral acids.

F. Phosphoric Acid Dips

The use of phosphoric acid in this area somewhat defies easy classification because such dips may serve one or more, or even all of three functions: (a) removal of organic soil, (b) removal of inorganic soil, and (c) deposition of phosphate films desirable for subsequent finishing operations, notably painting. Basic costs are generally higher than in sulfuric acid baths, lower than in hydrochloric acid baths. However, cost is very rarely a factor; phosphoric acid solutions are used primarily because of the specific application intended. For (a) and (b) above, practice is to use a mixture of phosphoric acid, low-molecular-weight organic polyethers, and anionic surfactants. For (c), phosphating formulas are used; these are beyond the scope of this text, but may be found in general texts on this subject. In general, ferrous substrates treated in phosphoric acid dips have excellent residual resistance to corrosion. Hence, inhibitors are only rarely used in such baths.

G. Formulation of Acid Pickles and Acid Dips

The most common solution is based on sulfuric acid. The time required for pickling is primarily a function of acid concentration and temperature.

Table 4 illustrates a typical example for a given pickling problem. Obviously, this cannot be generalized, but offers a representative illustration of the basic factors involved in sulfuric acid pickling. In the specific case of wire or strip pickling operations, which are continuous operations, higher H_2SO_4 concentrations are used, at temperatures as high as 200-210°F. For general plating operations, a concentration of 5% (wt) H_2SO_4 at 160-170°F is probably the best overall recommendation. In such operations, the buildup of end product consists primarily of $FeSO_4 \cdot xH_2O$. The bath is discarded when such buildup becomes excessive. When more concentrated baths are used (such as 20% H_2SO_4), periodic replenishment of the bath to replace drag-out losses is economically justified. In all such pickling baths, it is obvious that buildup of $FeSO_4$ will slow the rate of pickling action. Table 5 illustrates a single example of this point. As noted above, inhibitors are commonly used, and the latter increase the pickling time required to a moderate extent. Tables 4 and 5 are based on noninhibited pickles.

As indicated previously, hydrochloric acid is used less frequently than sulfuric acid because of higher costs. However, it is much more effective in activation application. It also is often more effective than sulfuric acid for generalized pickling applications when used at room temperature. Also, because of the good solubility of iron salts, hydrochloric acid pickles are

TABLE 4

Acid Pickling in Sulfuric Acid

H_2SO_4 (wt %)	Time required (min) at			
	$150^\circ F$	$170^\circ F$	$190^\circ F$	$210^\circ F$
5	13	7.5	4.5	2
12	9.5	5	3	1.5
16	8	4.5	2.5	1

TABLE 5

Effect of Iron in Sulfuric Acid Pickling Baths

H_2SO_4 (wt %)	Time required at $150^\circ F$ (min)		
	2% Fe	4% Fe	8% Fe
5	7.5	9	11
16	3	4	5.5

less sensitive to aging problems than sulfuric acid pickles. Because of equipment and ventilation duct and pump problems arising from corrosion, hydrochloric acid pickles are rarely used above about $125^\circ F$.

Fluoboric acid pickling offers advantages when dealing with cuprous, lead, tin, and solder substrates. The general principles offered above are applicable. If prior alkaline cleaners have led to formation of silicate residues, hydrofluoric acid is required in the pickle solution.

There exists a growing trend toward use of "powdered acid" formulations, for reasons of ease of handling, toxicology, and shipping regulations of the ICC and IATA. Such formulations are based on the use of powdered versions of sulfuric acid (e.g., $NaHSO_4$). There is no corresponding dry version of hydrochloric acid although it is possible to use NaCl in combination with other dry acid salts. If fluorides are needed (see above), then the dry acid must contain a powdered form of the fluoride ion, of which there are many examples.

H. Alkaline Descalers and Derusters

As a complete alternative to the use of acid pickles, suitable alkaline descalers and derusters may be used. Inorganic films on metal surfaces may be removed by use, generally electrolytically, and even more specifically, by use of periodic reverse current (PR), of solutions containing sodium hydroxide, sodium cyanide, and, in some cases, chelating agents effective in alkaline media. Surfactants may also be employed to accelerate the cleaning action. Generally speaking, such materials are most efficacious when treating ferrous substrates, in which case the anodic portion of the cycle is longer than the cathodic portion of the cycle (e.g., 30 sec reverse, 10 sec direct). A typical formula is given in Table 6.

With recent emphasis on effluent control, current developments are many in this field. They may be divided into two categories.

1. Low-Cyanide Alkaline Descalers

Such solutions comprise materials similar to those described above, except that no more than 1-2 oz/gal NaCN is required.

2. Noncyanide Descalers

These materials are so recent on the market that no formulas have been published. However, it should be noted that generally, chelating agents are employed. Especially in the case of NTA, chelation of toxic metals can present serious problems.

I. Bright Dipping and Electropolishing

Sometimes, especially in the case of cuprous substrates, the end purpose of acid dipping is to provide a very bright, reflective surface. When nonelectrolytic processes are employed, the term bright dipping is normally used. When electrolysis is required, the common term is electropolishing. In both cases, the chemistry is similar. The exact compositions employed range from the simple production of a bright, clean surface, to those that create truly brilliant surfaces from semilustrous substrates. Details of electropolishing and chemical polishing are available in the bibliography. Basically, the chemistry of such baths involves use of (a) a strong inorganic acid, (b) an oxidizing agent stable in acid, yet sufficiently controlled to minimize attack on the substrate, (c) a virtual lack of effect on the substrate, and (d) a brightening or levelling action during treatment.

VI. TESTS FOR CLEANLINESS

Tests for cleanliness in the case of metal cleaners are quite different from those discussed elsewhere in this volume for soft surface and laundry cleaners. In the case of metal cleaners, the end purpose of cleaning is the

TABLE 6

Alkaline Descaler Formula

Constituent	Amount (g/liter)
NaOH	180
NaCN	120
Chelating agent (such as EDTA, NTA, gluconates, heptogluconates, etc.)	80

production of a surface that permits maximum possible adhesion of subsequent metal-finishing treatments. As noted earlier, this may range from surfaces relatively free from extraneous substances in the case of electroplating operations, to surfaces containing desired films, such as phosphate coatings on ferrous articles prior to painting and enameling and anodized coatings on aluminium and magnesium alloys.

In all cases, however, the essential criterion is one of complete wettability of the surface with respect to the subsequent treatment. Since many metal-finishing operations are carried out in aqueous media, wetting tests are generally the most significant ones, and the most sensitive.

A. Water-Break Test

This is by far the oldest, and yet, to this day, one of the most simple, yet sensitive tests for metal surface cleanliness. In this test, the part is first rinsed in the purest possible water (preferably distilled or deionized water) after the final cleaning stage (the test is invalid if carried out after any alkaline cleaning stage; if such happens to be the final stage, a brief dip in 1-2% HCl or H_2SO_4 is required prior to rinsing for this test). It is noted visually whether or not, after removal from the rinsing stage, the part remains 100% wetted. Any evidence of "water break" is considered as a failure of the test. A standardized method for carrying out this test may be found in ASTM F 22-65.

B. Atomizer Test

This is a highly refined version of the water-break test. In this test, the metal surface is first prepared as described in the preceding subsection, except (and this is the critical difference between the two tests) that the surface is first allowed to dry completely prior to testing. When dry, the

TABLE 7

Sensitivity of Metal Cleaning Tests[a]

Type of contamination	Fatty acids		Fatty esters			Medium oils		Paraffinic oils	
Oil	Stearic, oleic acids		Tristearin, lard oil		Tripalmitin, olive oil	SAE 60 motor oil	SAE 50 oil, lubricating and cutting oils	Mineral oil; SAE 10 oil	
Surface finish	Polished	Matte	Polished	Matte	Polished	Polished	Matte	Polished	Matte
Test Used									
Water break	$< 2 \times 10^{-7}$	1.5×10^{-7}	3×10^{-7}	5×10^{-7}	—	1×10^{-6}	1.5×10^{-6}	1.5×10^{-6}	9×10^{-6}
Atomizer	—	2×10^{-8}	3×10^{-8}	6×10^{-8}	3×10^{-8}	—	1×10^{-7}	1×10^{-7}	4×10^{-7}
Fluorescent dye	—	—	—	3×10^{-5}	—	1×10^{-5}	4×10^{-6}	—	4×10^{-5}
Radioactive tracer	—	—	—	—	—	1.7×10^{-7}	—	—	—
Potassium ferricyanide	—	—	—	3×10^{-5}	—	—	—	—	1×10^{-4}
CuSO$_4$ dip	—	—	—	3.5×10^{-5}	—	4×10^{-6}	—	—	—

[a] All values are in grams per square centimeter.

726

surface is subjected to a fine mist of water from a simple atomizer (such as the type normally used for nasal spraying). The developing water-spreading pattern is observed. A "clean" surface will quickly develop a uniform film of water. An imperfectly cleaned surface will show incomplete water coverage. The reason for the greater sensitivity of this test is the fact that the advancing contact angle is much more sensitive than the receding contact angle with respect to metallic surface sensitivity. Specifically, the atomizer test will detect about 2×10^{-8} g/cm^2 of oleic acid on a metallic surface, which is considerably less than a monomolecular layer. A standardized method for carrying out this test may be found in ASTM F 21-65. Further details may be found in the bibliography.

C. Other Tests

There are many other tests for evaluating metal cleanliness, and these are detailed in the bibliography. The principal problem is that most, if not all, of these tests register identification of specific soils, rather than identification of all soils contributing to the overall problem of readying metallic surfaces for finishing. An estimate of test sensitivity is given in Table 7.

BIBLIOGRAPHY

Because so many people have contributed to the literature (and especially to the patent field)in recent years, it would be quite unfair to delineate a detailed bibliography. Instead, a few major references are appended, most of which offer very extensive bibliographies for further reading in this specialized area.

ASTM B322-68, Recommended Practice for Cleaning Metals Prior to Electroplating, Amer. Soc. Testing Mater., Philadelphia, Penn., 1968.

ASTM STP 310, Handbook of Vapor Degreasing, Amer. Soc. Testing Mater., Philadelphia, Penn., 1968.

A. K. Graham, ed., Electroplating Engineering Handbook, 2nd ed., Van Nostrand-Reinhold, Princeton, N.J., 1962 (new edition now in press).

H. B. Linford and E. B. Saubestre, American Electroplaters' Society Research Report, Serial No. 18, 26, 1951, 1953.

Metal Finishing Guidebook Directory, Metals and Plastics Publ., Westwood, N.J., 1971.

S. Spring, Metal Cleaning, Van Nostrand-Reinhold, Princeton, N.J., 1963.

S. Spring, Metal Finishing, 61, No. 11, 74; No. 12, 66 (1963).

W. Wiederholt, Chemical Surface Treatment of Metals, Draper, London, 1965.